Springer Series on Behavior Therapy and Behavioral Medicine

Series Editor: *Cyril M. Franks, Ph.D.*

Advisory Board: John Paul Brady, M.D., Robert P. Liberman, M.D., Neal E. Miller, PhD., and Stanley Rachman, Ph.D.

Vol. 1   **Multimodal Behavior Therapy**   *Arnold A. Lazarus*

Vol. 2   **Behavior Therapy Assessment**   *Er J. Mash and Leif G. Terdal, editors*

Vol. 3   **Behavioral Approaches to Weight Control**   *Edward E. Abramson, editor*

Vol. 4   **A Practical Guide to Behavioral Assessment (O.P.)**

Vol. 5   **Asthma Therapy:** A Behavioral Health Care System for Respiratory Disorders *Thomas L. Creer*

Vol. 6   **Behavioral Medicine:** Practical Applications in Health Care *Barbara G. Melamed and Lawrence J. Siegel*

Vol. 7   **Multimodal Handbook for a Mental Hospital:** Designing Specific Treatments for Specific Problems *Lillian F. Brunell and Wayne T. Young, editors*

Vol. 8   **Eating and Weight Disorders:** Advances in Treatment and Research *Richard K. Goldstein, editor*

Vol. 9   **Perspectives on Behavior Therapy in the Eighties** *Michael Rosenbaum, Cyril M. Franks, and Yoram Jaffe, editors*

Vol. 10   **Pediatric and Adolescent Behavioral Medicine:** Issues in Treatment *Patrick J. McGrath and Philip Firestone, editors*

Vol. 11   **Hypnosis and Behavior Therapy:** The Treatment of Anxiety and Phobias *J. Christopher Clarke and J. Arthur Jackson*

Vol. 12   **Child Obesity:** A New Frontier of Behavior Therapy *Michael D. LeBow*

Vol. 13   **Punishment and Its Alternatives:** A New Perspective for Behavior Modification *Johnny L. Matson and Thomas M. DiLorenzo*

Vol. 14   **The Binge-Purge Syndrome:** Diagnosis, Treatment and Research *Raymond C. Hawkins II, William J. Fremouw and Pamelia F. Clement, editors*

Vol. 15   **Behavioral Assessment in Behavioral Medicine** *Warren W. Tryon, editor*

Vol. 16   **Behavior Therapy Casebook** *Michel Hersen and Cynthia Last, editors*

Vol. 17   **The Covert Conditioning Handbook** *Joseph R. Cautela and Albert J. Kearney*

Vol. 18   **Problem-Solving Therapy:** A Social Competence Approach to Clinical Intervention ' *Thomas J. D'Zurilla*

Vol. 19   **The Psychological Management of Chronic Pain:** A Treatment Manual *H. Clare Philips*

Vol. 20   **Paradigms in Behavior Therapy:** Present and Promise *Daniel B. Fishman, Frederick Rotgers, and Cyril M. Franks, editors*

Vol. 21   **Innovations in Child Behavior Therapy** *Michel Hersen, Ph.D., editor*

Vol. 22   **Adolescent Behavior Therapy** *Eva L. Feindler and Grace R. Kalfus, editors*

Vol. 23   **Unifying Behavior Therapy:** Contributions of Paradigmatic Behaviorism *Georg Eifert and Ian Evans, editors*

Vol. 24   **Learned Resourcefulness:** On Coping Skills, Self-Control and Adaptive Behavior *Michael Rosenbaum, editor*

Vol. 25   **Aversive and Nonaversive Interventions:** Controlling Life-Threatening Behavior by the Developmentally Disabled *Sandra L. Harris and Jan S. Handleman, editors*

Vol. 26   **Anxiety Across the Lifespan:** A Developmental Perspective *Cynthia G. Last, editor*

Cynthia G. Last, PhD, is professor of psychology and director of the Anxiety Treatment Center in the Department of Psychology at Nova University. She is joint editor and founder of the *Journal of Anxiety Disorders.* She has coauthored/coedited eight books including *Handbook of Child and Adult Psychopathology* (1990), *Handbook of Anxiety Disorders* (1988), *Handbook of Child Psychiatric Diagnosis* (1989), and *Anxiety Disorders in Children* (1989). Dr. Last is the recipient of several research grants from the National Institute of Mental Health to study anxiety disorders in children and adolescents. She has published numerous journal articles and book chapters on the assessment, diagnosis, and treatment of anxiety disorders in both child and adult populations.

Anxiety Across the Lifespan

A Developmental Perspective

Cynthia G. Last
Editor

Springer Publishing Company
New York

Springer Publishing Company, Inc.
536 Broadway
New York, NY 10012-3955

93 94 95 96 97 / 5 4 3 2 1

Library of Congress Cataloging-in-Publication Data

Anxiety across the lifespan : a developmental perspective /
   Cynthia G. Last, editor.
      p. cm. — (Springer series on behavior therapy and behavioral
   medicine : v. 26)
      Includes bibliographical references and index.
      ISBN 0-8261-6460-9
      1. Anxiety.   2. Anxiety in children.   I. Last, Cynthia G.
   II. Series.
      [DNLM: 1. Anxiety.   2. Anxiety Disorders.   3. Human Development.
   W1 SP685NB v.26 / WM 172 A637123]
   RC531.A6115 1992
   616.85'223—dc20
   DNLM/DLC
   for Library of Congress   92-49675
                                                                    CIP

Printed in the United States of America

Contents

Preface   vii

Contributors   ix

1   Introduction   1
Cynthia G. Last

2   DSM and Classification of Anxiety Disorders in Children and Adults   7
Wendy K. Silverman

3   Anxiety Symptoms in Nonpsychiatrically Referred Children and Adolescents   37
Donna L. Moreau and *Myrna M. Weissman*

4   Developmental Differences in Expression of Anxiety Disorders in Children and Adolescents   63
Cyd C. Strauss

5   Aspects of School Phobia   78
Ian Berg

6   Relationship Between Familial and Childhood Anxiety Disorders   94
Cynthia G. Last

7   Relationship Between Adult and Childhood Anxiety Disorders: Genetic Hypothesis   113
Svenn Torgersen

8   Childhood Separation Anxiety Disorder and Adult-Onset Agoraphobia: Review of Evidence   128
Bruce A. Thyer

9   Expression and Treatment of Obsessive-Compulsive Disorder in Childhood, Adolescence, and Adulthood   148
Greta Francis and *Janet Borden*

10   Developmental Issues in Measurement of Anxiety   167
Deborah C. Beidel and *Melinda A. Stanley*

11   Conclusions and Future Directions   204
Cynthia G. Last

Index   215

Preface

Most books on anxiety disorders focus exclusively on either children or adults. In so doing, the flow and continuity (as well as discontinuity) between child and adult presentations of anxiety are lost. The purpose of this book, therefore, is to bridge the gap between what we know about childhood and adult anxiety disorders.

The book begins with a chapter by Wendy Silverman, which focuses on the *Diagnostic and Statistical Manual* (DSM) classification system for anxiety disorders, and how these disorders are applied to both children and adults. Next, Donna Moreau and Myrna Weissman review epidemiological data on anxiety symptoms in nonreferred children and adolescents. In chapter 4, developmental differences in the expression of anxiety disorders in children and adolescents is covered by Cyd Strauss. Ian Berg reviews the literature on school phobia in chapter 5. Next, family studies that deal with the relationship between childhood and adult anxiety disorders are summarized by Cynthia Last. In chapter 7, Svenn Torgersen reviews genetic data on the relationship between adult and childhood anxiety disorders. In the following chapter, the relationship between childhood separation anxiety disorder and adult-onset agoraphobia is covered by Bruce Thyer. In chapter 9, Greta Francis and Janet Borden address the similarities and differences in the expression and treatment of obsessive-compulsive disorder across the lifespan. In chapter 10, Deborah Beidel and Melinda Stanley discuss developmental considerations in the measurement of anxiety, comparing and contrasting techniques for use with children, adolescents, and adults. The book concluded with a "future directions" chapter, written by Cynthia Last.

Many people have contributed their time and effort to this book. First and foremost I thank the eminent contributors for sharing their expertise. Second, many thanks are in order for the technical assistance of Kim Sterner and Cynthia Park. Finally, my appreciation goes to Kathleen O'Malley, my editor at Springer, for her support and forebearance in the face of the inevitable delays.

Cynthia G. Last

Contributors

Deborah C. Beidel, PhD, is assistant professor of psychiatry at the University of Pittsburgh School of Medicine. She is director of the Childhood Text Anxiety Program, and codirector of the predoctoral psychology internship training program and a postdoctoral training program in clinical-research training for psychologists. Dr. Beidel received her PhD from the University of Pittsburgh in 1986, and completed her internship and postdoctoral training at Western Psychiatric Institute and Clinic, University of Pittsburgh School of Medicine. Her clinical-research interests, spanning both child and adult populations, primarily focus on the etiology and psychopathology of anxiety disorders.

Ian Berg, MD, is senior clinical lecturer at the University of Leeds and consultant in child and adolescent psychiatry, Leeds General Infirmary. He completed his psychiatric residency at the Royal Victoria Hospital and Children's Hospital in Montreal. He furthered his training at the Hospital for Sick Children in London and the Royal Hospital for Sick Children in Edinburgh. He is author of approximately 75 articles in various aspects of child psychiatry. He also is joint editor of two books, *Out of School* (1980) and *Off School in Court* (1988).

Janet Borden, PhD, is assistant professor in the Department of Psychology at the University of Louisville. She received her doctoral degree from Virginia Polytechnic Institute and State University in 1988. Dr. Borden completed a predoctoral internship and a postdoctoral research fellowship at Western Psychiatric Institute and Clinic at the University of Pittsburgh School of Medicine. Her clinical and research interests include anxiety and panic disorders in adults.

Greta Francis, PhD, is assistant professior in the Department of Psychiatry and Human Behavior at Brown University. She received her doctoral degree from Virginia Polytechnic Institute and State University in 1986. She completed a predoctoral internship and a postdoctoral research fellowship at Western Psychiatric Institute and Clinic at the University of Pittsburgh School of Medicine. Her clinical and research interests include anxiety and affective disorders in children and adolescents.

Donna L. Moreau, MD, is assistant clinical professor of psychiatry at Columbia University College of Physicians and Surgeons. She also is the director of the Child Anxiety and Depression Clinic at the Presbyterian Hospital in the City of New York. She specializes in the areas of anxiety and depression in children, and has published several articles in this area.

Wendy K. Silverman, PhD, is associate professor of psychology at Florida International University, the State University of Florida at Miami. She received her doctoral degree from Case Western Reserve University. Her research interests are in the child clinical area, focusing particularly on the assessment and treatment of childhood anxiety disorders.

Melinda A. Stanley, PhD, is assistant professor of Psychiatry at the University of Texas Medical School at Houston where she is director of the Anxiety Disorders Clinic and postdoctoral training program in clinical psychology. Dr. Stanley received her PhD in clinical psychology from Texas Tech University in 1987, and completed her internship and postdoctoral training at Western Psychiatric Institute and Clinic, University of Pittsburgh School of Medicine. Her primary clinical and research interests involve the psychopathology and treatment of the anxiety disorders.

Cyd C. Strauss, PhD, is clinical assistant professor in the Department of Psychiatry at the University of Florida. She also holds positions as clinical director of the Fear and Anxiety Clinic in the Department of Clinical and Health Psychology at the University of Florida and as codirector at the Center for Children and Families in Gainesville, Florida. She specializes in childhood anxiety disorders and has published numerous articles and chapters in this area.

Bruce A. Thyer, PhD, is professor of social work at the University of Georgia, and associate clinical professor with the Department of Psychiatry and Health Behavior at the Medical College of Georgia. Dr. Thyer received his PhD in social work and psychology from the University of Michigan in 1982.

Svenn Torgersen, PhD, is professor of clinical psychology and chairman of the Department of Psychology at the University of Oslo. He also is the research consultant at the Department of Psychiatry, University of Oslo. He received his doctoral degree from the University of Oslo. Dr. Torgersen's research area is genetic studies of anxiety, depression, and personality disorders.

Myrna M. Weissman, PhD, is professor of epidemiology in psychiatry, College of Physicians and Surgeons at Columbia University. She also is chief of the Department of Clinical-Genetic Epidemiology at New York State Psychiatric Institute. Dr. Weissman has authored or coauthored more than 300 scientific aritcles and chapters, and several books including *The Depressed Woman: A Study of Social Relationships* (1974), *Interpersonal Psychotherapy of Depression* (1984), and *Community Surveys of Psychiatric Disorders* (1986). Here professional discipline is psychiatric epidemiology, and her current research is on the epidemiology of psychiatric disorders in the community, and the treatment and guidelines of affective and anxiety disorders.

CHAPTER 1

Introduction

Cynthia G. Last

Historically, our understanding and classification of child psychopathology has been based on knowledge obtained from adult disorders. Children and adolescents were viewed as "miniature adults" (Ollendick & Hersen, 1983), and their assessment, diagnosis, and treatment "scaled down" from the existing adult literature.

This trend particularly is clear for the anxiety disorders. Commonly used assessment instruments are "child" versions of well-known adult anxiety instruments (e.g., State-Trait Anxiety Inventory—State-Trait Anxiety Inventory for Children; Taylor Manifest Anxiety Scale—Child Manifest Anxiety Scale, Fear Survey Schedule—Fear Survey Schedule for Children—see chapter 10). Although all three of these measures have been used extensively in clinical and research settings, their validity remains to be clearly established. In fact, recently Perrin and Last (1992) conducted a preliminary investigation of the discriminate validity of the three child anxiety measures by comparing clinic referred samples of boys with an anxiety disorder ($n = 105$) or attention deficit hyperactivity disorder (ADHD) ($n = 59$) with a community sample of never psychiatrically ill boys ($n = 49$). The results (see Table 1.1) indicate that the two patient groups did not differ on any of the three anxiety measures, suggesting that the measures may not be tapping the phenomenology of childhood anxiety per se, but rather may be assessing a more general or global index of psychopathology or distress.

The DSM diagnostic scheme uses the same diagnostic criteria for adults and children (e.g., panic disorder, obsessive-compulsive disorder, phobic disorder) or separate categories that are assumed to be related (phenomenologically or longitudinally) to adult counterparts (e.g., generalized anxiety disorder—overanxious disorder, panic disorder with agoraphobia; separation anxiety disorder, see chapter 2). For the most part, this classification system (for child anxiety) has not been based on empirically derived data but rather from clinical impressions. In fact, recent studies suggest that in many instances children do not express anxiety in ways that

1

TABLE 1.1 Mean Scores for FSSC-R, RCMAS, and STAIC-M

Measure	Group Anxiety (n = 105)	ADHD (n = 59)	Normal (n = 49)
FSSC-R			
Total fear score[a]	124.3	124.7	120.5
No. of intense fears[a]	11.3	12.3	8.3
Failure/criticism[a]	28.9	29.6	28.5
Fear of unknown[a]	27.4	26.2	24.9
Injury/small animals[a]	31.8	31.6	31.8
Fear of danger/death[a]	26.1	26.7	25.4
Medical fears[a]	10.2	9.9	9.8
RCMAS			
Total score	11.5*	11.3*	6.0
Physiological[a]	3.7*	4.1*	1.8
Worry/oversensitivity	4.9*	3.9*	2.8
Concentration anxiety	2.9*	3.2*	1.4
STAIC-State			
Total state anxiety[a]	33.1*	30.8	28.6
State—cognitive	12.1	12.4	11.6
State—somatic[a]	29.6*	27.5	25.6
STAIC-Trait			
Total trait anxiety	35.8*	34.1*	30.7
Trait—cognitive	15.1***	14.3	13.2
Trait—somatic[a]	27.5****	26.	24.3

Note. FSSC-R = Fear Survey Schedule for Children—Revised. RCMAS = Revised Child Manifest. Anxiety Scale. STAIC-M = State–Trait Anxiety Inventory for Children—Modified.
[a]Indicates age corrected mean.
*vs. Normal, $p < .0001$. **vs. Normal, $p < .015$. ***vs. Normal, $p < .0003$. ****vs. Normal, $p < .003$.

are similar to adults (see subsequent examples), and presumed relationships between "child" and "adult" anxiety disorders have not been supported by recent family and follow-up studies (Last, Hersen, Kazdin, Orvaschel, & Perrin, 1991; Last, Hersen, Kazdin, & Perrin, 1992).

Therapeutic interventions also, for the most part, have been adapted from research studies conducted with adult anxiety-disordered patients (e.g., see chapter 9). Pharmacological and behavioral interventions that have been found useful for treating adult anxiety-disordered patients have been applied clinically to children on a wide-scale basis. Few controlled empirical investigations of treatment efficacy, however, have been published for clinically referred anxious children. Thus, whether these adult-derived interventions similarly are effective for children and adolescents remains unanswered.

Whether children and adolescents manifest anxiety in ways that are similar to adults is an empirical question. Unfortunately, in this instance, we have put "the horse before the cart," by measuring, classifying, and treating anxiety in youngsters using constructs derived from adults.

The developmental or longitudinal approach to understanding psychopathology, including the anxiety disorders, does not presume constancy or similarities in the presentation of mental disorders throughout the lifespan. Rather, as individuals continue to grow and change (physically, socially, and cognitively), the manifestations of psychopathology are expected to vary.

Some examples from recent research on childhood anxiety disorders may prove helpful in further clarifying this concept.

PANIC DISORDER

It frequently has been reported that spontaneous panic attacks are rarely observed in prepubertal children (Alessi, Robbins, & Dilsaver, 1987; Last & Strauss, 1989; Macaulay & Kleinknecht, 1989; Von Korff, Eaton, & Keyl, 1985). Nelles and Barlow (1988) have proposed that the young child cognitively is incapable of identifying the physical sensations of panic as stemming from an internal source; rather, children tend to label external situations or events as causing the fear reaction.

GENERALIZED ANXIETY DISORDER

Research on somatic complaints in anxiety-disordered children suggest that stomachaches and headaches are the two most frequently offered symptoms (Last, 1991). Recent data suggest that the numerous specific physical complaints currently required for a DSM-III-R diagnosis of generalized anxiety disorder are almost never met by young children and those in early adolescence (Last, Perrin, Hersen, & Kazdin, 1991). More specifically, in a clinically referred sample of 188 anxiety-disordered children and adolescents, not one met criteria for the diagnosis (see Table 1.2). Similar findings have been observed in other clinic samples of anxiety-disordered youngsters (Kendall, personal communication; Silverman, personal communication).

TABLE 1.2 Frequency of Specific DSM-III-R Anxiety Disorders

DSM-III-R diagnosis	Primary at intake[a]		Lifetime[b]	
	n	%	n	%
Separation anxiety disorder	51	27.1	84	44.7
Simple phobia	37	19.7	80	42.6
Social phobia	28	14.9	61	32.4
Overanxious disorder	25	13.3	51	27.1
Panic disorder	18	9.6	24	12.8
Obsessive-compulsive disorder	13	6.9	28	14.9
Posttraumatic stress disorder	6	3.2	7	3.7
Avoidant disorder	5	2.7	20	10.6
Generalized anxiety disorder	0	0.0	0	0.0

[a]Five children received primary anxiety disorder diagnoses that are not addressed here: anxiety disorder not otherwise specified ($n = 3$), agoraphobia without a history of panic disorder ($n = 1$), and adjustment disorder with anxious mood ($n = 1$). [b]The number of diagnoses exceed the number of children (188) because most of the youngsters had a lifetime history of multiple anxiety disorders.

OVERANXIOUS DISORDER

Although worrying about future events appears to be the hallmark of the disorder in both children and adolescents, worrying about past events (another criterion of the disorder) is frequently seen among adolescents but not young children (Strauss, Lease, Last, & Francis, 1988). It is speculated that the young child cognitively is less able to deal with the concept of "past" as opposed to "future" (see chapter 4).

PHOBIC DISORDERS

The issue of developmental appropriateness is of central importance when assessing possible phobias in children and adolescents, because research indicates that certain fears are age appropriate (i.e., "normal") at different developmental stages (Ollendick, Matson, & Helsel, 1985). For instance, fear of the dark might be considered nonclinically significant in a 4-year-old child, but developmentally inappropriate (and clinically significant) in a 13-year-old (see chapters 3 and 4).

In addition to addressing the phenomenological differences between child, adolescent, and adult presentations of disorders, the lifespan approach concerns itself with "predictive links" between the different developmental stages. For example, does childhood separation anxiety increase the risk for adult-onset agoraphobia (see chapter 8)? Does adolescent overanxious disorder predict adult generalized anxiety disorder? What is the lifetime risk for depressive disorder in individuals with a childhood history of anxiety disorder?

Prospective, longitudinal studies are the most empirically rigorous means for assessing "predictive links" (i.e., the course and outcome of the anxiety disorders). Unfortunately, such studies tend to be costly and time-consuming, and, thus, rarely done. Last et al., (1992) recently have completed a blind, controlled, follow-up study of clinically referred anxiety-disordered children. Children were reassessed every 12 months for 3 to 5 years to determine clinical course and prognosis (outcome) as the children entered adolescence and young adulthood (the sample at study intake was aged 5 to 17 years). The investigators particularly were interested in determining whether the youngsters: (a) met DSM-III-R diagnostic criteria for any other psychiatric disorder at follow-up (e.g. major depression) and (b) showed similar outcomes at follow-up (e.g., completely well, no change, worse, etc.).

Preliminary analyses from the preceding investigation suggest that most of the anxiety-disordered youngsters were free from their initial anxiety disorders at follow-up. In addition, findings do not support the notion that anxiety-disordered children are at increased risk for depressive disorders—the risk was equally low among the anxiety-disordered probands, a psychopathological control group of ADHD children, and a "normal" control group of never psychiatrically ill children. Although a small percentage of the anxiety-disordered probands developed a new anxiety disorder during each year of the follow-up period, this rate does not differ significantly from that obtained for the behavior-disordered (ADHD) control group, possibly suggesting that the development of anxiety disorders is related to psychopathology per se rather than a history of anxiety disorder in particular.

Finally, the developmental perspective concerns itself with the intergenerational expression of similar disorders, either through environmental or genetic (hereditary) modes of transmission (see chapters 6 and 7). As discussed in detail in chapter 6, a recent family study of the relatives of anxiety-disordered children indicate an increased rate of anxiety disorders compared with the relatives of psychopathological (ADHD) and "normal" controls (Last, Hersen, Kazdin, Orvaschel, & Perrin, 1991). Also of interest is the fact that certain anxiety disorder subtypes (e.g., panic disorder, obsessive-compulsive disorder) appeared to have a specific relationship for parents and their children. These specific relationships have been supported further by findings from genetic research (see chapter 7).

In this book, we explore all three of these developmental issues—phenomenological differences/similarities among children, adolescents, and adults (chapters 2, 3, 4, 9, and 10); predictive links between developmental stages (chapters 5 and 8); and intergenerational expression of disorder (chapters 6 and 7)—in relationship to the anxiety disorders. In that anxiety disorders have received enormous attention in recent years, it is fitting that they, as have other disorders, should benefit from a "lifespan" examination or orientation.

REFERENCES

Alessi, D. E., Robbins, D. R., & Dilsaver, S. C. (1987). Panic and depressive disorders among psychiatrically hospitalized adolescents. *Psychiatric Research, 20,* 275–283.

Last, C. G. (1991). Somatic complaints in anxiety disordered children. *Journal of Anxiety Disorders, 5,* 125–138.

Last, C. G., Hersen, M., Kazdin, A. E., Orvaschel, H., & Perrin, S. (1991). Anxiety disorders in children and their families. *Archives of General Psychiatry, 48,* 928–934.

Last, C. G., Hersen, M., Kazdin, A. E., & Perrin, S. (1992). *Prospective study of anxiety disordered children.* Unpublished manuscript.

Last, C. G., Perrin, S., Hersen, M., & Kazdin, A. E. (1991). *DSM-III anxiety disorders in children: Sociodemographic and clinical characteristics.* Unpublished manuscript.

Last, C. G., & Strauss, C. C. (1989). Panic disorder in children and adolescents. *Journal of Anxiety Disorders, 3,* 87–95.

Macaulay, J. L., & Kleinknecht, R. A. (1989). Panic and panic attacks in adolescents. *Journal of Anxiety Disorders, 3,* 221–241.

Nelles, W. B., & Barlow, D. A. (1988). Do children panic? *Clinical Psychology Review, 8,* 359–372.

Ollendick, T. H., & Hersen, M. (1983). A historical overview of child psychopathology. In T. H. Ollendick and M. Hersen (Eds.), *Handbook of child psychopathology* (pp. 3–11). New York: Plenum.

Ollendick, T. H., Matson, J. L. & Helsel, W. J. (1985). Fears in children and adolescents: Normative data. *Behaviour Research and Therapy, 4,* 465–467.

Perrin, S., & Last, C. G. (1992). *Do childhood anxiety measures measure anxiety?* Unpublished manuscript.

Strauss, C. C., Lease, C. A., Last, C. G., & Francis, G. (1988). Overanxious disorder: An examination of developmental differences. *Journal of Abnormal Child Psychology, 4,* 433–443.

Von Korff, M. R., Eaton, W. W., & Keyl, P. M. (1985). The epidemiology of panic attacks and panic disorder. *American Journal of Epidemiology, 122,* 970–981.

CHAPTER 2

DSM and Classification of Anxiety Disorders in Children and Adults

Wendy K. Silverman

Classification refers to the process of forming groups from a large set of entities. In psychopathology, a classification system is an organizing system that allows clinicians to better understand the people who seek help from them (Blashfield, 1984). As discussed by Blashfield and Draguns (1976), a classification system has the following purposes: (a) it provides the language or agreed set of terms necessary for communication among researchers and clinicians; (b) it serves as a basis for information retrieval; (c) it provides descriptive information about the units being studied; (d) it provides a basis for making predictions (e.g., concerning etiology, prognosis, and response to treatment in the case of psychopathology); and (e) it provides the basic concepts required for theory formulation.

Although several classification systems exist for classifying psychopathology (e.g., International Classification of Diseases (ICD) of the World Health Organization), the system that is most widely used in America and that has attracted the most research attention is the American Psychiatric Association's DSM (American Psychiatric Association Committee on Nomenclature and Statistics, 1952; 1968, 1983, 1987). It is the latest edition of DSM, DSM-III-R, and the way in which it classifies childhood and adult anxiety disorders, that is the focus of this chapter.

We begin with a brief overview of DSM-III-R. This is followed by an evaluation of the DSM-III-R childhood and adult anxiety disorder subcategories, focusing particularly on their reliability and validity. Included in this section is a discussion of the major descriptive differences (e.g., demographic and psychometric variables, and patterns of comorbidity) that have been found among the various disorders. We also briefly describe other approaches to assessing diagnostic validity: family and follow-up studies. The complex nature of the relationship frequently observed between anxiety and depression is discussed next. We conclude the chapter with a brief discussion of alternative approaches to the classification of psychopathology, in general, and the anxiety disorders, in particular.

DSM-III-R

In contrast to DSM-II, DSM-III possessed several unique features that were retained in its revision, DSM-III-R. In short, DSM-III and DSM-III-R (a) possessed specific diagnostic criteria; (b) adopted a multiaxial approach to patient evaluation; (c) included expanded descriptive information about the categories; and (d) reorganized and increased the number of diagnostic categories. Each of these features is briefly discussed subsequently. (The reader is referred to Blashfield, 1984; Russell, Cantwell, Mattison, & Will, 1979; Rutter & Shaffer, 1980; Spitzer, Williams, & Skodol, 1979 for detailed discussions of these features.)

Diagnostic Criteria

A major difference between DSM-III/III-R and DSM-II is the use of diagnostic criteria. In contrast to DSM-II, DSM-III/III-R precisely specify to the clinician how many symptoms an individual must exhibit for him or her to receive that diagnosis. As indicated by Spitzer et al. (1979), diagnostic criteria help to increase reliability among clinicians by decreasing three major sources of variance: (a) information variance (i.e., the differences among clinicians in the information that they elicit from clients); (b) observation-interpretation variance (i.e., the differences among clinicians in what observations they make about a client and how these observations are interpreted); and (c) criterion variance (i.e., the different definitions that clinicians may associate with a diagnosiss). Despite these positive aspects of diagnostic criteria, the specific criteria contained in DSM-III were criticized for lacking empirical support for them. Indeed, a major rationale for revising DSM-III was to "fine-tune" the criteria to improve their sensitivity and specificity (DSM-III-R, pp. xx).

Multiaxial Approach

A complete diagnosis according to DSM-III/III-R involves evaluating the client along five dimensions or axes: Axis I—clinical syndrome; Axis II—personality disorder (adults) or developmental disorder (children); Axis III—medical disorder; Axis IV—severity of psychosocial stressor; and Axis V—highest level of adaptive functioning.

A multiaxial system provides more complete information about clients than a single-category classification system. Rutter, Shaffer, and Shepherd

(1975), in a test of a multiaxial system sponsored by the World Health Organization, reported that psychiatrists using the system found that it was easy to apply, that it made classification more uniform, and that it corresponded more closely to their usual clinical approach. Nevertheless, additional research on DSM's multiaxial system is necessary, especially regarding measurement issues associated with the various axes (e.g., reliability, validity, etc.).

Descriptive Information About Categories

Compared with DSM-II, there is a great deal more information presented in DSM-III and DSM-III-R about the characteristics of each disorder. "New" information found in DSM-III/III-R include "associated features," "age at onset," "course," "impairment," "complications," "prevalence," "sex ratio," and "differential diagnosis." Although this additional information provides a more comprehensive picture of the disorder, the empirical basis for some of the information provided is not always clear.

Diagnostic Categories

DSM-II versus DSM-III

There is a substantial increase in the number of diagnostic categories included in DSM-III relative to DSM-II. For example, DSM-II divided behavior disorders of childhood and adolescence into 7 categories, whereas DSM-III increased the number of specific childhood categories to 45. This increase in the number of childhood categories reflects the growing recognition that the historical, and common view, of extrapolating diagnostic constructs directly from adults to children is no longer adequate. Although, as Last (1987; see chapter 1) points out, this tradition of applying nosological constructs derived from adults to children is continued in DSM-III (and DSM-III-R) in two ways: (a) the same criteria are used for adults and children (e.g., phobic disorders, obsessive-compulsive disorder, posttraumatic stress disorder) and (b) the childhood diagnostic categories often are functionally equivalent to categories used for adults (e.g., separation anxiety disorder—agoraphobia, overanxious disorder—generalized anxiety disorder). Unfortunately, the advantage of the above two approaches, with respect to the anxiety disorders, is still not totally clear, and warrants continued investigation.

The major child and adult anxiety disorder categories present in each version of DSM appear in Table 2.1. Observation of this table reveals that although only one specific childhood anxiety category existed in DSM-II (i.e., "overanxious reaction"), DSM-III contained a new broad category

TABLE 2.1 Classification of Childhood and Adult Anxiety Disorders in DSM-II, DSM-III, and DSM-III-R

DSM-II	DSM-III	DSM-III-R
Overanxious reaction	Anxiety disorders of childhood and adolescence	Anxiety disorders of childhood and adolescence
	Separation anxiety disorder	Separation anxiety disorder
	Overanxious disorder	Overanxious disorder
	Avoidant disorder	Avoidant disorder
Phobic neurosis	Phobic disorders	Phobic disorders
	Agoraphobia with panic attacks	Agoraphobia without history of panic disorder
	Agoraphobia without panic attacks	
	Social phobia	Social phobia
	Simple phobia	Simple phobia
Anxiety neurosis	Anxiety states	Anxiety states
	Panic disorders	Panic disorder with agoraphobia
	Generalized anxiety disorder	Panic disorder without agoraphobia
Obsessive-compulsive neurosis	Obsessive-compulsive disorder	Obsessive-compulsive disorder
	Posttraumatic stress disorder	Posttraumataic stress disorder
	Acute chronic or delayed	Acute chronic or delayed
	Atypical anxiety disorder	Anxiety disorder not otherwise specified

called "anxiety disorders of childhood and adolescence," comprised of three subcategories: "separation anxiety disorder," "overanxious disorder," and "avoidant disorder." The establishment of this new category and subcategories (as well as many of the other categories—not just the anxiety categories) has been criticized for being overrefined, untested, and excessive in number. Later, we explore the extent to which this criticism has credence.

An additional major way in which DSM-III differs from its predecessor, DSM-II, is in the omission of the term "neurosis." There are several reasons for this omission. First, new etiological theories for anxiety disorders (see Barlow [1998] and Marks [1987] for excellent discussions of these theories) varied from previous theoretical conceptions underlying the term *neurosis.* Second, the neurosis was thought to be too vague and broad, thereby hindering research in classification.

In DSM-III only those "neurotic" disorders where anxiety is experienced directly (rather than being maintained unconsciously as in DSM-II) were classified in the new category "anxiety disorders." As mentioned earlier, this new category was comprised of more specific and narrower subcategories. For example, "phobic disorders," formerly classified broadly as "phobic neuroses" in DSM-II, was broken down further in DSM-III as "agoraphobia with panic attacks," "agoraphobia without panic attacks," "social phobia," and "simple phobia." Two new categories were also added to DSM-III: "panic disorder" and "posttraumatic stress disorder."

DSM-III versus DSM-III-R

In general, most of the changes made in the childhood and adult anxiety disorder categories from DSM-III to DSM-III-R dealt with clarifying some of the diagnostic criteria. There are a few exceptions, however. Substantial changes were made in DSM-III-R in the classification of panic disorders, agoraphobia with panic attacks, and generalized anxiety disorder. Specifically, agoraphobia with panic attacks was subsumed under panic disorder. Generalized anxiety disorder (GAD), a residual category in DSM-III, diagnosed only when no other anxiety disorders were identified, was specified in a great deal more detail in DSM-III-R. The result is that GAD is more likely to be identified, in addition to the other anxiety disorders, when using DSM-III-R than when using DSM-III (Barlow, Blanchard, Vermilyea, Vermilyea, & DiNardo, 1986).

Finally, the exclusionary rules of DSM-III were eliminated in the revision. That is, in DSM-III, a diagnosis of anxiety disorder could have been excluded in the presence of several other specific disorders or classes of disorders. For example, affective disorders occupied a higher position than anxiety disorders, so a diagnosis of major depression excluded a diagnosis of panic disorder if, in the clinician's judgment, the panic disorder was "due to" the major depression. As noted earlier, exclusionary rules also existed within the anxiety disorders. For instance, a diagnosis of GAD was automatically excluded by the presence of another anxiety disorder, such as panic disorder (Barlow, 1988).

These exclusionary rules were removed from DSM-III-R for several reasons. First, there was little empirical support for the assumptions underlying the hierarchies (DiNardo & Barlow, in press). Boyd et al. (1984) reported that when DSM-III diagnoses were assigned without exclusionary restrictions, the presence of any disorder increased the probability of the presence of other disorders that would normally be excluded. Sturt (1981), using data from the Present State Examination, showed that patients with infrequently occurring symptoms or syndromes exhibit a high number of other symptoms or syndromes. Sturt interpreted these results as evidence of a general tendency for the presence of any given symptom to be associated with the presence of several other symptoms.

A second reason for removing the exclusionary rules was that it became apparent that they resulted in a loss of potentially important information relevant to understanding relationships among the disorders and in identifying dimensions of pathology that underlie the categories (DiNardo & Barlow, in press). The presence of additional syndromes may differentiate homogeneous subgroups within a major diagnostic category that have different patterns of familial aggregation, course, or treatment responsiveness. In light of the preceding, DSM-III-R eliminated many automatic exclusions, and replaced others with decisions rules that are based on a case-by-case consideration of the relationship among the various symptom clusters in a patient (DiNardo & Barlow, in press).

RELIABILITY

A classification system is not very useful if it cannot be used in a reliable manner. Regarding a diagnostic system such as DSM-III-R, reliability implies that clinicians agree on diagnoses assigned to a particular patient.

As mentioned earlier, the use of diagnostic criteria helps to decrease information, interpretation, and criterion variance. The increased specificity and complexity of diagnostic criteria, however, also make it more important to use standardized interview protocols. Interview protocols ensure that the wide range of symptomatology present in each discrete category are in fact assessed and that each clinician inquires about the symptomatology in a consistent fashion.

The need to develop structured interview protocols specific to the anxiety disorders became apparent as evidence accumulated that the existing interview schedules for both children and adults (e.g., the SADS, the Diagnostic Interview Schedule [DIS], the K-SADS, the DISC, the CAS, etc.) did not provide sufficient detail for the differential diagnosis of anxiety disorders. Hence, reliably diagnosing the anxiety disorders using these interview schedules was problematic. For example, regarding the adult categories, Robins, Helzer, Croughan, and Ratcliff (1981) reported the following Kappa values for the anxiety disorders, based on the DIS: agoraphobia, .67; simple phobia, .47; obsessive-compulsive disorder, .60; and panic disorder, .56. In this study, the Kappa values reflected any instance in which the same diagnosis was derived from the same two interviews (rather than instances of an exact match between primary diagnoses).

The Kappa coefficients obtained for the child anxiety disorder categories using different structured interviews are found in Table 2.2. With the

TABLE 2.2 Kappa Coefficients Obtained for the Childhood Anxiety Disorders Using Structured Interviews

Childhood Disorders	Kappa
DSM-III field trials[a]	
Phase I ($n = 71$)	.25
Phase II ($n = 55$)	.44
Schedule for Affective Disorders and Schizophrenia[b] ($n = 95$)	.47
Diagnostic Interview Schedule for Children[c] ($n = 95$)	.27 to .39
Schedule for Affective Disorders and Schizophrenia for School Age Children[d] ($n = 52$)	.24
Interview Schedule for Children[e] ($n = 65$)	.84
Child Assessment Schedule[f] ($n = 30$)	
Child Version	.37
Parent Version	.51

Note. Adapted from [a]Williams & Spitzer (1980). [b]Strober, Green, & Carlson (1981). [c]Costello, Edelbrock, Kalas, Kessler, & Klaric (1984). [d]Chambers, Puig-Antich, Hirsch, Paez, Ambrosini, Tabrizi, & Davies (1985). [e]Last (1987). [f]Hodges, McKnew, Burbach, & Ruebuck (1987).

exception of the ISC (Last, 1987), all of these Kappa coefficients are in the unacceptable range (Chambers et al., 1985; Costello, Edelbrock, Dulcan, Kalas, & Klaric, 1984).

Although the research on the ISC is encouraging, the ISC is symptom oriented rather than syndrome oriented, thereby restricting its diagnostic utility. In addition, as noted by Last (1987), methodological factors may have inflated the Kappas found in their study using the ISC (e.g., the same two interviewers assessed all of the subjects; all children were suspected of having an anxiety problem, thereby leading to possible interviewer bias).

Although not included in Table 2.2 (because Kappas were not reported), but surely worthy of mention here, is the Children's Anxiety Evaluation Form (CAEF), developed by Hoehn-Saric, Maisami, and Wiegand (1987). Based on history, signs, and symptoms obtained through semistructured interviews, the CAEF was designed to measure anxiety in youngsters. Preliminary research with 63 child and adolescent inpatients suggested that the CAEF may be useful in differentiating patients independently diagnosed on discharge as having anxiety disorders from those who were given diagnoses as oppositional disorder, nonaggressive conduct disorders, aggressive conduct disorders, and dysthymic disorders. Although promising, the CAEF is also not without its shortcomings. First, the CAEF is based on interview data obtained from the child only—data from parents are not obtained. Second, like the ISC, the CAEF is also symptom oriented, consisting of the possible anxiety-related symptoms as enumerated in the Hamilton Anxiety Scale (Hamilton, 1960) rather than syn-drome oriented.

In light of the difficulties noted previously with these structured in-terviews, researchers working at the Center for Stress and Anxiety Dis-order—SUNY Albany, including this author, have focused their energies for several years on developing detailed structured interviews specifically for the anxiety disorders. This has resulted in the Anxiety Disorders Interview Schedule (ADIS; DiNardo, O'Brien, Barlow, Waddell, & Blanchard, 1983) and the Anxiety Disorders Interview Schedule for Children—Child and Parent versions—(ADIS-C and ADIS-P; Silverman & Nelles, 1988). A brief overview of these interview schedules, and the reliability studies that have been conducted on them, are presented subsequently.

ADIS

Description

The ADIS was designed to improve differential diagnosis among the DSM-III (and now the ADIS-R for DSM-III-R) anxiety disorder categories. The ADIS also obtains information regarding history of the problem, situational and cognitive factors influencing anxiety, and detailed symptom ratings to provide a data base for investigation of the clinical characteristics of the categories. Also embedded in the interview are the Hamilton Anxiety Scale and the Hamilton Depression Scale.

Reliability Studies

Individuals referred to the Anxiety Disorders Clinic at the Center for Stress and Anxiety Disorders were administered the ADIS at a different time by a different and independent interviewer, who was blind to the results of the first interviewer. Diagnostic agreement was defined as an exact match of the two clinicians' primary diagnosis, using DSM-III criteria. Table 2.3 presents the Kappa coefficients calculated on the first 125 consecutive admissions, with the exception of posttraumatic stress disorder, (PTSD) which had too small a N to compute Kappa.

Examination of Table 2.3 indicates that the Kappas for social phobia, agoraphobia, and obsessive-compulsive disorder were high. Panic disorder and GAD are relatively lower Kappas, not surprising given that there are fewer behavioral referents for these two disorders. Further, GAD was treated in this study as a residual diagnosis, to be diagnosed only when no other anxiety disorders are identified. Preliminary data, in which GAD is not treated as a residual diagnosis, as specified in DSM-III-R, are more encouraging (Barlow, 1988).

The difficulty in diagnosing simple phobia had to do with the fact that

TABLE 2.3 Kappa Coefficients for Specific Diagnostic Categories for ADIS After 125 Consecutive Admissions

Diagnosis	N	Kappa
Agoraphobia with panic	41	.85
Social phobia	19	.91
Simple phobia	7	.56
Panic disorder	17	.65
Generalized anxiety disorder	12	.57
Obsessive-compulsive disorder	6	.83

Note. From Barlow, D. H. (1987). The classification of anxiety disorders. In G. L. Tischler (Ed.), *Diagnoses and classification in psychiatry: A critical appraisal of DSM-III* (pp. 223–242). New York: Cambridge University Press. Reprinted by permission.

most individuals who present with simple phobia at the clinic display other anxiety disorders as well (e.g., simple phobia *and* agoraphobia). This made the clinical weighting of the primary and secondary disorders problematic (i.e., what should be primary—simple phobia or agoraphobia?). Disagreements between clinicians on this issue resulted in lower Kappa values (Barlow, 1988).

The reliability of PTSD was recently examined by Blanchard, Gerardi, Kolb and Barlow (1986). In this study, diagnoses determined by an ADIS interview were compared against a criterion diagnosis. A Kappa of .86 was obtained using this procedure.

ADIS-C and ADIS-P

Description

Similar to the ADIS, the ADIS-C and ADIS-P were developed to permit differential diagnosis among the DSM-III/III-R childhood anxiety disorder categories in youngsters 6 to 18 years of age. The interviews also permit the clinician to rule out alternative diagnoses, such as affective disorders, and to provide quantifiable data concerning anxiety symptomatology, etiology, course, and a functional analysis of the disorder. Because any of the adult anxiety categories (e.g., simple phobia) may also be used, when appropriate with children, questions regarding these categories were adopted (and modified) from questions contained in the ADIS. Questions about the childhood disorders were either developed by this author or were adapted from the Diagnostic Interview for Children and Adolescents (DICA; Herjanic & Campbell, 1977).

Although there is considerable overlap between the parent and child schedules, the parent schedule is more detailed in its questions about the history of the problem and about consequences that occur to the child after he or she displays the problem behavior (e.g., behavioral avoidance). There is also more detailed coverage of other childhood disorders, such as conduct disorder, sleep terror disorder, and attention deficit disorder, on the parent version than on the child version. The child version, conversely, is more detailed about symptomatology and phenomenology, and is simpler than the parent version in its form and content.

Reliability Studies

The first study to examine the reliability to the ADIS-C and ADIS-P was conducted on 51 children and adolescents (27 girls, 24 boys) and their mothers (Silverman & Nelles, in press). Forty-one percent of the sample were referred to the Child and Adolescent Fear and Anxiety Treatment Program within the Center for Stress and Anxiety Disorders and 59% of the sample were the offspring of parents with anxiety disorders being seen at the center. The child was interviewed first, followed by the parent interview.

Three separate (and independent) diagnoses were determined for three conditions: (a) the child inverview only; (b) the parent interview only; and (c) a composite of the child and parent interviews. Subjective judgment was employed to derive the composite diagnosis. (The reader is referred to Silverman & Nelles [in press] for the guidelines used to derive the composite diagnosis.)

Correlation coefficients were computed for each of the pairs of raters for all diagnostic subcategories that appear on the parent and child ADISs. The correlations for the child and parent interviews were .98 and .93, respectively, which reflect a very high reliability for total pathology. Interrater agreement was also very high for the specific anxiety disorder categories for both the child and parent schedules.

We also examined the overall measure of agreement between clinicians by calculating the Kappa for exact agreements between clinicians on specific categories. For the ADIS-C, the overall Kappa coefficient was .84, .83 for the ADIS-P, and .78 for the composite diagnosis. These Kappa coefficients indicate a high level of agreement for specific diagnostic categories.

Because the primary objective of the ADIS-C was to identify children with anxiety disorders, we examined how reliably clinicians could diagnose anxiety disorders versus all other diagnostic categories combined. With the ADIS-C, the Kappa agreement for classifying children as having either an "anxiety disorder" or "other" was .85; 1.0 with the ADIS-P, and .46 with both interview schedules combined.

Because of our small N's, we could compute Kappas for only the specific diagnoses of simple phobia and overanxious disorder. These were both in the moderate to high range (K = .64 and .54, respectively). The only exception to this was overanxious disorder, which had a low Kappa coefficient. Interestingly DiNardo et al. (1983) reported that the most difficult diagnosis to make with the ADIS was GAD. To explain these findings, DiNardo et al. speculated that because patients with specific phobias, agoraphobia, panic disorder, and so on, often report chronically high levels of anxiety, it is difficult to determine whether the chronic anxiety experienced by these patients is not merely anticipatory anxiety. As it is difficult to make this distinction between chronic versus anticipatory anxiety, errors are often made in the differential diagnoses of GAD and other anxiety disorders. Similarly, the children we see with anxiety problems, such as simple phobia, separation anxiety, and so on, also report high levels of anxiety; we too find it difficult to determine whether this anxiety is chronic or anticipatory in nature. Further research on examining the criteria for making differential diagnoses between overanxious disorder and other anxiety disorders would help clarify this issue.

We also have some preliminary data examining the test-retest reliability of the ADIS-C and ADIS-P. In this reliability study, the child and parent are administered each of the respective versions of the interview schedule (i.e., the ADIS-C and ADIS-P) on two separate (and independent) occasions, 10 days to 2 weeks apart by two different interviewers. Based on a N of 15 children, 7 of the children received the same primary diagnosis based on the child interview; 12 received the same primary diagnoses based on the parent interview; and 11 received the same primary diagnoses based on the composite (i.e., combining the parent and child data). Despite our rather small N's, preliminary correlation coeficients (based on correlating the parent and child interview responses, obtained at time 1 with their responses obtained at time 2), indicate that most of these correlations were significant, with r's ranging from .44 ($p < .10$) to 1.00 ($p < .01$). Interestingly, both simple phobia and overanxious disorder had poor test-retest reliabilities, based on both the child and parent ADISs. This may reflect the point raised earlier regarding the difficulty in distinguishing between chronic versus anticipatory anxiety. As we accumulate a larger N, we hope to obtain a better picture of the test-retest reliability of parent and child responses to the ADIS-C and ADIS-P, respectively, as well as a determination of how this reliability may vary as a function of the diagnostic category and the child's age and gender.

Overall, the results of our reliability studies are encouraging and indicate that when childhood anxiety disorders are diagnosed with a syndrome-oriented interview protocol that is detailed in its coverage of anxiety disorders, such as the ADIS-C and ADIS-P, then these disorders can be diagnosed reliably.

VALIDITY

With the development of the child and adult ADISs, research on the validity of the anxiety disorders is likely to proliferate. In general, studies (many of which were conducted before the development of the ADIS) tend to support the construct validity of the adult categories (i.e., whether the various features that describe a disorder form a unified whole) (Barlow, 1988). (The reader is referred to Barlow [1988] for a summary of this literature.) Unfortunately, there is a paucity of research examining the construct validity of the childhood categories.

Our focus in this section is on the discriminant validity (i.e., the distinctiveness of each disorder). We present evidence that will help shed light on the question: Do differences exist among the various anxiety disorders that support the distinctiveness of each disorder? To examine this question, we present some of the major descriptive differences (e.g., demographic and psychometric variables, and patterns of comorbidity) that have been found among the various disorders. Following this, we note two other approaches to assess the validity of diagnostic categories: family and follow-up studies.

Descriptive Differences Found Among Adult Anxiety Disorders

In our discussion of descriptive differences found among the adult anxiety disorders, we will refer to the data displayed in Table 2.4.

Age of Onset

Table 2.4 indicates that several of the adult anxiety disorders differ in their age of onset. The most common simple phobias—animal and blood—usually start in early childhood, at about age 6. The age of onset of other simple phobias vary widely from early childhood to old age (Marks, 1987). Social phobias usually develop after puberty, with a peak in late adolescence. The anxiety states, specifically, panic disorder and GAD, have a later onset, usually in the mid-20s to early 30s. Obsessive–compulsive disorder (OCD) begins somewhat earlier, usually at about age 22.

Treatment Age

The age range for when adults with anxiety disorders who present for treatment is between 27 (for social phobias) to 44 (for GAD), with most seeking treatment in their 30s.

TABLE 2.4 Summary of Descriptive and Psychometric Data for Adult Anxiety Disorders

	Simple phobias	Social phobias	Panic disorders	AG	GAD	OCD
Age of onset	Childhood (animal and blood) to old age (others)	Late adolescence	Mid-20s to early 50's	24	Mid-20s to early 30s	22
Age when treated	30	27	36	32	43	34
Percent female	76	60	80	75	64	60
SES	Not associated with SES	Higher SES	Lower SES	Lower SES		Higher SES
Hamilton Anxiety	14.1	17.8	18.9	20.7	20.0	20.0
Hamilton Depression	9.3	15.3	15.5	16.6	15.8	19.3
STAIC						
State	33.18	51.57	46.03	48.77	58.20	49.75
Trait	35.18	57.64	48.80	50.62	55.67	51.58
BDI	7.7	15.09	14.48	15.85	17.27	17.00
CSAQS						
Cognitive	15.20	21.46	19.32	22.50	20.60	21.75
Somatic	12.00	20.62	20.35	20.12	19.73	16.67
PSSS	16.90	37.85	60.13	52.12	58.67	54.83
FQ						
Agoraphobia	7.07	5.20	7.43	21.75	4.75	11.00
Social	7.43	19.95	12.03	16.47	11.25	14.71

Note. Data are compiled from several studies. Main sources: Barlow (1988); DiNardo & Barlow (in press); Marks (1987).

Gender

Several of the anxiety disorders are clearly more prevalent in women than in men. This is true for simple phobias, especially animal phobias, agoraphobia, and panic disorders, particularly those patients with severe avoidance. The prevalences of social phobias, OCD, and GAD are almost equally distributed between the sexes.

Socioeconomic Status (SES)

The various anxiety disorders observed among adults appear to differ in their distribution among the social classes. For example, although simple phobias in adults are not associated with specific social classes, social phobias are more prevalent in higher social classes. Panic disorder with agoraphobia, conversely, is more prevalent among individuals of lower SES. Studies indicate that the social class of OCDs vary, although several suggest that OCDs are of above-average social class (Rachman & Hodgson, 1980; Yaryura-Tobias & Neziroglu, 1983). Because these findings are from hospital (not community) samples, however, they may reflect features of individuals who seek treatment, in general, rather than OCDs, specifically. Future studies using more careful sampling procedures can clarify this issue.

Psychometric Variables

Table 2.4 reveals several interesting differences among adult anxiety disorder patients in their scores on various psychometric instruments. Differences have been found in severity of anxiety and depression, as measured on the Hamilton Scales. In general, the Hamilton scales indicate that simple and social phobias are associated with the lowest levels of anxious and depressive symptomatology. Agoraphobia is associated with higher levels of anxiety than the other anxiety disorders; OCD is associated with higher levels of depression (DiNardo & Barlow, in press).

Table 2.4 also displays the scores among the different anxiety disorder patients on the State Trait Anxiety Inventory (STAI; Spielberger, Gorsuch, & Lushene, 1970), the Fear Questionnaire (FQ; Marks & Mathews, 1978), the Cognitive-Somatic Anxiety Questionnaires (CSAQS; Schwartz, Davidson, & Goleman, 1978), the Beck Depression Inventory (BDI; Beck, Ward, Mendelson, Mock, & Erbaugh, 1961), and the Psychosomatic Symptom Survey (PSSS; Cox, Freundlich, & Meyer, 1975). Table 2.4 reveals that simple phobia is associated with the lowest scores on measures of state anxiety, trait anxiety, and depression. No other differences among the groups emerged on the measures of trait anxiety and depression. GAD patients, however, have significantly higher state anxiety scores than patients with panic disorder or simple phobia (DiNardo & Barlow, in press).

Different patterns of scores emerge among the groups on the two measures of somatic symptoms, the CSAQS and the PSSS. On the CSAQS, simple phobia and OCD have lower scores than any other group, with no other significant differences among the groups. On the PSSS, panic disorder and GAD have the highest mean scores, though not significantly higher than OCD disorder or agoraphobia, whereas simple and social phobia have the lowest mean scores. Because the PSSS assesses a broader range of somatic symptoms than the CSAQS, the different pattern of scores observed may reflect the broader somatic symptomatology of panic disorder and GAD, and the tendency of social and simple phobics to experience somatic symptoms that are focused on specific situations (DiNardo & Barlow, in press).

Table 2.4 also presents the scores on the subscales of the FQ (agoraphobic and social fears). Table 2.4 indicates that these subscales may be sensitive in identifying the groups for which they are intended, but they do not have very good specificity (DiNardo & Barlow, in press). For example, on the agoraphobic subscale, the agoraphobic group has significantly higher scores than any other group. The scores of the OCD, panic, and simple phobic groups, however, are significantly higher than the GAD or social phobic groups.

Table 2.5 shows the data obtained by Turner, McCann, Beidel, and Mezzich (1986), which provide further evidence for the distinctiveness of the adult anxiety disorders. Turner et al. (1986) administered several questionnaires to the following three patient groups: (a) simple and social phobics, (b) agoraphobics, and (c) an Anxiety State group (GAD, OCD, and panic disorder). The results revealed that the anxiety state patients reported similar levels of anxiety as the agoraphobic patients, with both groups reporting more anxiety on the questionnaires than the social and simple phobia groups. Further, patients with DSM-III panic disorder (part of the anxiety state group) experienced severe panic and milder agoraphobic fear than the agoraphobia groups, and two groups (i.e., agoraphobia and anxiety states) overlapped with respect to both kinds of symptoms. According to Turner et al. (1986), these data support the DSM-III-R differentiation of anxiety states from phobic disorder, in addition to the reclassification of agoraphobia as an anxiety state.

Descriptive Differences Found Among the Childhood Anxiety Disorders

In terms of the discriminant validity of the childhood categories, significant differences have been found among several of the subcategories along the following descriptive variables: age presenting for treatment (see also chapter 4), gender, and SES. With respect to the age in which these children

TABLE 2.5 One-Way Analysis of Variance on Agoraphobia, Simple and Social Phobias, and Anxiety State Groups

Measure	Simple and social phobia (n = 44)		Agoraphobia (n = 18)		Generalized anxiety disorder; panic disorder; obsessive-compulsive disorder (n = 27)		F
	M	SD	M	SD	M	SD	
State-Trait Anxiety Inventory,							
A—State	37.46	11.49	51.06	12.34	55.93	10.56	24.39***
A—Trait	37.68	11.07	51.83	15.38	58.37	14.42	22.61***
Beck Depression Inventory	7.50	7.37	16.94	9.78	21.78	9.53	23.88***
Cornell Medical Index	24.00	14.06	39.89	23.17	52.22	22.90	18.86***
Maudsley Obsessive-Compulsive Inventory	4.80	3.83	8.22	7.06	10.85	6.71	10.27**
Fear Survey Schedule	66.84	44.42	145.83	77.00	140.93	48.77	22.40***
Social Avoidance and Distress Scale	7.73	7.61	17.94	8.67	17.48	7.69	17.83***
Fear of Negative Evaluation Scale	12.52	9.38	19.33	9.79	18.41	8.29	5.26*

Note. From Turner, S M., McCann, B. S., Beidel, D. C., & Mezzich, J. E. (1986). DSM-III classification of the anxiety disorders: A psychiatric study. *Journal of Abnormal Psychology, 95,* 168–172. Reprinted by permission.
*p < .01. **p < .001. ***p < .0001.

(accompanied by their parents) present for treatment, Last, Francis, Hersen, Kazdin, and Strauss (1987) found that children with phobic disorder—school, tend to be older (mean age = 14 years) than children with overanxious disorder (OAD) (mean age = 10.8 years) and separation anxiety disorder (SAD) (mean age - 8.9 years). In terms of gender differences, Last, Strauss, and Francis (1987) and Last, Francis, Hersen, Kazdin, and Strauss (1987) reported that SAD was more prevalent in females than in males, whereas OAD and phobic disorder—school were more prevalent among males than females. In contrast to the gender prevalence of simple phobia observed among adults (more prevalent in females than in males), simple phobias appear to be just as common in boys as in girls among prepubertal children.

The childhood disorders also demonstrate different prevalences, as a function of SES. Last, Francis, Hersen, Kazdin and Strauss (1987) and Last, Hersen, Kazdin, Finkelstein, and Strauss (1987) reported that children with SAD tend to come from families of lower socioeconomic levels than children with OAD and phobic disorder—school. Youngsters with OAD tend to come predominantly from families of middle to upper socioeconomic status; youngsters with phobic disorder—school—are predominantly from families of high SES.

Whether the childhood anxiety disorders may be differentiated on the basis of psychometric measures has also been investigated (see also chapter 10). The results of these efforts have been more mixed, as compared with the adult work. This may be more reflective of the global nature of the questionnaire measures used in childhood assessment, however, rather than problems with the classification scheme per se. For example, Hoehn-Saric et al. (1987) found that scores on an interview schedule that they developed, the CAEF mentioned earlier, could differentiate patients independently diagnosed on discharge as having anxiety disorders from those diagnosed with disorders other than anxiety. Furthermore, positive correlations were found between the CAEF and STAIC Trait scores and Revised Children's Manifest Anxiety Scale (RCMAS) scores. The RCMAS and the STAIC, however, failed to differentiate among the diagnostic groups. The authors interpreted their data as demonstrating that currently available self-report measures of anxiety are not very useful in their ability to discriminate among various forms of childhood psychopathology.

Last, Francis, Hersen, Kazdin, and Strauss (1987) also reported that the STAIC, the RCMAS, and the revised Fear Survey Schedule for Children (FSSC-R) failed to differentiate children with SAD and phobic disorder—school. Similarly, Strauss, Last, Hersen, and Kazdin (1988) found that these three measures could not distinguish children with anxiety disorder from a group of psychopathological control children. We have also found the child self-report measures of anxiety to be rather insensitive in detecting meaningful differences among various groups (Silverman, Cerny, Nelles, & Burke, in press).

In an important exception to the preceding, Last, Francis, and Strauss (1989) recently demonstrated that the FSSC-R could discriminate children with SAD, OAD, and phobic disorder—school, using a qualitative index of fearfulness (patterns of intense fears) rather than a standard quantitative score (total score, factor scores). Specifically, the primary fear of the SAD children was of getting lost. OAD children's fears focused on social evaluative and performance concerns (being criticized, being teased, and making mistakes). The children with phobic disorder—school differed from SAD and OAD children in the number of intense fears reported, with going to school being the only fear reported by at least one third of the group.

Although not a study of the discriminant validity of the various childhood anxiety disorder categories, Mattison and Bagnato's (1987) investigation of the convergent and discriminant validity of OAD is worthy of mention. These investigators examined whether the Child Behavior Checklist (CBCL) and the RCMAS could differentiate boys (8 to 12 years old) with OAD from boys with dysthymic disorder or attention deficit disorder with hyperactivity. The results revealed that the OAD group demonstrated the greatest number of high correlations with the Schizoid or Anxious subscales of the CBCL (for convergent validity), whereas none of the overanxious boys had a hyperactive- or delinquent-type profile on the CBCL (for discriminant validity). The overanxious boys were also more severely elevated on the Internalizing factors. Finally, on the RCMAS, the OAD children scored higher than the dysthymic and attention deficit disorder boys on the worry/oversensitivity and physiological factors. Overall, therefore Mattison and Bagnato's (1987) data support the validity of OAD among boys between the ages of 8 to 12.

Comorbidity

Another step toward determining the validity of the anxiety disorders is to examine the extent to which they overlap or discriminate among themselves. Indeed, in daily clinical practice, it is more usual than not to see clients—both children and adults—who present with more than one clinical disorder. In such instances, it is difficult, if not impossible, to "pigeonhole" a client into one specific category.

The studies of comorbidity support the omission of the former hierarchical rules of DSM-III, mentioned earlier. In these studies, summarized subsequently, clinicians assigned diagnoses based on DSM-III criteria, but they were not required to exclude diagnoses based on hierarchical rules for the anxiety and affective disorders.

Barlow, DiNardo, Vermilyea, Vermilyea, and Blanchard (1986) examined the patterns of additional diagnoses among 108 adult anxiety disorder patients. They found that at least one concurrent diagnosis was assigned in many cases, with the number of additional diagnoses varying with the primary diagnosis. Specifically, almost all cases of panic disorder, GAD, and OCD were assigned a concurrent diagnosis. In about half of the cases of social phobia and agoraphobia, no additional diagnoses were assigned. In terms of the specific diagnoses that tended to be "concurrent" ones, the results revealed that social and simple phobia were the most frequently occurring additional diagnoses for all disorders except OCD. For OCD, depressive disorder was most common. Depressive disorder was also a common additional diagnosis for all disorders except simple phobia.

DiNardo and Barlow (in press) recently reported comorbidity data based on the last 300 patients seen at the center. Table 2.6 presents the number of additional diagnoses among the anxiety and affective disorders. Excluding agoraphobia without panic (which had one case), additional diagnoses were assigned in 44% of the anxiety disorder cases. These additional diagnoses were differentially distributed among the primary diagnoses. Specifically, simple phobia occurred most frequently among cases of agoraphobia, GAD, and dysthymia. The concurrent diagnosis of social phobia occurred most frequently among cases of dysthymia, whereas a concurrent diagnosis of dysthymia occurred most frequently among affective disorder cases.

Patterns of comorbidity among child and adolescent anxiety disorder patients were reported by Last, Strauss, and Francis (1987). The number of concurrent anxiety disorders for each diagnostic group is presented in Table 2.7. The results revealed that children who received a primary diagnosis of SAD were most likely to receive the concurrent diagnosis of OAD. Children with the primary diagnosis of OAD were most likely to receive a diagnosis of social phobia or avoidant disorder. The phobic disorder—school group had a wide range of additional diagnoses, with no apparent pattern. The two most common concurrent diagnoses for the major depressive group were social phobia and OAD. In addition, more than one quarter of this group was assigned a concurrent diagnosis of SAD and avoidant disorder.

Thus, similarities as well as differences appear in the patterns of comorbidity that exist among anxious children and adults. Like adults, social phobia (or avoidant disorder) emerged as a common concurrent diagnosis among children. Also similar to adults, a concurrent diagnosis of depressive disorder was common among children. Further, in Last, Hersen, Kazdin, Finkelstein, and Strauss's (1987) comparison of SAD versus OAD children, it is reported that OAD children were more likely than SAD children to present with an additional concurrent anxiety disorder, usually simple phobia or panic disorder. To the extent that SAD is the functional

TABLE 2.6 Number (%) of Anxiety Disorder Cases in Which Additional Diagnoses Were Assigned

	Primary diagnosis								
Additional diagnoses	Agoraphobia with panic	Agoraphobia without panic	Social phobia	Simple phobia	Panic disorder	GAD	Obsessive-compulsive	Major depression	Dysthymia
0	47(55)	1	28(58)	16(67)	36(54)	17(55)	8(53)	3(27)	2(22)
1	27(31)		13(27)	7(29)	20(30)	8(26)	5(33)	5(45)	3(33)
2	8(9)		7(15)	1(4)	8(12)	4(13)	1(7)	3(27)	3(33)
3	3(3)			1(1)	2(6)	1(7)		1(11)	
4	1(1)			2(3)					
Total 292	86	1	48	24	67	31	15	11	9

Note. From DiNardo, P. A., & Barlow, D. H. (in Press). Sydrome and symptom comorbidity in the anxiety disorders. In J. D. Maser & C. R. Cloninger (Eds.), *Comorbidity in anxiety and mood disorders.* Washington, DC: American Psychiatric Press. Reprinted by permission.

TABLE 2.7 Number of Concurrent Anxiety Disorders by Primary Diagnosis

No. of concurrent anxiety disorders	Primary diagnosis[a]							
	SAD ($N = 24$)		OAD ($N = 11$)		SP ($N = 11$)		MD ($N = 11$)	
	N	%	N	%	N	%	N	%
None	14	58.3	5	45.4	4	36.4	0	0
One	4	16.7	4	36.4	4	36.4	6	54.5
Two	4	16.7	1	19.1	3	27.3	1	9.1
Three or more	2	8.3	1	9.1	0	0	4	36.4

Note. From Last, C. E., Strauss, C. C., & Francis, G. (1987). Comorbidity among childhood anxiety disorders. *Journal of Nervous and Mental Disease, 175,* 726–730. Reprinted by permission.
[a]Primary diagnoses for which $N < 4$ has been omitted from this table.

equivalent of panic disorder and OAD is the functional equivalent of GAD, this result is similar to Barlow, DiNardo, Vermilyea, Vermilyea, and Blanchard's (1986) finding among adult anxiety disorder patients that a common concurrent diagnosis of GAD is panic disorder. In terms of differences between the child and adult patterns of comorbidity, although simple phobia emerged as a common concurrent diagnosis among adults, this was not found to be true among children. Further, although GAD was rarely found to be a concurrent diagnosis among adults, except in the affective disorder cases, OAD was a common concurrent diagnosis among children.

In sum, as mentioned earlier, the comorbidity data support DSM-III-R's deletion of the hierarchical rules for the anxiety and affective disorders. The data also indicate that overlap does occur among several of the anxiety disorders in both children and adults. Further studies are needed to determine if the presence of additional diagnoses increases the discriminant validity of the diagnostic system. For example, does the presence of additional diagnoses identify subgroups within any particular category that are homogenous with respect to clinical or psychometric characteristics, course of illness, or treatment response? One potential approach for further examining the issue of comorbidity, as suggested by Last, Strauss, and Francis (1987), would be to employ a multitrait-multimethod assessment strategy. This would allow for a more detailed evaluation of convergent and discriminant validity among the various disorders.

Other Approaches to Assessing Diagnostic Validity: Family and Follow-Up Studies

There are other useful approaches for determining the validity of the DSM diagnostic categories, in addition to the ways mentioned previously. These include family and follow-up studies. (The reader is referred to Last [1987] for a discussion of the contribution of these kinds of studies to research on diagnostic validity.) Unfortunately, because of limited space, we cannot review the data obtained from family (see chapter 6) and follow-up (see chapter 5) studies with respect to the anxiety disorders. Suffice it to say that the research suggests a familial influence in the anxiety disorders (see Silverman, Cerny, & Nelles [in press] for a review). Specifically, there appears to be an increased prevalence of certain anxiety disorders among the close relatives of an index case, thereby providing further support for the validity of some of these disorders. Of course, the extent to which this familial influence is affected by genetic, environmental, or other factors requires additional study (see chapter 7). In terms of follow-up studies, the evidence indicates that the adult anxiety disorders vary in their course, providing further evidence for their distinctiveness. Unfortunately, follow-up studies on the childhood disorders is dearth, though such research is currently in progress (Last, Hersen, Kazdin, & Perrin, 1991; Silverman, Cerny, & Nelles, in press).

ANXIETY AND DEPRESSION

A frequent clinical observation is that many anxious patients appear depressed and many depressed patients appear anxious. This observation is reflected by DSM-III-R, which classifies anxiety and depression as separate disorders. In fact, however, the nature of the relationship existing between anxiety and depression is complex, and much of the research findings examining this relationship is contradictory. It is beyond the scope of this chapter to review in detail all the studies that have been conducted that have examined the anxiety-depression relationship. Rather, we briefly summarize the major methodological limitations of these studies and draw some general conclusions from this research.

The major methodological limitations, which caution against direct comparisons, include the following: different samples have been employed in these studies (e.g., inpatients versus outpatients; children versus adolescents; a broad range of anxiety disorder patients versus specific diagnostic groups, and so forth) and different assessment measures have been used (e.g., clinical interview, observer-rated scales, patient-rated scales, etc.) Indeed, continued development of instruments that clearly measure anxiety specifically versus depression specifically is crucial if progress is to be realized in this area. Recent research by Riskind, Beck, and Brown (in press), which focused upon revising the two Hamilton scales to distinguish major depressive disorder and GAD more clearly, is an excellent example of the kind of work that is needed.

Another methodological limitation is that variable levels of interpretation have been made across studies. In some investigations the level of interpretation pertains to the relationship of anxiety and depression at the symptom level (e.g., Clancy, Noyes, Hoenk, & Slymen, 1979; Dealy, Ishiki, Avery, Wilson, & Dunner, 1981), whereas in others it is at the level of factors (e.g., Mendels, Weinstein, & Cochrane, 1972; Prusoff, Klerman, & Paykel, 1972). As Stavrakaki and Vargo (1986) point out, discussion at one interpretational level is not necessarily comparable with discussion at a different level.

With the preceding limitations in mind, some general comments can be made. First, among both children and adults, different patterns of overlap and separation occur between anxiety and depression. Although some studies have found overlap existing between anxiety and depression, thereby supporting the notion that anxiety and depression are variants of the same disorder differing quantitatively (e.g. Lesses, 1982; Roth, Gurney, Garside, & Kerr, 1972) (the unitary position), others have found separation existing between anxiety and depression, thus supporting the position that anxiety and depression are distinct disorders differing qualitatively (Gurney, Roth, Garside, Kerr, & Schapira, 1972; Prusoff, Klerman, & Paykel, 1972) (the pluralistic position) (Stavrakaki & Vargo, 1986). A mixture of the two syndromes that appears to be phenomenologically different from either primary anxiety or primary depressive disorder has been reported in still other investigations (e.g., Clancy, et al., 1979; Schapira, Roth, Kerr, & Gurney, 1972). Given the various patterns noted above, it is possible that there are several forms of anxiety and depression, of differing origins that exist, with the presence of one being a predisposition to the development of the other, in some cases (Marks, 1987).

Second, in terms of the "frequency" of a particular type of overlap, the research suggests that although depression is nearly always associated with anxiety, anxiety often occurs without depression (Marks, 1987). Third, the overlap existing between anxiety and depression has been better delineated in samples selected for affective disorders than for anxiety disorders (Puig-Antich & Rabinovich, 1986). Fourth, the research indicates that when anxiety and depression coexist, there is increased severity of symptomatology, increased chronicity of the disorders, reduced responsiveness to treatment, and a poorer prognosis (e.g., Clancy et al., 1979; Schapira et al., 1972; Strauss et al., 1988).

Fifth, at present, an understanding about the nature of the association existing between anxiety and depression (when an association emerges), is non-existent. One potentially promising strategy for better understanding the nature of this relationship is to combine family studies and follow-up of children and adolescents with "pure" major depressive disorder, "pure" anxiety disorder, and with both disorders (Puig-Antich & Rabinovich,

1986). To the extent that childhood and adult psychopathology are continuous, an examination of the nature of the relationship in children might help to clarify the relationship in adults (Stavrakaki & Vargo, 1986).

Finally, and perhaps most relevant to this chapter, it remains for future investigations to ascertain what impact the coexistence of anxiety and depressive disorder has on the *classification* of psychopathology, as well as treatment and prognosis.

CONCLUSION

This chapter presents the current state of knowledge regarding the DSM classification of anxiety disorders in children and adults. The most important conclusion to be drawn from this review is that the classification of these disorders requires further refinement and research. This is especially true regarding the application of the adult criteria to children with respect to some of the anxiety disorder subcategories (e.g., OCD, simple phobia, PTSD, etc.). As far as we are aware, the validity of these adult diagnostic criteria applied to youngsters has not been systematically evaluated with respect to parallels in symptomatology, etiology, course, prognosis, and treatment response.

In addition, the validity of the childhood anxiety subcategories (i.e., SAD, OAD, and avoidant disorder) requires greater examination. It is hoped that this issue will be examined not just by comparing these groups along various demographic and psychometric variables, but also through family and follow-up studies. Certainly, the important work of Last and her colleagues, which encompasses all of the preceding methods, is an example of the type of research that is needed.

Interestingly, *none* of the studies that the author reviews in this chapter include a sample of children diagnosed with avoidant disorder. This is consistent with the author's research and clinical experience, as well as that of others, that it is uncommon for children to receive avoidant disorder as a primary diagnosis. An issue that will certainly deserve greater scrutiny, as work gets under way on DSM-IV, is whether or not avoidant disorder should continue to be included in the DSM as a childhood anxiety disorder.

Another important issue discussed in this chapter is that of comorbidity. The comorbidity data that the author reviews here clearly show that overlap occurs among several of the anxiety disorders in children and adults. Now what is needed is to determine whether the distribution of certain additional diagnoses improves the discriminant validity of the classification system. That is, does the presence of additional diagnoses identify subgroups within any particular category that are homogenous with respect to clinical or psychometric characteristics, course of illness, or treatment response? Adequate resolution of this issue will certainly assist in improving the classification of the anxiety and related disorders.

Also evident from this chapter is the fact that the nature of the relationship between anxiety and depression is complex as well as intriguing. Precisely how anxiety and depression relate, in both children and adults, at the syndrome and symptom level, and how this impacts on classification, requires clarification.

Despite all the unresolved issues raised previously, one point can be made fairly definitively at this time. That is that DSM-III-R, and most likely even the categorical approach of the DSM system, is not the last word in the classification of psychopathology. Indeed, an increasing number of theorists and investigators have been calling for alternative approaches to classification (e.g., Achenback, 1985; Cantor, Smith, French, & Mezzich, 1980; Greenspan, Lourie, & Nover, 1979; Sneath & Sokal, 1973) or at least to combine the categorical approach of the DSM with other approaches (Barlow, 1988; Carlson & Garber, 1986).

Barlow (1988), for example, argues that a classification scheme that is a combination of a categorical and dimensional approach best represents clinical reality. A dimensional approach to classification is concerned with the question: Which important features are prominent across the anxiety disorders? Research is accumulating that salient anxiety-related features across patients with various anxiety disorders include social phobic features, panic, intrusive thoughts, and ritualistic checking (Barlow, 1988). Thus, in a "combined" categorical and dimensional classification, the categories are defined by the convergence of several dimensions. Although a single dimension may be the central defining feature of a category, it may be more accurate to conceptualize patients in a category as having a similar profile on several dimensions. DiNardo and Barlow (in press) give the example of panic disorder, which is characterized as having high levels of symptomatology on the somatic and panic dimensions, but low levels on worry and avoidance. Although the preceding profile may be generally accurate for panic disorder patients, important variations may exist among the patients, and these differences can only emerge with consideration of hierarchy-free additional diagnoses or symptom dimensions.

Greenspan et al. (1979) have argued for a developmental approach to classification that would emphasize individuals' patterns of processing, organizing, and integrating information, as well as their adaptive pathological capacities. In contrast to the DSM approach of emphasizing specific and static behaviors, a developmental approach is sensitive to structural changes of the organism, resulting from development that may facilitate or hinder functioning. Silverman (1987) cited examples of several developmental tasks that are likely to influence children's experience of anxiety. These include the development of mastery and competence, the development of a future time perspective, the development of person perception, entry into the peer group, and so on. Silverman (1987) also called for more basic research on how developmental processes in attention, retention, motor representations, and motivation operate in rendering anxiety in youngsters. The results of such developmental research, as Carlson and Garber (1986) also point out, may then be used to broaden the existing definitions of symptoms to reflect developmental differences in phenomenology. Beyond symptoms, these authors also called for a classification that would include individual's adaptation and competence within the context of crucial developmental tasks.

It is beyond our scope here to elaborate further on other approaches to classification, such as taxometric (Achenbach, 1985) and ecological approaches (Hobbs, 1975; Salzinger, Antrobus, & Glick, 1980). Suffice it to say that despite the improvements seen in the DSM system over the years, DSM's categorical approach, in the minds of many, is not a fait accompli. It is not yet clear what impact these other, alternative approaches will have on the classification of psychpathology, in general, and the anxiety disorders, in particular. What is clear is that these alternative approaches will result in a flurry of research activity, leading to exciting discussion and probably controversy in the years to come.

REFERENCES

Achenbach, T. R. (1985). *Assessment and taxonomy of child and adolescent psychopathology.* California: Sage.

American Psychiatric Association Committee on Nomenclature and Statistics. (1952). *Diagnostic and statistical manual of mental disorders* (1st ed.). Washington, DC: American Psychiatric Association.

American Psychiatric Association Committee on Nomenclature and Statistics. (1968). *Diagnostic and statistical manual of mental disorders* (2nd ed.). Washington, DC: American Psychiatric Association.

American Psychiatric Association Committee on Nomenclature and Statistics. (1983). *Diagnostic and statistical manual of mental disorders* (3rd ed.). Washington, DC: American Psychiatric Association.

American Psychiatric Association Committee on Nomenclature and Statistics. (1987). *Diagnostic and statistical manual of mental disorders* (3rd ed. rev.). Washington, DC: American Psychiatric Association.

Barlow, D. H. (1987). The classification of anxiety disorders. In G. L. Tischler (Ed.), *Diagnoses and classification in psychiatry: A critical appraisal of DSM-III* (pp. 223–242). New York: Cambridge University Press.

Barlow, D. H. (1988). *Anxiety and its disorders: The nature of anxiety and panic.* New York: Guilford.

Barlow, D. H., Blanchard, E. B., Vermilyea, J. A., Vermilyea, B. B. & DiNardo, P. A. (1986). Generalized anxiety and generalized anxiety disorder: Description and reconceptualization. *American Journal of Psychiatry, 143,* 40–44.

Barlow, D. H., DiNardo, P. A., Vermilyea, B. B., Vermilyea, J. A., & Blanchard, E. B. (1986). Co-morbidity and depression among the anxiety disorders: Issues in classification and diagnosis. *Journal of Nervous and Mental Disease, 174,* 63–72.

Beck, A. T., Ward, C. H., Mendelson, M., Mock, J., & Erbaugh, J. (1961). An inventory for measuring depression. *Archives of General Psychiatry, 4,* 567–571.

Blanchard, E. B., Gerardi, R. J., Kolb, L. C., & Barlow, D. H. (1986). The utility of the Anxiety Disorders Interview Schedule (ADIS) in the diagnosis of post-traumatic stress disorder (PTSD) in Vietnam veterans. *Behaviour Research and Therapy, 24,* 577–580.

Blashfield, R. K. (1984). *The classification of psychopathology: Neo-Kraepelinian and quantitative approaches.* New York: Plenum.

Blashfield, R. K., & Draguns, J. G. (1976). Toward a taxonomy of psychopathology: The purpose of psychiatric classification. *British Journal of Psychiatry, 129,* 574–583.

Boyd, J. M., Burke, J. D., Gruenberg, E., Holzer, C. E., Rae, J. S., George, L. K., Karno, M., Stoltzman, R., McEvoy, M. A., & Nestadt, G. (1984). Exclusion criteria of DSM-III: A study of co-occurrence of hierarchy—free syndromes. *Archives of General Psychiatry, 41,* 983–989.

Cantor, N., Smith, E. E., French, R., & Mezzich, J. (1980). Psychiatric diagnosis as prototype categorization. *Journal of Abnormal Psychology, 89,* 181–193.

Carlson, G. A., & Garber, J. (1986). Developmental issues in the classification of depression in children. In M. Rutter, C. E. Izard, & P. B. Read (Eds.), *Depression in young people: Developmental and clinical perspectives* (pp. 399–434). New York: Guilford.

Chambers, W. J., Puig-Antich, J., Hirsch, M., Paez, P., Ambrosini, P. J., Tabrizi, M. S., & Davies, M. (1985). The assessment of affective disorders in children and adolescents by semi-structured interview. *Archives of General Psychiatry, 42,* 696–702.

Clancy, J., Noyes, R., Hoenk, P. R., & Slymen, D. J. (1979). Secondary depression in anxiety neurosis. *Journal of Nervous and Mental Disease, 166,* 846–850.

Costello, A. J., Edelbrock, C., Dulcan, M., Kalas, R., & Klaric, S. H. (1984). Report on the NIMH Diagnostic Interview Schedule for Children (DISC). Unpublished manuscript.

Cox, D. J., Freundlich, A., & Meyer, B. G. (1975). Differential effectiveness of electromyographic feedback, verbal relaxation instructions, and medication placebo with tension headache. *Journal of Consulting and Clinical Psychology, 43,* 892–898.

Dealy, R. S., Ishiki, D. M., Avery, D. H., Wilson, L. G., & Dunner, D. L. (1981). Secondary depression in anxiety disorders. *Comprehensive Psychiatry, 22,* 612–618.

DiNardo, P. A., & Barlow, D. H. (in press). Syndrome and symptom comorbidity in the anxiety disorders. In J. D. Maser & C. R. Cloninger (Eds.), *Comorbidity in anxiety and mood disorders.* Washington, DC: American Psychiatric Press.

DiNardo, P. A., O'Brien, G. T., Barlow, D. M., Waddel, M. T., & Blanchard, E. B. (1983). Reliability of DSM-III anxiety disorder categories using a new structured interview. *Archives of General Psychiatry, 40,* 1070–1079.

Greenspan, S. I., Lourie, R. S., & Nover, R. A. (1979). A developmental approach to the classification of psychopathology in infancy and early childhood. In J. Noshpitz (Eds.), *Handbook of child psychiatry.* New York: Basic Books.

Gurney, C., Roth, M., Garside, R. F., Kerr, T. A., & Shapira, K. (1972). The relationship between anxiety states and depressive illnesses. *British Journal of Psychiatry, 121,* 162–166.

Hamilton, M. (1960). A rating scale for depression. *Journal of Neurology, Neurosurgery and Psychiatry, 23,* 56–62.

Herjanic, B., & Campbell, W. (1977). Differentiating psychiatrically disturbed children on the basis of a structured interview. *Journal of Abnormal Child Psychology, 5,* 127–134.

Hershberg, S. G., Carlson, G. A., Cantwell, D. P., & Strober, M. (1982). Anxiety and depressive disorders in psychiatrically disturbed children. *Journal of Clinical Psychiatry, 43,* 358–361.

Hobbs, N. (1975). *Issues in the classification of children.* San Francisco: Jossey-Bass.

Hodges, K., McKnew, D., Burbach, D. J., & Ruebuck, L. (1987). Diagnostic concordance between two structured child interviews using lay examiners: The Child Assessment Schedule and the Kiddie-SADS, *Journal of the American Academy of Child Psychiatry, 26,* 654–661.

Hoehn-Saric, E., Maisami, M., & Wiegand, D. (1987). Measurement of anxiety in children and adolescents using semi-structured interviews. *Journal of the American Academy of Child & Adolescent Psychiatry, 26,* 511–545.

Kolvin, I., Berney, P., & Bhate, R. (1984). Classification and diagnosis of depression in school phobia. *British Journal of Psychiatry, 145,* 347–357.

Last, C. G. (1987). Developmental considerations. In C. G. Last & M. Hersen (Eds.), *Issues in diagnostic research.* New York: Plenum.

Last, C. G., Francis, G., Hersen, M., Kazdin, A. E., & Strauss, C. C. (1987). Separation anxiety and school phobia: A comparison using DSM-III criteria. *American Journal of Psychiatry, 144,* 653–657.

Last, C. G., Francis, G., & Strauss, C. C. (1989). Assessing fears in anxiety disordered children with the Revised Fear Survey Schedule for children (FSSC-R). *Journal of Clinical Child Psychology, 18,* 137–141.

Last, C. G., Hersen, H., Kazdin, A. E., & Finkelstein, R. (1985). Reliability and validity of DSM-III anxiety disorders of childhood and adolescence: A preliminary report, unpublished manuscript.

Last C. G., Hersen, M., Kazdin, A. E., Finkelstein, R., & Strauss, C. D. (1987). Comparison of DSM-III separation anxiety and overanxious disorders: Demographic characteristics and patterns of comorbidity. *Journal of the American Academy of Child and Adolescent Psychiatry, 26,* 527–531.

Last, C. G., Hersen, M., Kazdin, A., & Perrin, S. (1991). Prospective study of anxiety disordered children. Manuscript submitted for publication.

Last, C. G., Strauss, C. C., & Francis, G. (1987). Comorbidity among child-hood anxiety disorders. *Journal of Nervous and Mental Disease, 175,* 726–730.

Lesses, S. (1982). The relationship of anxiety to depression. *American Journal of Psychotherapy, 36,* 332–348.

Marks. (1987). *Fears, phobias, and rituals.* New York: Oxford University Press.

Marks, I. M., & Mathews, A. M. (1978). Brief standard self-rating for phobic patients. *Behaviour Research and Therapy, 17,* 263–267.

Mattison, R. E., & Bagnato, S. J. (1987). Empirical measurement of overanxious disorder in boys 8 to 12 years old. *Journal of the American Academy of Child and Adolescent Psychiatry, 26,* 536–540.

Mendels, J., Weinstein, N., & Cochrane, C. (1972). The relationship between anxiety and depression. *Archives of General Psychiatry, 27,* 649–653.

Prusoff, B. A., Klerman, G. L., & Paykel, E. S. (1972). Concordance between clinical assessments and patients' self-report in depression. *Archives of General Psychiatry, 26,* 546–552.

Puig-Antich, J., & Rabinovich, H. (1986). Relationship between affective and anxiety disorders in childhood. In R. Gittelman (Ed.), *Anxiety disorders of childhood* (pp. 136–156). New York: Guilford.

Rachman, S. J., & Hodgson, R. (1980): *Obsessions and compulsions.* Englewood Cliifs, NJ: Prentice Hall.

Riskind, J. E., Beck, A. R., & Brown, G. B. (in press). Taking the measure of anxiety and depression: Validity of reconstructed Hamilton scales. *Journal of Nervous and Mental Disease.*

Robins, L. N., Helzer, J. E., Croughan, J., & Ratcliff, K. S. (1981). National Institute of Mental Health Diagnostic Interview Schedules: Its history, characteristics, and validity. *Archives of General Psychiatry, 38,* 381–389.

Roth, M., Gurney, C., Garside, R. F., & Kerr, T. A. (1972). The relationship between anxiety states and depressive illnesses: 1. *British Journal of Psychiatry, 121,* 147–161.

Russell, A. T., Cantwell, D. P., Mattison, R., & Will, L. (1979). A comparison of DSM-II and DSM-III in the diagnosis of childhood psychiatric disorders: 3. Multiaxial features. *Archives of General Psychiatry, 36,* 1223–1226.

Rutter, M., & Shaffer, D. (1980). DSM-III: A step forward or back in terms of the classification of child psychiatric disorder? *Journal of the American Academy of Child and Adolescent Psychiatry, 19,* 371–394.

Rutter, M., Shaffer, D., & Shepherd, M. (1975). A multiaxial classification of child psychiatric disorders. Geneva: World Health Organization.

Salzinger, S., Antrobus, J., & Glick, J. (Eds.). (1980). *The ecosystem of the "sick" child.* New York: Academic Press.

Schapira, K., Roth, M., Kerr, T. A., & Gurney, C. (1972). The prognosis of affective disorders: The differentiation of anxiety states and depressive illnesses. *British Journal of Psychiatry, 121,* 175–181.

Schwartz, G. E., Davidson, R. J., & Goleman, D. J. (1978). Patterning of cognitive and somatic processes in the self-regulation of anxiety: Effects of medication versus exercise. *Psychosomatic Medicine, 40,* 321–328.

Silverman, W. K. (1987). Childhood anxiety disorders: Diagnostic issues, empirical support and future research. *Journal of Child and Adolescent Psychotherapy, 4,* 121–126.

Silverman, W. K., Cerny, J. A., & Nelles, W. B. (in press). The familial influence in anxiety disorders: Studies on the offspring of patients with anxiety disorders. In B. B. Lahey & A. E. Kazdin (Eds.), *Advances in Clinical Child Psychology* (Vol. 11). New York: Plenum.

Silverman, W. K., Cerny, J. A., Nelles, W. B., & Burke, A. E. (in press). Behavior problems in children of parents with anxiety disorders. *Journal of the American Academy of Child and Adolescent Psychiatry.*

Silverman, W. K., & Nelles, W. B. (1988). The Anxiety Disorders Interview Schedule for Children. *Journal of the American Academy of Child and Adolescent Psychiatry, 27,* 772–778.

Sneath, P. H. A., & Sokal, R. R. (1973). *Numerical taxonomy: The principles and practice of numerical classification.* San Francisco: Freeman.

Spielberger, C. D., Gorsuch, R. L., & Lushene, R. E. (1970). *Manual for the STAT.* Palo Alto: Consulting Psychologists Press.

Spitzer, R. L., Williams, J. B. W., & Skodol, A. E. (1979). DSM-III: A major achievement and an overview. *American Journal of Psychiatry, 137,* 151–164.

Stavrakaki, C., & Vargo, B. (1986). The relationship of anxiety and depression: A review of the literature. *British Journal of Psychiatry, 149,* 7–16.

Strauss, C. C., Last, C. G., Hersen, M., & Kazdin, A. E. (1988). Association between anxiety and depression in children and adolescents with anxiety disorders. *Journal of Abnormal Child Psychology, 15,* 57–68.

Strober, M., Green, J., & Carlson, G. (1981). Reliability of psychiatric diagnosis in hospitalized adolescents. *Archives of General Psychiatry, 38,* 141–145.

Sturt, E. (1981). Hierarchical patterns in the distribution of psychiatric symptoms. *Psychological Medicine, 11,* 783–794.

Turner, S. M., McCann, B. S., Beidel, D. C., & Mezzich, J. E. (1986). DSM-III classification of the anxiety disorders: A psychiatric study. *Journal of Abnormal Psychology, 95,* 168–172.

Williams, J. B. W., & Spitzer, R. L. (1980). Appendix F. In American Psychiatric Association. *Diagnostic and statistical manual of mental disorders* (3rd ed., (pp. 467–481). Washington, DC: Author.

Yaryura-Tobias, J. A., & Neziroglu, F. A. (1983). *Obsessive-compulsive disorders: Pathogenesis-diagnosis-treatment.* Basel: Marcel Dekker.

CHAPTER 3

Anxiety Symptoms in Nonpsychiatrically Referred Children and Adolescents

Donna L. Moreau and Myrna M. Weissman

The purpose of this chapter is to examine anxiety symptons and disorders in nonpsychiatric child populations of different ages using the approach of epidemiology. Epidemiology is the study of patterns of distribution of disease in a population. Incidence is the rate at which new cases develop. Prevalence is the rate of existing cases present in the population at any one given time. True estimates of prevalence are based on studying the total population at risk, both treated and untreated cases. The ultimate goal of epidemiological studies is to identify risk factors that, if altered, can prevent the occurrence and the spread of disease.

There are methodological problems in epidemiological studies of psychiatric disorders that may make comparisons among studies difficult. These include use of noncomparable instruments to obtain data, lack of standardized criteria to make diagnoses, variable definitions of "caseness," and variable populations (Orvaschel & Weissman, 1986).

In addition, there are particular problems associated with epidemiological studies of childhood psychopathology and the evolution of psychopathology across the lifetime (Chiland, 1977). First and foremost, there are no epidemiological studies of children with anxiety followed longitudinally into adulthood. This information would be useful because behavior that is normal at one age may be a symptom of psychopathology at another age. Because children are more vulnerable to environmental and family stresses and have fewer coping skills than adults, symptoms may be reactive and self-limited. At what age does a symptom stop being transient and become the target of treatment? A symptom can be subjectively and objectively described. Who decides what is a symptom, child or parent or teacher?

Systematic assessment of diagnoses are critical for obtaining epidemiological data that are reliable (Orvaschel & Weissman, 1986). The use of structured and semistructured diagnostic interviews is new to the field of child psychiatric research (see chapter 2). Commonly used interviews include DICA (Herjanic & Campbell, 1977), DISC (Costello, Edelbrook, & Costello, 1985), and Schedule for Affective Disorders and Schizophrenia for School-age Children (K-SADS: Chambers et al., 1985).

Because children may behave differently at home and at school, information from multiple sources is important (Rutter, 1977). Children can be reliable informants about their own symptoms, and, in fact, recent reports suggest that mothers tend to underreport psychopathology in their children (Weissman, Wickramaratne, Warner, John, Prusoff, Merikangas, & Gammon, 1987).

Prevalence rates from treated populations may be quite biased. Children who seek treatment are not necessarily representative of those who have the disorder. They may be the most disabled or come from families of higher SES. Children with "quiet" nondisruptive disorders, such as depression, anxiety, or phobias, may not be readily referred and may be underrepresented in treated populations.

The current taxonomic system of psychiatric disorders (DSM-III and DSM-III-R) used in the United States delineates gross developmental differences in psychiatric illness in that there is a special category for disorders diagnosed only in childhood, but it does not address the lifetime evolution of these disorders or the relationship of them to the adult disorders. Nor does it differentiate disorders in children from disorders in adolescents. Thus, disorders found across the lifespan are diagnosed with the same criteria, irrespective of age or development. There are 11 different diagnostic categories for anxiety symptoms, 3 of which are diagnosed only in childhood (see chapter 2). The latter include separation anxiety disorder, overanxious disorder, and avoidant disorder. Studies of nonreferred populations that contribute to the delineation and definition of anxiety disorders in children are reviewed and discussed. The studies are cross-sectional by age. A review of studies predating DSM-III will be followed by more recent studies using DSM-III diagnostic criteria.

ANXIETY SYMPTOMS: STUDIES PRE-DATING DSM-III

There is a dearth of epidemiological data on childhood anxiety disorders, and the bulk of this research antedates the DSM-III classification system. Orvaschel and Weissman (1986) extensively reviewed the epidemiological studies predating DSM-III on childhood anxiety disorders (see Table 3.1). These studies were necessarily of anxiety symptoms, not disorders. In

TABLE 3.1 Studies Reporting Prevalence of Anxiety in Children

Study	Location	Sample source	Sample size	Age of Sample (years)	Informant	Fears/ worries (%)	Separation concerns (%)	Other anxiety (%)
Lapouse & Monk	United States	Community	482	6–12	Mother	43	41	
Agras et al.	United States	Community	325	Children and adults	Subject or mother	7.7		
Werry & Quay	United States	School	1,753	5–8	Teacher	16.5		18 (tension) 18 (nerves)
Richman et al.	United Kingdom	Community	705	3	Mother	12.8 (fears) 26 (worries)		
Earls et al.	United States	Community	100	3	Mother	14 (fears) 8 (worries)		
Kastrup	Denmark	Community	175	5–6	Parent	4	13.7	8 (nightmares)
Abe & Masui	Japan	Community	2,500	11–12	Subject	2–43 (fears) 4–33 (worries)		

Note. From Orvaschel, H., & Weissman, M. M. (1986). Epidemiology of anxiety disorders in children: A review. In R. Gittelman (Ed.), *Anxiety disorders of childhood* (pp. 58–72). New York: Guilford. Reprinted by permission.

seven community studies anxiety symptoms were noted to be prevalent at all ages and common to both sexes. Three of the studies looked at anxiety symptoms across the age span; two were of behavioral disturbance in preschool children, and suggested a link between fears and worries to overall psychopathology; and two were cross-sectional surveys of children reporting no connection between fears and anxieties and psychopathology. Only two of the studies used semistructured interviews, and the child was directly interviewed in only one study.

The data suggest that anxiety symptoms are more common in girls, decrease with age, and are more prevalent in blacks and children from lower SES. Comorbidity is common. The significance of such symptoms in childhood is unclear, and the prognosis for symptomatic children is un- known (Orvaschel & Weissman, 1986).

Lapouse and Monk (1959) interviewed 482 mothers from randomly selected homes with children 6 to 12 years. There were 49% boys and 51% girls in the sample. A prevalence rate of 43% was reported for "many fears and worries," defined as seven or more. More girls (57%) than boys (36%) and more 6- to 8-years-olds (48%) than 9- to 12-year-olds (37%) reported fears and worries. Girls had fears and worries about snakes, strangers, dirt, and animals. Younger children had fears and worries about little cuts and bruises, thunder and lightning, blood, bugs, staying home alone, the dark, and animals, whereas older children feared tests and examinations at school. There was a greater percentage of black children (63%) than white children (44%) and greater percentage of children from low socioeconom- ic background (50%) than high socioeconomic background (36%) in the fearful group. Blacks reported fears and worries about using other people's utensils, germs, animals, going into the water, and people in authority. Children from lower socioeconomic backgrounds had fears and worries about using other people's utensils, school marks, world catastrophes, being kidnapped, and people from other ethnic or racial backgrounds. When compared with the child's report, mothers underreported the num- ber of fears and worries by 41%. The presence of fears and worries was found to be unrelated to other psychopathology.

Agras, Sylvester, and Oliveau (1969) studied a random community sam- ple of 325 adults and children, directly interviewing subjects 14 years and older, and interviewing mothers about the children under 14 years. They found three categories of fears corresponding to different age ranges. Fears of doctors, injections, darkness, and strangers occurred in childhood and showed a sharply declining prevalence, suggesting they are relatively short-lived. From childhood to early adulthood, fears of animals, heights, storms, enclosed places, and social situations were predominant and showed a slowly declining prevalence, suggesting that once acquired they tend to persist. Fears of crowds, death, injury and illness, and separation had their onset in adulthood, with the greatest prevalence in late adult life. Phobias had an overall prevalence of 7.7% and were severely disabling in 0.2%. Psychiatrists saw approximately 5.7% of the more severely disabled phobics.

Werry and Quay (1971) distributed questionnaires to the teachers of 1753 children, 926 boys and 827 girls aged 5 to 8 years, about behavior problems and fears common in child guidance clinic populations. Sixteen percent of the boys and 17% of the girls were anxious/fearful; 23.1% of boys and 12.3% of girls were described as tense; and 21.9% of boys and 15.5% of girls were nervous. There was a steady decline in anxiety symptoms in children from 5 to 7 years. Boys had a resurgence of anxiety symptoms at 8 years. The latter could represent a true increase in prevalence or could be a reverse halo effect associated with other behavioral disturbances (Orvaschel & Weissman, 1986). The authors conclude that "the prevalence of many symptoms of psychopathology in the general 5 to 8 year old population is quite high and their individual diagnostic value is therefore very limited."

In the following two studies the mothers of a random sample of 3-year-olds were interviewed about fears and worries in the children. In the first of these studies (Richman, Stevenson, & Graham, 1975) 2.6% of the total sample were described as worriers, and 12.8% of the total sample had fears. When the relationship between worries/fears and behavior problems was examined, it was found that 7.1% of the children with behavior problems were worriers, and 44.4% of them had fears. Girls outnumbered boys 3 to 1 in worrying and 6 to 1 for fears.

Earls (1980) conducted a similarly designed study on 100 3-year-olds in a small rural community. Mothers' reports were used to determine the prevalence of behavior problems and fears in their children. Eight percent of the children were worriers, and 14% had fears. Of this latter group, girls outnumbered boys seven to one. Fears and worries were more common in the behavior problem group of children.

The following two studies were cross-sectional surveys of children. In the first of these (Kastrup, 1976), parents of 175 Danish preschool children, 95 boys and 80 girls 5 to 6 years old, were asked about fears and anxieties in their children. Eleven percent of the boys and 5% of the girls had nightmares. Three percent of the boys and 5% of the girls had fears, and 12% of the boys and 16% of the girls had fears of separation. No relationship between fears and behavior problems was found.

In the final study, Abe and Masui (1981) asked 2,500 school children, 1,290 boys and 1,210 girls 11 to 12, to fill out a 49-item questionnaire that included 11 items on fears and anxieties. Answers were positive if the subject was troubled by any symptoms at the time of investigation or in the preceding 6 months. Anxiety symptoms were equally present in boys and girls except frequency of micturition, which was more common in boys. Anxiety symptoms, fear of blushing and fear of being looked at, were greatest in midadolescence and peaked in girls 2 years earlier than in boys. Fear of going out of doors alone and feelings of impending death tended to decrease with age. Girls outnumbered boys in all fears except the fear of talking. Orvaschel and Weissman (1986) extrapolated prevalence rates from this report and found that 2% of boys and 7% of girls were afraid of going out alone, and 38% of boys and 43% of girls were afraid of being looked at. Anxiety about impending death was present in 5% of the boys and 4% of the girls. Hypochondriasis was present in 33% of boys and 31% of girls. No data were reported on degeee of impairment.

Orvaschel and Weissman (1986) point out the difficulties comparing these seven studies. They occurred in four different countries: four in the United States, one in Great Britain, one in Denmark, and one in Japan. The age range was wide, 3 to 23 years, and one of the studies included adults as well as children. Although none of the studies followed the children longitudinally, the data support a decrease in the number of fears and a change in the type of fears with age.

ANXIETY DISORDERS: STUDIES USING DSM-III CRITERIA

There are 16 studies in the literature using DSM-III criteria to establish psychiatric diagnoses in nonpsychiatrically referred children. Some of these studies are of community or school samples of children; others are of children at risk for the development of psychiatric disorders by virtue of their parents' diagnosis; and two are of children seen in medical practices.

These studies addressed some of the methodological problems associated with the earlier studies: a consistent nosological system (DSM-III) was employed; semistructured interviews were used; and the children themselves were interviewed. All the studies documented prevalence rates of anxiety disorder, some specific as to type of anxiety disorders, and several probed for a specific anxiety disorder. A review of the epidemiological studies of community and school samples of children is followed by a review of the studies from pediatric practices. Finally, the high-risk studies are reviewed.

Epidemiological Studies of Community/School Samples

Anxiety Disorders.

The eight studies reviewed are heterogeneous regarding sample size, age, instruments, country, period for prevalence rates, and definition of caseness (see Table 3.2). The DICA was used in all but three studies. In those studies the DISC or questionnaires were used.

Five studies determined the prevalence of psychiatric disorders, including anxiety disorders, in samples of children: a school study of an adolescent population; two community studies of preadolescent children; a community sample of adolescents 11 to 20 years; and a community study of children and adolescents, 4 to 16 years, in Puerto Rico. A longitudinal study reported on the lifetime prevalence of psychiatric disorders, including anxiety disorders, many years later in previously normal preschool children rated for behavior problems. Two studies reported lifetime rates for a specific anxiety disorder, OCD, and panic disorder in community samples of adolescents.

The 6- to 12-month prevalence rate of psychiatric disorders ranged from 17.6% to 49.5%. If stricter definitions of caseness are used the rates ranged from 7.3% to 18.7%. Lifetime incidence of psychiatric disorders in the longitudinal study was 71%. The 6- to 12-month prevalence of anxiety disorders ranged from 7.3% to 8.7%, and the lifetime incidence was reported to be 30%. There was little difference between the prevalence rates of anxiety disorders in adolescents (8.7%) and in prepubertal children (8%). The type of disorder was predicted by age, however.

Table 3.3 presents rates of specific disorders in children from community or school samples. The 6- to 12-month prevalence rates of attention deficit disorder or behavior disorders were higher than anxiety disorders in prepubertal children (Anderson, Williams, McGee, & Silva, 1987; Bird, Gould, Yager, Staghezza, & Canino, 1988), whereas in adolescents anxiety disorders were equally as common as depression or conduct disorder (Kashani et al., 1987; Kashani & Orvaschel, 1988). Separation anxiety disorder was more prevalent in prepubertal children (3.5% to 5.4%) than in adolescents (.7%). Overanxious disorder occurred more frequently in adolescents (7.3%) than in children (2.9% to 4.6%). The lifetime rate for any anxiety disorder was the same as the rate for conduct disorder in the longitudinal study. Prevalence of panic disorder (2.1% lifetime rate) was reported only in adolescents. Lifetime rates of OCD in adolescents ranged from 1.9% to 6% in the longitudinal study. Avoidant disorder (6% lifetime rate) was only reported in the longitudinal study. Phobias were reported in 2.4% to 9.2% of children and 4.7% of adolescents. A lifetime rate of 17% for phobias was reported in the longitudinal study. Comorbidity was common. Girls outnumbered boys in all anxiety disorders except for preadolescent boys who had higher rates of overanxious disorder than girls.

Kashani et al. (1987) and Kashani and Orvaschel (1988) reported on the 6-month prevalence rates for anxiety disorders in a school sample of 150 adolescents 14 to 16 years old. There were 50 adolescents, 25 girls and 25 boys, in each age group. Subjects, whose names were systematically drawn from a pool of 1,703 students, were recruited from a community school.

TABLE 3.2 Epidemiological Studies of Community or School Samples of Children Yielding DSM-III Diagnoses

Study	Location	Sample source	Sample size	Age of Sample (years)	Informant	Instrument	% DSM-III diagnosis	% Cases[a]	% Anxiety disorders
Kashani et al.	United States	School	150	14–16	Child and parent	DICA	41.3	18.7	8.7
Anderson et al.	New Zealand	Community	792	11	child	DISC-C	17.6	7.3	8
Bird et al.	PR	Community	386	4–16	Teacher, child, and parent	CBCL and DISC	49.5	17.8	7.3
Lerner et al.[b]	United States	School	80	10–22	Teacher, child and parent	DICA	71		30
Velez et al.	United States	Community	776	11–20	Child & parent	Interview			8.1
Costello	United States	Community	789	7–11	Child and parent	Interview			17.9
Hayward et al.[b]	United States	School	95	14	Child	SCL-90-R and interview			2.1[c]
Flament et al.[b]	United States	School	356	14–18	Child	LOI-CV and DICA			1.9[d]

[a]Cases refers to children whose symptoms meet criteria for DSM-III diagnosis, and who are impaired or in need of treatment. [b]Lifetime rates (all other rates are for 6 or 12 months). [c]Panic Disorder. [d]OCD.

TABLE 3.3 Prevalence Rates of DSM-III Diagnosis in Community or School Samples of Children

Study	SAD (%)	OAD (%)	Avoidant disorder (%)	Panic disorder (%)	Phobia (%)	OCD (%)	Conduct (%)	ADD disorder (%)	Depression (%)
Kashani et al.	0.7	7.3			4.7		8.7		8
Anderson et al.	3.5	2.9			2.4		3.4	6.7	1.8
Bird et al.	4.7				2.6		1.5	9.5	5.9
Lerner et al.	3[a]	1[a]	6[a]		17[a]	6[a]	33[a]		
Velez et al.	5.4	2.7							
Costello	4.1	4.6			9.2				
Hayward et al.				2.1[a]					
Flament et al.						1.9[a]			

Note. SAD = separation anxiety disorder. OAD = overanxious disorder. OCD = obsessive-compulsive disorder. ADD = Attention deficit disorder.

[a]Lifetime rates (all other rates are for 6 or 12 months).

The sample represented 7% of all adolescents aged 14 to 16 years attending public school in one city.

The students were 95% white, 4% black, and 1% oriental. DSM-III diagnoses were based on direct structured interview (DICA) with the adolescents. The parent was interviewed with the DICA—Parent Version. "Caseness" was based on parental reports of impairment and determined by clinician and psychiatrist agreement on definite or serious need for treatment.

In this study, 41.3% of the students met DSM-III criteria for at least one psychiatric disorder, but only 18.7% met the definition for caseness. The most common disorders occurring in the sample were anxiety disorders (8.7%), conduct disorder (8.7%), and depression (8%). Twenty-six adolescents (17%), 17 girls and 9 boys, had enough symptoms to meet DSM-III criteria for at least one anxiety disorder, but only 13 (8.7%), 10 girls and 3 boys, were sufficiently impaired and in need of treatment to meet the definition of caseness.

Eight adolescents had one disorder. Four adolescents had two disorders, and one adolescent had three disorders. Eleven adolescents (7.3%) were diagnosed as having overanxious disorder. Seven adolescents (4.7%) were diagnosed as having phobic disorder, and one adolescent (.7%) was diagnosed with separation anxiety disorder. Comorbidity was most commonly depression.

There was no association between sex, SES, race, divorce, or parental separation and the presence of a psychiatric disorder. Although specific risk factors were related to the presence or absence of a psychiatric disorder, none was directly linked with anxiety disorders. When anxious adolescents were compared with nonanxious adolescents on methods of dealing with stress, anxious adolescents used fantasy, wishful thinking, denial, and displacement significantly more often than nonanxious adolescents.

Anderson et al.'s (1987) study was similar to Kashani and Orvaschel (1988) and Kashani et al.'s (1987) studies but was designed to measure the 12-month prevalence of DSM-III disorders in a large sample of preadolescent children in the general population. The children were part of a longitudinal study of a large representative sample of New Zealand children born during a 1-year period at Dunedin's only obstetric hospital. When this cohort was 3 years old, those still living in the region were recruited for the study. Assessments were conducted at ages 5, 7, 9 and 11 years.

Of the 925 children 11 years of age who were enrolled in the Dunedin Multidisciplinary Health and Development Research Unit, 792 participated in this study. There were 416 boys and 376 girls. The sample represented 41% of 11-years-olds attending Dunedin's intermediate schools. Children of single mothers, lower SES, and Polynesian ethnic origins were underrepresented. The children were interviewed with the DISC-C, version XIII-III.

Case identification using DSM-III criteria was based on information from three sources (parent, child, and teacher), alone or in combination. Four levels of agreement based on pervasiveness and confirmation of symptoms were used to identify a case. Level 1 consisted of those children whose symptoms independently met criteria as reported by more than one source. Level 2 involved those children whose symptoms met criteria by one source and had some symptoms confirmed by one or both other sources. Children in level 3 had symptoms that met criteria as reported by one source without confirmation from other sources. Children in level 4 had symptoms that met criteria when symptoms from all three sources were combined. Symptoms were counted only once even when reported by several sources. Children with symptoms in levels 1 and 2 were defined as cases.

Seven children (0.9%) who had IQs less than 70 were excluded from the data analysis. The overall prevalence for psychiatric disorders was 17.6% but dropped to 7.3% when strict definition of caseness was used. Forty-five percent of the disorders occurred singly. The ratio of boys to girls was 1.7:1.

There were eight categories of disorders, four of which were anxious/phobic disorders. Attention deficit disorder was the single most prevalent diagnosis (5.7%) followed by anxious/phobic disorders (combined rate of 8%). Fifty-nine children had a total of 80 anxious/phobic disorders. Separation anxiety disorder was diagnosed in 28 children (3.5%), but only 10 met the definition for caseness. Overanxious disorder was diagnosed in 23 children (2.9%), but only 4 fit the definition of caseness. Simple phobia was diagnosed in 19 children (2.4%), but none of these was defined as a case. Seven children (.9%) were diagnosed as having social phobia, but none fit the definition for caseness. There was no evidence for avoidant disorder in any of the children.

Overanxious disorder was the only category with a higher ratio of boys to girls (1.7:1). Aggressivity decreased with age for anxious-phobic children. Families with children diagnosed as having attention deficit, conduct-oppositional, and multiple disorders sought consultation most frequently.

Bird et al. (1988) used a two-stage design to study a random sample of households with children 4 to 16 years. The CBCL was administered to the parents and to the teacher if the child was 6 years or older. All households with CBCL results above the cutoff point were selected for further study. The DISC and Child-Global Assessment Scale (C-GAS) were completed for one child from each of these homes and for 20% of the children with CBCL scores below the cutoff point. There were 386 children, 197 boys and 189 girls, assessed in stage 2. Final DSM-III diagnoses were by consensus. Cases were defined as those children whose symptoms fit DSM-III criteria for a disorder and whose functioning was impaired as determined by a C-GAS score < 61.

Forty-nine percent of the children had at least one DSM-III diagnosis, but 17.8% met stricter definition for caseness. The 6-month prevalence rate for anxiety disorders was 7.3% and was superseded by attention deficit disorder (9.5%). Separation anxiety disorder (4.7%) peaked in the 6- to 11-year range and was the most common anxiety disorder overall. Phobias were present in 2.6% of the children. Comorbidity was common (46%). Low SES and male sex were associated with all diagnostic categories except separation anxiety disorder.

Lerner, Inui, Trupin, and Douglas's study (1985) is the first longitudinal study to determine lifetime DSM-III diagnoses in a sample of previously normal children when originally assessed an average of 11.5 years previously. The initial cohort consisted of 174 children 3 to 5 years attending a 2-year preschool serving a university community. Eighty-eight children were assessed at follow-up. Fifty-two percent of the subjects were male.

The initial assessment consisted of information obtained from the teachers who saw each child during the 2-year period. The charts were abstracted to determine the presence of verbal aggression, physical aggression, hyperactivity-distractibility, social withdrawal, speech problems, and language problems. Sixty-six subjects (75%) had behavior problems rated as mild or greater. Social withdrawal was the most frequent behavior problem recorded and occurred in 38% of the children, more commonly in girls.

At follow-up the DICA was used to interview 88 children and their parents. Sixty-two children (71%) met DSM-III criteria for at least one psychiatric disorder in the intervening period, and 50 children (57%) had undergone an evaluation or received treatment. Behavior disorders slightly exceeded anxiety disorders in frequency and occurred in 29 subjects (33%). Twenty-six children (30%) had anxiety disorders: 3 (3%) separation anxiety disorder, 5 (6%) avoidant disorder, 1 (1%) overanxious disorder, 15 (17%) simple phobia, and 5 (6%) OCD. Although children with moderate or severe scores on behavior profiles had a twofold greater chance of developing a specific psychiatric disorder than children who scored lower, there was no association between certain behavior problems and specific psychiatric disorders.

The lifetime incidence of disorders seems high, but the authors point out that the rates reflect cummulative rates that were augmented by substance abuse disorders and disorders that are frequently transient (i.e., enuresis). The authors note that using DSM-III criteria to screen the general population may result in an overestimate of prevalence rates for psychiatric disorders.

Panic Disorder

Evidence that panic disorder can occur in children is supported by isolated clinical reports (Herskowitz, 1986; Van Winter & Stickler, 1984; Vitielo, Behar, Wolfson, & Delaney 1987) and by a report of the disorder in psychiatrically treated patients (Alessi & Magen, 1988) (see also chapter 1). In a report from the National Institute of Mental Health (NIMH) Epidemiological Cachment Area (ECA) study, retrospective reports from a probability sample of 3,000 adults 18 years or older cited the peak age of onset of panic disorder between 15 and 19 years (Von Korff, Eaton, & Keyl, 1985).

Hayward, Taylor, and Killen (1989) distributed a survey questionnaire (SCL-90-R for depression and anxiety, modified version of Anxiety Sensitivity Index) to ninth-grade students attending a physical education class in a local school district (see Table 3.2). This was followed by a 5- to 10-minute structured interview conducted by a clinician blind to questionnaire answers. DSM-III inclusion criteria were used to determine the prevalence of panic attacks.

There were 95 ninth graders (49 male, 46 female), mean age 14 years, in the study. The ethnic background of the students was 55% white, 7% black, 25% Asian, 14% Hispanic, 3% Pacific Islander, 3% Native American, 7% other. The lifetime prevalence of DSM-III panic disorders was 2.1% but increased to 6.3% if DSM-III-R criteria were used. Fourteen children (14.7%), 10 girls and 4 boys, experienced at least one four-symptom attack. Four boys (4.2%) reported at least one symptom-limited panic attack. Overall lifetime frequency of panic attacks was 18.9%. Fourteen adolescents (14.7%) reported spontaneous autonomic symptoms without fear.

Attacks were more frequent in girls. Substance abuse patterns were the same for panic and nonpanic groups. The panic group had higher scores than the nonpanic group on anxiety measures, avoidant personality traits, and depression scales. The group with spontaneous autonomic symptoms without fear was similar to normals on measures of anxiety, depression, avoidant personality traits, and anxiety sensitivity.

OCD

One third to one half of adults with OCD report onsets by 15 years (Black, 1977; Flament et al 1988). Although OCD is an accepted diagnostic entity in adolescents with symptoms the same as in the adult disorder, (see also chapter 9) there is only one epidemiological study of a community sample that uses DSM-III criteria to make the diagnosis (Flament et al., 1988). Earlier studies on psychiatrically referred children based on retrospective chart reviews report prevalence rates of 0.2% to 1.2% (Berman 1942; Hollingsworth, Tanguay, Grossman, & Pabst, 1980; Judd, 1965; Rutter, Tizard, & Whitmore, 1970; cited in Flament, 1988).

Flament et al.'s (1988) study was part of a larger two-stage epidemiological survey conducted by Whitaker et al. (1990) to measure eating, depressive, and anxiety symptoms in an entire high school student population (9th through 12th grades) of a semirural, predominantly middle-class community (see Table 3.2). The first stage consisted of several survey questionnaires, including the Leyton Obsessive Inventory—Child Version (LOI-CV), and was followed by clinician-administered semistructured interviews (including the OCD section of the DICA and Addendum for Compulsive Personality Disorder from the DISC). There were 356 students, selected by stratified random sample from stage 1, interviewed during stage 2. Students with high LOI-CV scores were divided into two groups based on impaired functioning: those who exhibited low interference and those with high interference. Thirty-five students (1% of the stage–sample) were in the low-interference group and 81 students (2% of the stage one sample) were in the high-interference group. Eighty percent of the 116 students participated in stage 2.

Eighteen students met DSM-III criteria for current OCD, and two students met criteria for past history of OCD. Point prevalence of OCD was 0.35% and lifetime prevalence was 0.4%. If the sample is weighted to reflect the sampling design, prevalence rates were $1 \pm 0.5\%$ for current episode of OCD and $1.9 \pm 0.7\%$ for lifetime history of OCD. Of the 18 students with current OCD, there were 11 boys and 9 girls. The mean age at the time of the interview was 16.2 years with a range of 14 to 18 years. Mean age of onset of the disorder was 12.8 years with a range of 7 to 18 years. Most adolescents described a gradual onset of symptoms, but some described sudden onsets. Symptom duration ranged from 6 months to 7 years. Only one of these students had been under psychiatric care for OCD symptoms.

All but one boy described obsessions with associated rituals. Obsessive thoughts were related to fears of contamination (35%) or fears of hurting self or familiar persons (30%). The most commonly reported rituals were washing and cleaning (85%), checking (40%), straightening (35%), repetition of actions (15%), and doing things "just right" (15%). Seventy percent had multiple obsessions and compulsions.

Comorbidity was common. Fifteen of the 20 students with a lifetime diagnosis of OCD had one or more other lifetime psychiatric diagnoses, and 10 of these students had a current psychiatric diagnosis. Major depression was most common, occurring in five of the students. This was followed by overanxious disorder and subclinical panic attacks in four students each, bulemia in three students, and phobic disorder in two students. When students with either OCD or compulsive personality disorder were compared with the population as a whole, no differences were found in SES, race, religion, grade-point average, or current physical health.

The authors believe that the reported prevalence rates are an underestimate of the true prevalence of the disorder in adolescents. Because the sample population were adolescents attending school, more severely disturbed teens not attending school were not included in the study. Also, it is likely that some of those not filling out the questionnaire would have obsessive-compulsive symptoms. Because the LOI-CV only asks for current symptoms, a portion of the sample with past symptoms of OCD may have been missed.

Epidemiological Studies of Pediatric Patients

The prevalence rates of DSM-III psychiatric disorders were reported in a pediatric patient population at a primary care outpatient facility and in patients who were part of a longitudinal, prospective study of school-aged children with newly diagnosed insulin-dependent diabetes mellitus (IDDM). Both studies used semistructured interviews with the children and with the parents about the children. Prevalence rates for anxiety disorders were similar in both studies: 5.3% based on parent report and 8.9% based on child report in one study (Costello et al., 1988) and 8% by consensus in the other study (Kovacs, Feinberg, Paulauskas, Finkelstein, Pollock, & Crouse-Novak, 1985).

During a 15-month period, all parents of children aged 7 to 11 years who made a visit to one of two health maintenance organizations affiliated with a large city and its surrounding suburb were screened with the CBcL (Costello, 1988). All those with scores above the cutoff point and a random sample of those with scores at or below the cutoff point were interviewed with the DISC. Both parent and child were interviewed. DSM-III diagnoses were computer generated based on algorithms. One-year prevalence rates were determined from the weighted data. A total of 798 children, 51.5% girls, was screened. Of these, 300 children (126 high scores and 174 low scores) were selected for further assessment.

Consistent with other studies, there was a discrepancy between child and parent reports (see Table 3.4). The weighted prevalence rate for psychiatric disorders based on parental interview was 11.8% and based on child interview was 13.8%. The prevalence rate based on combined reports was 22%. The weighted prevalence for anxiety disorders was 5.3% based on parental interview and 8.9% based on child interview. Simple phobia (9.2%) was most prevalent of all the anxiety disorders and social phobia (1%) least prevalent. Separation anxiety disorder (4.1%), which was re-

TABLE 3.4 One-Year Prevalence of DSM-III Anxiety Disorders in Pediatric Patients by Parent and Child Reports

Diagnosis	Prevalence by parent (%)	Prevalence by child (%)	Prevalence by both (%)
Anxiety disorders	5.3	8.9	
Separation anxiety	0.4	4.1	4.1
Avoidant	1	0.6	1.6
Overanxious	2.8	2	4.6
Simple phobia	3	6.7	9.2
Social phobia		1	1
Agoraphobia		1.2	1.2
Panic disorder	—	—	—

ported predominantly by the children, was as frequent as overanxious disorder (4.6%), which was reported predominantly by the parents. Children reported simple phobias more than twice as often as the parents and reported agoraphobia (1.2%), which the parents did not report at all. In general, girls were more likely to report anxiety disorders than boys.

There were several risk factors significantly associated with emotional disorders (anxiety and depression). Both parent and child reports of increased stress in the life of the child were associated with increased probability of an emotional disorder. The mother's current state of mental health was a significant risk factor for boys. Emotional disorders occurred more frequently in the 7- to 9-year-olds than the 10- to 11-year-olds. Separation anxiety disorder in the younger group accounted for this.

Kovacs et al. (1985) assessed 74 children, 8 to 13 years, who had IDDM for the presence of psychiatric disorders before onset and after diagnosis of their medical illness. The child and parent (about the child) were interviewed with the Interview Schedule for Children. Symptoms were counted as positive if they were ≥ 1 standard deviation of the symptom's rating distribution for the cohort. At study intake 8% of children had an anxiety disorder that predated onset of IDDM.

Epidemiological Studies of High-Risk Children

There are seven studies in the literature that use DSM-III criteria to make psychiatric diagnoses in the children of depressed or anxious parents (see Table 3.5). The studies have in common the use of structured diagnostic interviews with the child and parent (about the child). Interviews included the DICA (two studies), the DISC (one study), the CAS (one study), and the K-SADS (three studies). The diagnoses in the children were determined by

TABLE 3.5 Seven Studies of Children at Risk for Psychiatric Disorders Based on Diagnoses of Depression or Anxiety in the Parents[a]

Study	Sample size	Control size	Age of sample (years)	Control group	Instrument	% Any anxiety disorder (proband) (%)	% Any anxiety disorder (control) (%)
Parents with major depression							
Orvaschel	61	45	6–17	Normal	K-SADS	19.7	8.7
Keller	72		6–19	Normal	DICA	19	
Hammen	19	35	8–16	Normal	K-SADS	21	12
	12			Bipolar		41	
	18			Medical			22
Weissman	153	67	6–23	Normal	K-SADS	39.9	17.9
Breslau	[b]	84	116	8–17	Normal	DISC	
	40%	16%					
Sylvester	27	48	7–17	Normal	DICA	44	3
Parents with dysthymic disorder							
Turner	14	29	7–12	Normal	CAS	21	9
Parents with anxiety disorders							
Breslau	[c]	54	116	6–17	Normal	DICA	
	20%	16%					
Sylvester[d]	50	48	7–17	Normal	DICA	42	3
Turner	16	29	7–12	Normal	CAS	37	9

Note. From Weissman, M. M. (1988). Psychopathology in the children of depressed parents: Direct interview studies. In D. L. Gershon & J. E. Barret (Eds.), *Relatives at risk for mental disorder* (pp. 143–159). New York: Raven. Reprinted by permission.
[a]Each author represents one study, although data from the Breslau, Sylvester, and Turner studies are listed separately under children of depressed or dysthymic parents and children of anxious parents. All rates are lifetime except annual rates reported by Breslau. [b]Probands have depression with or without generalized anxiety. [c]Probands have generalized anxiety disorder. [d]Probands have panic disorder.

consensus or best estimate. The raters were blind to the parents' diagnosis. Control groups were the children of parents without any psychiatric disorder and, in one study, children of medically ill parents.

The children of depressed or anxious parents are at significantly greater risk for the development of psychiatric disorders, particularly depression and anxiety disorders. The most common psychiatric diagnoses in these children are major depression, anxiety disorders, and substance abuse. The lifetime prevalence rates for anxiety disorders range from 19% to 44% in the children at risk and from 3% to 12% in the low-risk children and are 22% in the children of medically ill parents. The rates for anxiety disorders in the high-risk group are similar to the rates for major depression.

Separation anxiety disorder and overanxious disorder were the most commonly reported anxiety disorders (see Table 3.6). Prevalence rates for separation anxiety disorder ranged from 3% to 25% in the children of depressed/anxious parents, and the rate for children of bipolar parents was 25%. Rates for children of normal parents ranged from 4% to 9%. Prevalence rates for overanxious disorder ranged from 5% to 27% in the children at risk and from 3% to 12% in the children of normals. Prevalence rates for simple phobias ranged from 0.9% to 12% in the high-risk children. Prevalence rates for OCD ranged from 1% to 7%. Panic disorder and avoidant disorder were reported in one study each and had prevalence rates of 1.9% and 3%, respectively.

Weissman, Prusoff, Gammon, Merikangas, Leckman, and Kidd (1984) reported on lifetime prevalence rates of DSM-III diagnoses in the children of depressed parents based on interviews with the parent about the child and, in two later studies (Moreau, Weissman, & Warner, 1989; Weissman, Gammon, John, Merikangas, Prusoff, & Scholomskas, 1987), reported prevalence rates based on information that included a direct interview with the child. Children of nonbipolar depressed parents were age and sex matched to normal controls. There was a total of 220 subjects, 153 children of depressed parents and 67 children of normal controls. The children and the parents were interviewed about the children with K–SADS–E (Schedule for Affective Disorders and Schizophrenia for School–Aged Children—Epidemiological Version). A child psychiatrist blind to the parents' diagnosis determined DSM-III diagnoses in the children by best-estimate method.

Based on interviews with the parents about the children, DSM-III disorders were diagnosed in the high-risk children 3 times more frequently than in the children of normals. Children with both parents depressed were at the greatest risk for development of psychiatric disorder. The most commonly diagnosed disorders in the high-risk children were major depression (13.1%), attention deficit disorder (11.3%), and separation anxiety disorder (10.3%). None of the children of normal parents had separation anxiety disorder or major depression. School phobia was diagnosed in 2.8% of the

TABLE 3.6 Prevalence Rates of DSM-III Anxiety Disorders in Children of Depressed and/or Anxious Parents

Study	SAD (%)	OAD (%)	School phobia (%)	Avoidant disorder (%)	Panic disorder (%)	Agoraphobia (%)	Simple phobia (%)	OCD (%)
Weissman								
Depression	10.3		2.8		1.9	1.9	.9	1
Control			1.2					1.2
Breslau								
GAD	9	11						
Depression	13	27						
Normal	4	12						
Hammen								
Depression	16	5						
Bipolar	25	8					8	
Medical	11	11						
Normal	9	3						3
Keller								
Depression	3	7		3			6	
Orvaschel								
High risk	8						12	7
Low risk	4						7	0
Turner								
Anxious	25	12						
Dysthymic	7	7	7					

Note. SAD = separation anxiety disorder. OAD = overanxious disorder. OCD = obsessive compulsive disorder. GAD = general anxiety disorder.

high-risk group and 1.2% of the normal group. Panic disorder (1.9%), agoraphobia (1/9%), and simple phobia (.9%) were only diagnosed in the children at risk. OCD was estimated to occur in 1% of the high-risk children and 1.2% of the low-risk children.

When the children were interviewed directly, anxiety disorders occurred in 39.9% of the high-risk children and 27.4% of children of normal controls. The relative risk of developing any anxiety disorder for the children at risk was 2.2 ($p < .05$). There was no further specification as to the type of anxiety disorder.

Seven cases of panic attacks, six of which met DSM-III criteria for panic disorder, were diagnosed in the high-risk children (Moreau et al., 1989). Symptom profiles were similar to those found in adults with the disorder. Comorbidity was high, most commonly major depression and separation anxiety disorder.

Orvaschel, Walsh-Allis, and Ye (1988) compared lifetime prevalence rates of psychiatric disorders in 61 children of depressed parents with 45 children of nonpsychiatrically disordered parents. The children were 6 to 17 years. The children and parents (about the children) were interviewed with K-SADS.

The high-risk children were at greater risk for the development of DSM-III diagnoses and had more comorbidity than the low-risk children. There was a nonsignificant trend for high-risk children to have anxiety disorders compared with low-risk children. Separation anxiety disorder was diagnosed in 8% of the high-risk children and 4% of the low-risk children. Phobias in the high-risk children compared with low-risk children were 12% and 7%, respectively. OCD was only diagnosed in the high-risk children (7%). There was no association between anxiety disorders in the children and sex of depressed parent or age of onset of the parent's depression.

Breslau, Davis, and Prabucki (1986) reported on the annual prevalence of psychiatric disorders in 200 children, 8 to 17 years, of a geographically based probability sample of 331 families who had participated as normal controls in a study on childhood disability. Mothers' diagnoses were based on interviews with DIS. One child was randomly selected from each of the families and was interviewed with the DISC to generate diagnoses of major depression, separation anxiety disorder, and overanxious disorder. Children of mothers with major depression or generalized anxiety disorder were compared with the children of normal mothers.

The prevalence rate for anxiety disorders in the 200 children was 21%, 14% overanxious disorder, and 7% separation anxiety disorder. Prevalence rates for anxiety disorders in the children of mothers with either major depression or major depression and generalized anxiety disorder was 40%, in the children of mothers with generalized anxiety disorder was 20%, and in the children of normal mothers was 16%. Children of mothers with generalized anxiety disorder were not at increased risk for the development of any anxiety disorders, but the children of mothers with depression were at increased risk for the development of overanxious disorder.

Hammen, Gordon, Burge, Adrian, Jaenicke, and Hiroto (1987) interviewed 84 children of mothers with either unipolar or recurrent depression, bipolar disorder, chronic medical illness, or no psychiatric disorder. The children were 8 to 16 years. The children of mothers with affective disorders had more lifetime psychiatric disorders than the children of medically ill or normal mothers. Children of medically ill mothers had moderate rates of psychiatric disorders. Anxiety disorders were present in 21% of the children of depressed mothers, 41% of the children of bipolar mothers, 22% of the children of medically ill mothers, and 12% of the children of normal mothers. Rates of separation anxiety disorder were highest in children of bipolar mothers (25%) and lowest (9%) in children of normal mothers, and were 16% in children of depressed mothers and 11% in children of medically ill mothers. Overanxious disorder was more frequent in children of medically ill mothers (11%) than in the children of depressed mothers (5%), bipolar mothers (8%), or normals (3%).

Keller, Beardslee, Dorer, Lavori, Samuelson, and Klerman (1986) reported on the lifetime prevalence rates of psychiatric disorders in 72 children, 6 to 19 years, of parents with affective disorders. The parents were a subsample of subjects who had participated in the Children at Risk for Affective Disorders Study at Massachusetts General Hospital, a site of the NIMH Clinical Research Branch Collaborative Psychobiology of Depression Study. Diagnoses for the children were based on the DICA. Nineteen percent of the children had anxiety disorders: 3% separation anxiety disorder, 7% overanxious disorder, 3% avoidant disorder, and 6% simple phobia.

Sylvester, Hyde, and Reichler (1988) studied 125 children, 7 to 17 years, of parents with either panic disorder, major depression, or no psychiatric disorder. The children were diagnosed with data obtained from the DICA. The children of depressed parents and panic disorder parents had significantly higher lifetime rates of anxiety disorders, 44% and 42%, respectively, than did the children of normals (3%).

Turner, Beidel, and Costello (1987) reported prevalence rates of anxiety disorders in 16 children of anxiety-disordered patients, 14 children of dysthymic patients, 13 children of normal parents recruited from an announcement, and 16 normal school children enrolled in an elementary school. The 59 children, 38 boys and 24 girls, were 7 to 12 years old. Children and parents (about the children) were interviewed with the CAS, and, in addition, the children filled out self-report inventories. The children of anxious parents reported more anxiety, fears, worries, school problems, and somatic complaints than the normal children, or the children of dysthymic or normal parents. These children were 7 times more likely to meet criteria for any anxiety disorder, most commonly separation anxiety disorder and overanxious disorders, than the normal children and were 2 times more likely to have any anxiety disorder than the children of dysthymic parents.

CONCLUSION

The newer epidemiological studies cited since Orvaschel and Weissman's review (1986) are more sophisticated in their methodology and include structured diagnostic interviews, information from the child and from parent about the child, a consistent nosological system (DSM-III), and prevalence rates for specific anxiety disorders. Prevalence rates for anxiety disorders in the general population, however, are high unless information provided by the parent is used to define stricter diagnostic criteria based on degree of impairment and need for treatment. Even with stricter criteria, most children with anxiety disorders do not seek psychiatric services.

Although there currently are no published longitudinal epidemiological studies of anxiety disorders first diagnosed in childhood, a review of the multiple cross-sectional studies of children at different ages yields certain trends. Six to 12-month prevalence rates of anxiety disorders are similar for prepubertal children and adolescents. Separation anxiety disorder is more frequent in children than adolescents, and the reverse is true for overanxious disorder. There are conflicting reports on phobias, but rates seem to be highest in the 7- to 11-year age group.

Children at risk for psychiatric disorder by virtue of depression or anxiety in their parents compared with children of nonpsychiatrically ill parents have higher rates of anxiety disorders, particularly separation anxiety disorder, overanxious disorder, and simple phobias. The offspring of low-risk controls in these studies have rates comparable with the rates in community or school samples of children.

The epidemiological data in children are still limited, however. Many questions about anxiety disorders and symptoms in nonpsychiatric samples of children remain. The natural history of anxiety disorders in childhood and the relationship of childhood anxiety disorders to the adult disorders are unclear. The epidemiological data still rest on small cross-section samples of interviewed children. Longitudinal studies are necessary to determine the differences of anxiety disorders across the lifespan and to understand the relationship of childhood disorders to adult disorders. Therefore, all conclusions are subject to future findings.

Acknowledgment: The preparation of this chapter was supported in part by the NIMH grants #36197, #37592, and #28274. Portions of this manuscript appeared in "Epidemiology of Anxiety Disorders in Children: A Review" in *Anxiety Disorders of Childhood,* edited by Rachel Gittelman, PhD, Guilford Press, New York, and in "Psychopathology in the Children of Depressed Parents: Direct Interview Studies" in *Relatives at Risk for Mental Disorders,* edited by D. L. Dunner, E. S. Gershon, and J. E. Barret, Raven Press, New York.

REFERENCES

Abe, K., & Masui, T. (1981). Age-sex trends of phobic and anxiety symptoms in adolescents. *British Journal of Psychiatry, 138,* 297–302.

Agras, S., Sylvester, D., & Oliveau, D. (1969). The epidemiology of common fears and phobias. *Comprehensive Psychiatry, 10,* 151–156.

Alessi, N. E., & Magen, J. (1988). Panic disorder in psychiatrically hospitalized children. *The American Journal of Psychiatry, 145,* 1450–1453.

Anderson, J. C., Williams, S., McGee, R., & Silva, P. A. (1987). DSM-III disorders in preadolescent children. *Archives of General Psychiatry, 44,* 69–81.

Berman, L. (1942). The obsessive-compulsive neurosis in children. *Journal of Nervous and Mental Disorders, 85,* 26–39.

Bird, H. R. (1989). Risk factors of maladjustment in Puerto Rican children. *Journal of American Academy of Child and Adolescent Psychiatry.*

Bird, H. R., Canino, G., Rubio-Stipec, M., Gould, M. S., Ribera, J., Sesman, M., Woodbury, M., Heurtas-Goldman, S., Pagan, A., Sanchez-Lacay, R., & Moscoso, M. (1988). Estimates of the prevalence of childhood maladjustment in a community survey in Puerto Rico: The use of combined measures. *Archives of General Psychiatry, 45,* 1120–1126.

Black, A. (1974). The natural history of obsessional neurosis. In Hock, P. H., & Zubin, J. (Eds.), *Obsessional states* (pp 19–54). London: Methuen.

Breslau, N., Davis, G. C., & Prabucki, K. (1987). Searching for evidence on the validity of generalized anxiety disorder: Psychopathology in children of anxious mothers. *Psychiatry Research, 20,* 285–297.

Chambers, W. J., Puig-Antich, J., Hirsch, M., Paez, P., Ambrosini, P. J., Tabrizi, M. A., & Davies, M. (1985). The assessment of affective disorders in children and adolescents by semistructured interview: Test-retest reliability of the Schedule for Affective Disorders and Schizophrenia for School-age Children, Present Episode Version. *Archives of General Psychiatry, 42,* 696–702.

Chiland, C. (1977). Problems in child psychiatric epidemiology—contributions from a longitudinal study in epidemiological approaches. In *Child psychiatry* (pp. 45–55). New York: Academic Press.

Costello, E. J. (1989). Developments of child psychiatric epidemiology. *Journal of the American Academy of Child and Adolescent Psychiatry.*

Costello, E. J., Costello, A. J., Edelbrock, C., Burns, B. J., Dulcan, M. K., Brent, D., Janiszewski, S. (1988). Psychiatric disorders in pediatric primary care. *Archives of General Psychiatry, 45 (12),* 1107–1117.

Costello, E. J., Edelbrook, C. S., & Costello, A. J. (1985). Validity of the NIMH Diagnostic Interview Schedule for children: A comparison between psychiatric and pediatric patients. *Journal of Abnormal Child Psychology, 13,* 579–596.

Earls, F. (1980). Prevalence of behavior problems in 3-year-old children: A cross-national replication. *Archives of General Psychiatry, 37,* 1153–1157.

Flament, M. F., Whitaker, A., Rappoport, J. L., Davies, M., Berg, C. Z., Kalikow, K., Sceery, W., & Shaffer, D. (1988). Obsessive compulsive disorder in adolescence: An epidemiological study. *Journal of the American Academy of Child and Adolescent Psychiatry, 27,* 764–772.

Hammen, C., Gordon, D., Burge, D., Adrian, C., Jaenicke, C., & Hiroto, D. (1987). Maternal affective disorders, illness and stress: Risk for children's psychopathology. *American Journal of Psychiatry, 144,* 736–741.

Hayward, C., Taylor, C. B., Killen, J. D. (1989). Panic attacks in young adolescents. *American Journal of Psychiatry, 146,* 1061–1062.

Herjanic, B., & Campbell, W. (1977). Differentiating psychiatrically disturbed children on the basis of a structured interview. *Journal of Abnormal Child Psychology, 5,* 127–134.

Herskowitz, J. (1986). Neurologic presentations of panic disorder in childhood and adolescence. *Dev Med Child Neurol, 28,* 617–623.

Hollingsworth, C. E., Tanguay, P. E., Grossman, L., & Pabst, P. (1980). Long-term outcome of obsessive-compulsive disorder in childhood. *Journal of American Academy of Child and Adolescent Psychiatry, 19,* 134–144.

Judd, L. L. (1965). Obsessive compulsive neurosis in children. *Archives of General Psychiatry, 12,* 136–143.

Kashani, J. H., Beck, N. C., Hoeper, E. W., Fallahi, C., Corcoran, C. M., McAllster, J. A., Rosenberg, T. K., & Reid, J. C. (1987). Psychiatric disorders in a community sample of adolescents. *American Journal of Psychiatry, 144,* 584–589.

Kashani, J. H., & Orvaschel, H. (1988). Anxiety disorders in mid-adolescence: A community sample. *American Journal of Psychiatry 145,* 960–964.

Kastrup, M. (1976). Psychic disorders among pre-school children in a geographically delimited area of Aarhus county, Denmark. *Acta Psychiatric Scandanavian, 54,* 29–42.

Keller, M. B., Beardslee, W. R., Dorer, D. J., Lavori, P. W., Samuelson, H., & Klerman, G. L. (1986). Impact of severity and chronicity of parental affective illness on adaptive functioning and psychopathology in children. *Archives of General Psychiatry, 43,* 930–937.

Kovacs, Feinberg, Paulauskas, Finkelstein, Pollock, & Crouse-Novak (1985) Initial coping responses and psychosocial characteristics of children with insulin-dependent diabetes mellitus. *Journal of Pediatrics, 106,* 827–834.

Lapouse, R., & Monk, M. A. (1959). Fears and worries in a representative sample of children. *American Journal of Orthopsychiatry, 19,* 803–813.

Lerner, J. A., Inui, T. S., Trupin, E. W., & Douglas, E. (1985). Preschool behavior can predict future psychiatric disorders. *Journal of the American Academy of Child Psychiatry, 24,* 42–48.

Marks, I., & Lader, M, (1973). Anxiety states (anxiety neurosis): A review. *Journal of Nervous and Mental Disorder, 156,* 3–18.

Moreau, D. M., Weissman, M. M. & Warner, V. (1989). Panic disorder in children. *American Journal of Psychiatry.*

Orvaschel, H., Walsh-Allis, G., & Ye, W. (1988). Psychopathology in children of parents with recurrent depression. *Journal of Abnormal Psychiatry, 16,* 17–28.

Orvaschel, H., & Weissman, M. M. (1986)l Epidemiology of anxiety disorders in children: A review. In R. Gittelman (Ed.), *Anxiety disorders of childhood* (pp. 58–72). New York: Guilford.

Richman, N., Stevenson, J. E., & Graham, P. J. (1975). Prevalence of behavior problems in three-year old children: An epidemiologic study in a London borough. *Journal of Child Psychology and Psychiatry, 16,* 277–287.

Rutter, M. (1977). Surveys to answer questions: Some methodological considerations. In P. J. Graham, (Ed.), *Epidemiological approaches in child psychiatry* (pp. 1–31). New York: Academic Press.

Rutrter, M., Tizard, J., & Whitmore, K. (1970). *Education, health and behavior.* London: Longman.

Sylvester, G., Hyde, T. S., & Reichler, R. J. (1988). Clinical psychopathology among children of adults with panic disorder. In D. L. Dunner, E. S. Gershon, & J. Barret (Eds.), *Relatives at risk for mental Disorders* (pp. 87–102). New York: Raven.

Turner, S. M., Beidel, D. C., & Costello, A. (1987). Psychopathology in the offspring of anxiety disorders patients. *Journal of Consulting and Clinical Psychology, 55,* 229–235.

Van Winter, J. T., & Stickler, G. B. (1984). Panic attack syndrome. *Journal of Pediatrics, 105,* 661–665.

Velez, C. N., Johnson, J., & Cohen, P. (1989). The children in the community project: A longitudinal analysis of selected risk factors for childhood psychopathology. *Journal of the American Academy of Child and Adolescent Psychiatry, 27,* 349–356.

Vitielo, B., Behar, D., Wolfson, S., & Delaney, M. A. (1987). Panic disorder in prepubertal children. *American Journal of Psychiatry, 144,* 525–526.

Von Korff, M. R., Eaton, W. W., & Keyl, P. M. (1985). The epidemiology of panic attacks and panic disorder: Results of three community surveys. *American Journal of Epidemiology, 122,* 970–981.

Weissman, M. M. (1988). Psychopathology in the children of depressed parents: Direct interview studies. In D. L. Dunner, E. S. Gershon, & J. E. Barret (Eds.), *Relatives at risk for mental disorder* (pp. 143–159). New York: Raven.

Weissman, M. M., Gammon, G. D., John, K., Merikangas, K. R., Prusoff, B. A., & Scholomskas, D. (1987). Children of depressed parents: Increased psychopathology and early onset of major depression. *Archives of General Psychiatry, 44,* 847–853.

Weissman, M. M., & Merikangas, K. R. (1986). The epidemiology of anxiety and panic disorders: An update. *The Journal of Clinical Psychiatry, 47* (Suppl.), 11–18.

Weissman, M. M., Prusoff, B. A., Gammon, G. D., Merikangas, K. R., Leckman, J. F., & Kidd, K. K. (1984). Psychopathology in the children (ages 6–18) of depressed and normal parents. *Journal of the American Academy of Child Psychiatry, 23,* 78–84.

Weissman, M. M., Wickramaratne, P., Warner, V., John, K., Prusoff, B. A., Merikangas, K. R., & Gammon, G. D. (1987). Assessing psychiatric disorders in children: Discrepancies between mothers' and children's reports. *Archives General Psychiatry, 44,* 747–753.

Werry, J. S., & Quay, H. C. (1971). The prevalence of behavior symptoms in younger elementary school children. *American Journal Orthopsychiatry, 41,* 136–143.

Whitaker, A., Johnson, J., Shaffer, D., Rapport, I. L., et al. (1990). Uncommon troubles in young people: Prevalence estimate of selected psychiatric disorders in a nonreferred adolescent population: *Archives of General Psychiatry, 47,* 487–496.

CHAPTER 4

Developmental Differences in Expression of Anxiety Disorders in Children and Adolescents

Cyd C. Strauss

As discussed at length in the previous chapter, there has been an extensive literature demonstrating that anxiety symptoms and fears change over the course of childhood and adolescence (Graziano, DeGiovanni, & Garcia, 1979). In particular, differences in the number and types of fears occur in children of various ages (e.g., Jersild & Holmes, 1935). In their review of the literature, Graziano et al. (1979) noted that the number of reported fears generally declines from young childhood to adolescence (MacFarlane, Allen, & Honzik, 1954; Scherer & Nakamura, 1968). The percentage of children reporting one or more fears also appears to decrease with age (see Graziano et al., 1979). Regarding variations in types of fears according to age, there appear to be age-related decreases in fears of separation, animals, the dark, and imaginary creatures, and age-related increases in school and social anxieties (Graziano et al., 1979). It should be noted that investigations that have demonstrated changes in anxiety symptomatology over the course of development have primarily been conducted in non-referred samples, thus describing the natural course of fears in children who do not demonstrate significant psychopathology for the most part (see chapter 2 for a review of the literature in this area).

With the advent of the DSM-III (American Psychiatric Association, 1980), research attention has increasingly shifted to children and adolescents with clinically significant anxiety disorders. In particular, clinic-referred youngsters diagnosis with anxiety disorders described in DSM-III and DSM-III-R (American Psychiatric Association, 1987) as first evident in childhood (i.e., separation anxiety disorder, overanxious disorder, and avoidant disorder) have been the subject of recent empirical work. In contrast to prior data, recent studies have shown that anxiety disorders can be assessed reliably using structured interviews, can be enduring, and are associated with serious forms of impairment (Last, Hersen, Kazdin, Finkel-stein, & Strauss, 1987; Silverman & Nelles, 1988; Strauss, Lahey, Frick, Frame, & Hynd, 1988; Strauss, Last, Hersen, & Kazdin, 1988).

Support for the reliability and validity of anxiety disorder subtypes in childhood and adolescence has laid the groundwork for further study of research questions of interest. One particular area of investigation has been the examination of developmental changes that occur in the man-ifestation of different anxiety disorder subtypes in childhood and adoles-cence. This area of research was spurred by the prior data demonstrating changes in subclinical fears over time in nonpsychopathological children and by the importance of identifying any changes that may occur in anxiety symptomatology for the diagnosis, assessment, and treatment of children with clinically significant anxiety disorders. Recently, several reports have appeared in the literature evaluating the change in anxiety disorder symp-toms in clinic samples of anxious children of different ages. Specifically, developmental differences in children with separation anxiety disorder, overanxious disorder, phobias, and anxiety-based school refusal have been examined. This chapter reviews the studies that have been conducted to date, discusses the implications of the results of these investigations, and outlines directions for future research in this important research area.

REVIEW OF THE LITERATURE

Studies conducted to date have employed a cross-sectional approach to examine age differences in the manifestation of specific anxiety disorder subtypes in childhood. Although this approach is not as satisfactory as following children over time, these data provide preliminary initial in-formation regarding changes in anxiety that may occur over the course of childhood and adolescence.

Separation Anxiety Disorder

The roles of age and gender in the symptom expression of separation anxiety disorder were examined in a study conducted by Francis, Last, and Strauss (1987). In this investigation, 45 clinic-referred youngsters (14 male, 31 female) between the ages of 5 and 16 were diagnosed with separation anxiety disorder on the basis of summary ratings derived from parent and child semistructured interviews using the ISC. Children were assigned to one of three age groups: (a) the *young* group consisted of children between the ages of 5 and 8 years ($n = 20$; 6 male, 14 female); (b) the *middle* group included children between the ages of 9 and 12 years ($n = 16$; 8 male, 8 female); and (c) the *adolescent* group contained children between the ages of 13 and 16 years ($n = 9$; all female).

The dependent variables examined in this study were ISC summary ratings for the nine individual symptoms included in the DSM-III diagnostic criteria for separation anxiety disorder. A diagnosis of separation anxiety disorder requires at least three of the following nine DSM-III criteria: (a) unrealistic worry about possible harm befalling major attachment figure(s) or fear that the major attachment figure(s) will leave and not return; (b) unrealistic worry that an untoward calamitous event will separate the child from a major attachment figure (e.g., the child will be lost, kidnapped, killed, or be the victim of an accident); (c) persistent reluctance or refusal to go to school in order to stay with major attachment figure(s) or at home; (d) persistent reluctance or refusal to go to sleep without being next to a major attachment figure or to go to sleep away from home; (e) persistent avoidance of being alone in the home and emotional upset if unable to follow the major attachment figure around the home; (f) repeated night-mares involving a theme of separation; (g) complaints of physical symp-toms on school days (e.g., stomachaches, headaches, nausea, vomiting); (h) signs of excessive distress on separation, or when anticipating separa-tion, from major attachment figure(s) (e.g., temper trantrums, crying, pleading with the parents not to leave); (i) social withdrawal, apathy, sadness, or difficulty concentrating on work or play when not with a major attachment figure. For the purposes of the study, each stymptom was scored as "present" (a clinically significant rating of "3" or greater) or "absent" (a nonsignificant rating of below "3").

Although males and females did not differ significantly from one another in their rates of any of the separation anxiety symptoms, age differences did emerge for the frequency of specific symptoms and for the total number of clinically significant symptoms. Specifically, young children (60%) were significantly more likely than middle children (13%) to present with "nightmares involving a theme of separation." In addition, young children (65%) and middle children (79%) were more likely to display "excessive distress upon separation" than were adolescents (13%). A trend toward significance ($p < .08$) was observed for "physical complaints on school days," with 100% of separation anxious adolescents reporting physical complaints on school days compared with 69% of middle children and 58% of young children having this symptom.

In terms of the total number of separation anxiety symptoms presented by children in each group, young children (100%) were significantly more likely to present with four or more total symptoms than were middle children (69%). That is, 31% of middle children met the minimum of three diagnostic criteria for the disorder. In contrast, young children never met the minimum number of criteria for separation anxiety disorder. No such differences emerged between the adolescent group and the other two groups.

The authors also calculated the most frequently co-occurring symptoms for each age group. Adolescents (79%) tended to present with both "reluctance or refusal to go to school" and "physical complaints on school days." The most common concurrent symptoms for middle children were "excessive distress upon separation" and "withdrawal, apathy, sadness, or poor concentration when separated," with 50% of this group displaying these two symptoms simultaneously. Two patterns of symptoms were found in the young group: 65 percent displayed both "worry about harm befalling an attachment figure" and "worry that a calamitous event will separate the child from an attachment figure" and 65 percent presented simultaneously with "worry about harm befalling an attachment figure" and "relutance or refusal to go to school."

These findings provide initial descriptive information regarding differences in the manifestation of separation anxiety disorder in children of different ages. One interesting observation in this fairly large clinic sample of separation anxious children was that the percentage of children found in each group declined with age (i.e., 44% of the sample were in the young group, 36% were in the middle group, and 20% were adolescents). Consistent with this finding was the observation that young children tended to present with more symptoms of separation anxiety disorder than did older children.

Last, Hersen, Kazdin, Finkelstein, and Strauss (1987) and Last, Francis, Hersen, Kazdin, and Strauss (1987) further examined age differences in a set of studies comparing separation anxiety disorder children with children diagnosed with other anxiety disorders including overanxious disorder and school phobia. In the first study, demographic characteristics and patterns of comorbidity associated with separation anxiety disorder and overanxious disorder were contrasted in a sample of 69 children between the ages of 5 and 18 (Last, Hersen, Kazdin, Finkelstein, & Strauss, 1987). For the purposes of this chapter, age at intake will be examined. Three groups were compared in this study: children with both SAD and OAD ($n = 21$), children with SAD but not OAD ($n = 22$), and those with OAD but not SAD ($n = 26$). Findings revealed that SAD (mean age = 9.1 years), and SAD and OAD (mean age = 9.6 years) children were significantly younger on average than OAD children (mean age = 13.4 years) at the time of referral. Conversely, SAD, and SAD and OAD groups did not differ from one another in terms of age at intake. Most children in both SAD groups (SAD = 91%, SAD and OAD = 71%) were under 13 years of age, whereas most OAD children (69%) were 13 years of age or older.

Last, Francis, Hersen, Kazdin, and Strauss (1987) similarly showed that separation anxious children ($n = 48$, mean age = 9.4 years) were significantly younger than children diagnosed with a phobic disorder of school ($n = 19$, mean age = 14.3 years). In addition, the school phobic group (79%) contained a significantly higher percentage of children 13 years and older than the SAD group (19%).

Overall, these investigations suggest that SAD occurs primarily in younger children (i.e., less than 13 years of age), although this disorder also exists in adolescence. This early occurrence of SAD in childhood contrasts with the age at intake observed in the two other most common anxiety disorder subtypes leading to referral to a child outpatient clinic (i.e., overanxious disorder and a phobic disorder of school). The finding that SAD is more common in young children may be related to the observation that separation concerns *normally* occur in young children in the general population. One possible hypothesis for the development of pathological levels of separation anxiety in young children is that children may be more susceptible to separation-related stressors during this period when they are more inclined to experience separation anxiety normally. That is, those children who develop clinically significant separation anxiety may have experienced stressors such as the death of a major attachment figure, prolonged hospitalization of an attachment figure, or physical/psychological absence of a parental figure during a normal developmental stage when they typically experience anxiety about separation.

Even when occurring at pathological levels, SAD symptoms may dissipate as development progresses with exposure to nonthreatening separation from attachment figures. Thus, SAD may exist primarily in young children, as the available data suggest. Alternatively, it may be that separation concerns are reported as more common in young children because older children are unwilling to reveal symptomatology associated with separation anxiety (e.g., distress on separation from parents), even though the symptoms indeed are present. Instead, it may be more developmentally acceptable to express somatic complaints and to remain home from school, which may then be interpreted as a phobic disorder of school rather than as separation anxiety disorder. Longitudinal studies investigating whether young separation anxious children later are more prone to display phobic disorders of school would be of interest to evaluate this hypothesis. Overall, interpretation of the preceding data clearly is speculative and awaits further empirical investigation.

It also should be noted that the data described earler indicate *age at intake* for each of the anxiety disorder groups. In contrast to the supposition that separation anxiety primarily is present in younger children, it may be that children with separation anxiety disorder are *referred* for evaluation at a younger age than other anxiety-disordered children, although these subtypes may be equally common among the different age groups in the general population. Epidemiological studies conducted in nonreferred samples and follow-up investigations of clinically referred anxious children will enable greater understanding of separation anxiety symptomatology in children.

Overanxious Disorder

Strauss and her colleagues (Strauss, Lease, Last, & Francis, 1988) studied developmental patterns in 55 consecutive clinic-referred children and adolescents who were diagnosed with overanxious disorder. To evaluate developmental differences among youngsters with overanxious disorder, two groups were formed: (a) children younger than 12 years of age at the time of referral ($n = 23$), and (b) children 12 years of age and older at intake ($n = 32$). The mean age was 8 years (SD = 1.64) for children in the younger group and 15 years (SD = 1.80) for children in the older group. The two age groups did not differ significantly in the number of children in each group, (i.e., overanxious disorder did not occur at different rates in younger versus older children referred for clinical services). This finding is similar to results obtained in the Last, Hersen, Kazdin, Finkelstein, and Strauss (1987) sample, in which SAD, SAD and OAD, and OAD groups were contrasted in terms of age at intake. When both OAD groups are considered, overanxious disorder was found both in younger (younger than 13 years old) and older (13 years and older) children.

In addition to evaluation of the rate of overanxious disorder in younger versus older clinic-referred children, the two age groups of overanxious children were compared on numerous variables: sociodemographic variables, overanxious disorder symptom ratings, concurrent diagnoses, and self-reported anxiety and depression. First, comparison of the younger and older overanxious groups revealed no significant differences in sex ratio, racial composition, or SES. Fifty-six percent of the younger and 62% of the older children were female. Almost all in both groups were white, and most families of both age groups were of middle to upper SES.

Next, younger and older overanxious disorder children were compared on the frequency (presence or absence) of each of the seven individual symptoms comprising the DSM-III diagnosis of overanxious disorder. Overanxious disorder symptoms include unrealistic worry about future events, preoccupation with the appropriateness of past behavior, overconcern about competence in one or more areas, somatic complaints for which no physical basis can be established, marked self-consciousness or susceptibility to embarrassment or humiliation, excessive need for reassurance about a variety of concerns, and marked feelings of tension. Symptoms were evaluated using clinician summary ratings derived from ISC parent and child interviews. Findings revealed that older overanxious children were significantly more likely than younger overanxious children to express preoccupation with the appropriateness of past behavior, although there were no significant differences between the two groups in the rate at which they presented with each of the remaining six diagnostic symptoms. Of note, all but one child in each group demonstrated unrealistic worries about future events. A comparison of the total number of overanxious disorder symptoms displayed by each child in the two age groups (a minimum of four of the seven symptoms are required for the diagnosis) indicated that older children were significantly more likely to have a greater number of symptoms than were younger children. Older children (66%) presented with six or seven symptoms significantly more often than the younger children (35%). In fact, as many as 28% of older children met all seven DSM-III criteria for the disorder, whereas only 4% of the younger group presented with all overanxious disorder symptoms.

Younger and older overanxious disorder groups also were contrasted in their rates of concurrent DSM-III diagnoses including coexisting anxiety disorders, major depression, oppositional disorder, conduct disorder, and attention deficit disorder. Younger children more commonly had a co-morbid anxiety diagnosis of separation anxiety disorder, whereas older children were more likely to receive a concurrent anxiety disorder diagnosis of simple phobia. Older overanxious disorder children (47%) also were significantly more likely than younger children (17%) to meet diagnostic criteria for major depression. Finally, younger children (35%) more frequently displayed a concurrent diagnosis of attention deficit disorder than older children (9%).

Data derived from self-report inventories of anxiety and depression demonstrated significantly more state and trait anxiety, greater worry and oversensitivity, and higher levels of depression in older than younger children with overanxious disorder. Owing to the possibility that the differing total number of overanxious symptoms found in the two age groups may have presented a confound for findings on self-report measures, additional analyses were conducted in which the number of overanxious symptoms served as a covariate. Analyses of covariance again revealed that the older group received significantly higher scores on measures of state anxiety, worry and oversensitivity, and depression when the effect of number of symptoms was statistically controlled.

In sum, age differences were found in clinic-referred children with overanxious disorder. Younger and older children were dissimilar in (a) the number of overanxious symptoms displayed, (b) patterns of comorbidity, and (c) severity of self-reported anxiety and depression. Although several important differences emerged between the two age groups, notable similarities also were found. The rate of overanxious disorder diagnoses in younger versus older clinic-referred children did not differ. The two age groups also resembled one another in demographic characteristics.

Moreover, the frequency of specific overanxious symptoms did not appear to change over the course of childhood.

The observation that overanxious disorder is equally likely to occur across younger and older age groups is of interest. Children who are overanxious may innately have a higher baseline of arousal that is associated with excessive worries and elevated tension. This high baseline of arousal may then make overanxious children more susceptible to develop developmentally appropriate fears/phobias at various stages (e.g., separation anxiety in young childhood).

The finding that older overanxious children are more pathological in their severity of overanxious symptoms and self-reported anxiety and depression is worthy of discussion. Possible explanations for this finding include the hypothesis that older children may merely be better informants, and, thus, better able to describe their anxiety and depressive symptomatology than younger overanxious children, despite the fact that the actual severity of symptoms is comparable. An alternative interpretation is that older overanxious children may indeed experience severer symptomatology as a result of having had overanxious symptoms over a longer period or as a consequence of having to face more serious concerns over the course of development. The greater degree of pathology found in overanxious adolescents is suggestive that symptoms may well persist and lead to later diagnoses of generalized anxiety disorder in adulthood. Again these ideas are speculative but are suggestive of directions for future research in this area of investigation.

Phobias

As noted previously, studies of subclinical fears indicate variation in the number and types of fears demonstrated by children at different ages (see Graziano et al., 1979). Although the number of fears reported generally declines from young childhood to adolescence, some studies have demonstrated an increase in the number of reported fears between the ages of 9 and 11 (e.g., MacFarlane et al., 1954), with a peak occurring at age 11 (e.g., Chazan, 1962). Not all studies, however, have obtained significant correlations between number of fears and age (e.g., Croake & Knox, 1973; Lapouse & Monk, 1959).

It also has been observed that children in different age groups tend to display differing types of fears. Young children report fears of animals, the dark, and imaginary creatures. For example, 80% of 5- to 6-year-olds were found to express a fear of animals, whereas 23% of 13- to 14-year-olds reported this fear (Maurer, 1965). Conversely, realistic fears (e.g., physical danger, natural hazards, school achievement, loss, and social realtionship problems) are infrequent in young children, but become more common by early adolescence (Bauer, 1976; Maurer, 1965). An epidemiological study conducted by Agras, Sylvester, and Oliveau (1969) substantiated this latter finding. From childhood to adulthood, there was a marked increase in the rate of subclinical fears of snakes, crowds, injection, and other realistic fears. Most of these fears *began* in childhood, however, and persisted into adolescence; therefore, the increased prevalence of realistic fears in adolescence appears to reflect an accumulation of fears over age rather than a peak onset during adolescence.

In terms of findings for clinical phobias, distinct types of phobias also appear to be associated with different ages of onset. The association between age of onset and the development of specific types of phobias in childhood has primarily been demonstrated in follow-up studies of adults with clinical phobias. The less disabling phobias (e.g., simple) tend to have an earlier onset than more disabling ones (e.g., agoraphobia). Sheehan, Sheehan, and Minichello (1981) found that 31% of adults with simple phobias reported an onet before 9 years of age, and 26% reported onset between ages 10 and 19. In contrast, they found that only 4% of adult agoraphobics reported the onset of their disorder before age 9, with 26% reporting onset between 10 and 19 years of age. Marks and Gelder (1966) similarly found that adult patients with specific animal phobias reported a mean age of onset of 4.4 years, whereas most adults with specific situation phobias, social anxieties, and agoraphobia reported an onset in adolescence or later.

Ost (1987) conducted a large-scale study investigating the age of onset of various phobias in a sample of adult clinic phobic patients ($n = 370$). Results demonstrated that animal phobics had the earliest mean age of onset (7 years), followed by blood phobics (9 years), dental phobics (12 years), social phobics (16 years), claustrophobics (20 years), and agoraphobics (28 years). This investigator also provided data suggesting that the mode of acquiring the phobia may be associated with age of onset. Phobics in their sample reporting an early onset indicated that they acquired their phobias through instruction/information or modeling, whereas those acquiring their phobias through conditioning did so significantly later.

Other studies of adult agoraphobics have demonstrated that school phobia may be a significant precursor to its development. Klein (1964) and Berg (1976) found that agoraphobia that begins in late adolescence or early adulthood is often preceded by school phobia in early adolescence. Two other studies, however, suggest that the relationship between adolescent school phobia and adult anxiety disorders is not a specific one. Berg, marks, McGuire, and Lipsedge (1974) found that about one fourth of both adult agoraphobics and adults with other neurotic disorders reported adolescent school phobia. Similarly, Tyrer and Tyrer (1974) showed that school phobia was more common in the developmental histories of phobic, anxious, and depressed adults than normal adults, but the three psychiatric groups did not differ in this respect. It must be noted that these follow-back studies of adults have important limitations, and prospective studies are needed before reaching definitive conclusions.

Recently, data have been collected that directly examine age differences among clinic-referred youngsters with different phobic disorder subtypes (i.e., those with simple versus social phobias) (Strauss & Last, 1991). Children with simple phobias and those with social phobias were compared with one another in their ages of onset and ages at the time of referral. The entire phobic sample consisted of 67 children between the ages of 4 and 17 years who were referred for clinical services at an outpatient clinic for children and adolescents with anxiety disorders, and who met DSM-III-R diagnostic criteria for either simple or social phobia. Twenty-nine children were identified who had social phobia and 38 children were simple phobics. Consistent with findings from retrospective studies of phobic adults, social phobic youngsters were significantly older at intake and at onset of their phobias than children in the simple phobic group. Children in the social phobic group had a mean age at intake of 14.9 years and a mean age of onset of their disorder of 12.3 years. In contrast, simple phobic children were referred for clinical services at age 11.1 years on average and reported an onset of their phobias at a mean age of 7.8 years. The mean duration of phobias at the time of referral was 2.6 years for social phobias and 3.3 years for simple phobias, which was not statistically different.

A frequency distribution of ages at intake for the two phobic disorder groups revealed that simple phobic children presented with simple phobias throughout the entire 4- to 17-year age range, with peaks occurring during the 10- to 11- and 12- to 13-year intervals. In contrast, children were not referred for clinical services with a social phobia before age 10. Indeed, all but one child presented with social phobia between the ages of 12 and 17 years.

Interestingly, agoraphobia was so rare in this sample that the youngsters were not studied, as only four youngsters were identified as agoraphobic from among a total of 138 referrals. Again, this low rate of agoraphobia in a child sample corroborated findings from studies of adult phobics that have indicated an onset of agoraphobia in late adolescence and adulthood.

Age of onset of phobias seems to be related to their stability over time. Agras, Chapin, and Oliveau (1972) found that phobias for persons under age 20 were far less persistent than for adults. In fact, 100% of untreated phobias of children and adolescents had remitted within 5 years. In contrast, there are preliminary data that some fears are more persistent than others. Agras et al. (1972) indicated that more specific and focused fears were associated with better long-tern outcome.

Overall, findings from various sources (i.e., epidemiological studies of subclinical fears in general population of children, retrospective reports obtained from adult phobics, and direct examination of age differences in phobic youngsters) consistently indicate that different types of fears and phobias tend to have their onset at particular points in development. Simple phobias (such as fears of animals, the dark, and heights) tend to occur earlier than social phobias, which are more likely to onset at a younger age than agoraphobia.

The change in type of phobias evident over the course of childhood again may be related to the child's developmental readiness for these fears. Young children normally tend to have subclinical fears of animals, the dark, and so on; such phobias may be learned at developmental stages when a child is most likley to have such fears normally. Learning may result from observation of fearful adults or children, a traumatic experience with the fear stimuli, or misinformation about the feared stimuli.

Anxiety-Based School Refusal

Finally, Last and Strauss (1990) recently conducted a study investigating the characteristics of anxiety-disordered children with school refusal, a subgroup of anxious children not distinguished in DSM-III or DSM-III-R but that constitutes a large proportion of anxiety-disordered children referred for clinical services. In this investigation, the sample consisted of 63 children with school refusal who were identified from among a total of 145 children evaluated at the Child and Adolescent Anxiety Disorder Clinic, Western Psychiatric Institute and Clinic during a 21-month period. The age at intake for the anxiety-disordered children with school refusal ranged from 7 to 17 years, with a mean age of 13.5 years. The peak ages at intake in this sample occurred between 13 and 15 years of age. Very few children younger than 10 years old were referred with school refusal. Age of onset for the DSM-III-R anxiety disorder diagnoses associated with school refusal also was evaluated. On average, onset was 2 years prior to referral (mean = 11.3 years, SD = 3.3 years).

The ages of intake and onset were examined further in three subgroups of school refusers: those with separation anxiety disorder ($n = 24$), social phobia ($n = 19$), and simple phobia ($n = 14$), which were the most common anxiety diagnoses associated with school refusal in this sample. Results indicated that the separation anxiety disorder children with school refusal were significantly younger at intake (11.7 years) and at onset (8.7 years) on average than youngsters in the social phobic (14.8 and 12.4

years) and simple phobic (14.2 and 12.9 years) groups. The two phobic subgroups did not differ significantly with respect to the two age variables. The findings demonstrating the early onset of school refusal associated with separation anxiety disorder relative to phobic disorder school refusers was not surprising in light of prior age trends observed in this diagnostic subgroup generally (i.e., not limited to those presenting with school refusal). As suggested previously, it may be that young children with separation-based school refusal later are those adolescents diagnosed with a phobic disorder of school. The absence of age differences between simple and social phobias of school was not consistent with the overall prior findings for phobic disorders (see preceding section).

CONCLUSIONS

The studies conducted to date indicate that different anxiety disorder subtypes tend to onset at different ages. To summarize, separation anxiety disorder most commonly occurs in young children, regardless of whether the disorder occcurs in the presence or absence of a coexisting diagnosis of overanxious disorder. Different patterns of symptom expression were found in young, middle, and adolescent separation anxiety-disordered youngsters. Overanxious disorder does not appear to be more common in either younger or older children, although the disorder manifests itself somewhat differently in children younger than age 12 compared with those 12 years and older. Older overanxious youngsters showed more significant pathology including more symptoms of the disorder, a greater likelihood of a comorbid major depression, and higher levels of anxiety. When overanxious disorder did occur in younger children, it was more likely to coexist with separation anxiety disorder. Regarding phobic disorders, phobias generally appeared to present during the entire course of childhood, but there was considerable evidence to suggest that specific subcategories of phobias are more likely to occur during particular age intervals. The onset of simple phobias generally precedes the occurrence of social phobias, both of which have earlier onsets than agoraphobia. Research to date also suggests that the onset of anxiety-based school refusal occurs across a broad age range; the onset of school refusal appears to be dependent largely on the type of anxiety disorder diagnosis that is associated with school nonattendance.

Interpretations of age differences found in the expression of anxiety disorder subtypes across childhood have been offered. In particular, the occurrence of overanxious disorder throughout childhood and adolescence may be related to an "innate" higher baseline of arousal. Appearance of specific fears or phobias may then occur as a result of learning (e.g., conditioning, modeling) at particular stages of development in children who have this heightened level of arousal. Perhaps children are more likely to develop specific *phobias* at times when these fears occur normally in the general population.

These conclusions must be tempered by several limitations of the available data base. First, *age at intake* was the only variable available in several of the studies, rather than age of onset, so that it is not clear whether the different age patterns observed reflect different ages at which children with alternative anxiety disorder subtypes are referred for clinical services or whether these differences represent actual age variations for the various anxiety disorder subtypes.

Second, these data are cross-sectional and thus do not provide information concerning the course of the disorders over time. As a result, we still know little about the natural history of the various anxiety disorders. For instance, do young separation anxious children later develop into overanxious disorder adolescents, with the focus of anxiety shifting from separation situations during young childhood to situations involving social and performance following puberty? Or are these separate disorders that are more likely first to appear at particular ages owing to developmental factors such as cognitive and social changes? Although many questions remain unanswered at present, data currently available point to interesting age differences that can be investigated using the preferred, but more costly, longitudinal approach.

For the most part, these investigations studied whether specific anxiety disorder subtypes were present or absent at particular ages, without examining important variables such as the intensity, duration, or patterns of comorbidity associated with each of the anxiety disorders at various ages. Future studies need to focus on these additional variables to provide a comprehensive picture of the development of anxiety disorders in childhood.

REFERENCES

Agras, W. S., Chapin, H. H., & Oliveau, D. C. (1972). The natural history of phobia. *Archives of General Psychiatry, 26,* 315–317.

Agras, W. S., Sylvester, D., & Oliveau, D. (1969). The epidemiology of common fears and phobia. *Comprehensive Psychiatry, 10,* 151–156.

American Psychiatric Association (1980). *Diagnostic and statistical manual of mental disorders* (3rd ed.). Washington, DC: Author.

American Psychiatric Association. (1987). *Diagnostic and statistical manual for mental disorders* (3rd ed., rev.). Washington, DC: Author.

Bauer, D. H. (1976). An exploratory study of developmental changes in children's fears. *Journal of Child Psychology and Psychiatry, 17,* 69–74.

Berg, I. (1976). School phobia in children of agoraphobic women. *British Journal of Psychiatry, 128,* 86–89.

Berg, I., Marks, I., McGuire, R., & Lipsedge, M. (1974). School phobia and agoraphobia. *Psychological Medicine, 4,* 428–434.

Chazan, M. (1962). School phobia. *British Journal of Educational Psychology, 32,* 200–217.

Croake, J. W., & Knox, F. H. (1973). The changing nature of children's fears. *Child Study Journal, 3,* 91–105.

Francis, G., Last, C. G., & Strauss, C. C. (1987). Expression of separation anxiety disorder: The roles of age and gender. *Child Psychiatry and Human Development, 87,* 82–89.

Graziano, A., DeGiovanni, I. S., & Garcia, K. (1979). Behavioral treatment of children's fears: A review. *Psychological Bulletin, 86,* 804–830.

Jersild, A. T., & Holmes, F. B. (1935). Children's fears. *Child development* [Monograph 20]. New York: Teachers' College, Columbia University.

Klein, D. F. (1964). Delineation of two-drug-responsive anxiety syndrome. *Psychopharmacologia, 3,* 397–408.

Lapouse, R., & Monk, M. A. (1959). Fears and worries in a representative sample of children. *American Journal of Orthopsychiatry, 29,* 803–818.

Last, C. G., Francis, G., Hersen, M., Kazdin, A. E., & Strauss, C. C. (1987). Separation anxiety and school phobia: A comparison using DSM-III criteria. *American Journal of Psychiatry, 144,* 653–657.

Last, C. G., Hersen, M., Kazdin, A. E., Finkelstein, R., & Strauss, C. C. (1987). Comparison of DSM-III separation anxiety and overanxious disorders: Demographic characteristics and patterns of comorbidity. *Journal of the American Academy of Child Psychiatry, 26,* 527–531.

Last, C. G., & Strauss, C. C. (1990). School refusal in anxiety disordered children and adolescents. *Journal of the American Academy of Child and Adolsecent Psychiatry, 29,* 31–35.

MacFarlane, J. W., Allen, L., & Honzik, M. P. (1954). *A developmental study of the behavior problems of normal children between twenty-one months and fourteen years.* University of California Press: Berkeley.

Marks, I. M., & Gelder, M. G. (1966). Different ages of onset in varieties of phobia. *American Journal of Psychiatry, 123,* 218–221.

Maurer, A. (1965). What children fear. *Journal of Genetic Psychology, 106,* 265–277.

Ost, L.-G. (1987). Age of onset in different phobias. *Journal of Abnormal Psychology, 96,* 223–229.

Scherer, M. W., & Nakamura, C. Y. (1968). A fear survey schedule for children (FSS-FC): A factor analytic comparison with manifest anxiety. *Behaviour Research and Therapy, 6,* 173–182.

Sheehan, D. V., Sheehan, K. E., Minichello, N. E. (1981). Age of onset of phobic disorders: A reevaluation. *Comprehensive Psychiatry, 6,* 544–553.

Silverman, W. K., & Nelles, W. B. (1988). The Anxiety Disorders Interview Schedule for Children. *Journal of the American Academy of Child and Adolescent Psychiatry, 27,* 772–778.

Strauss, C. C., Lahey, B. B., Frick, P., Frame, C. L., & Hynd, G. W. (1988). Peer social status of children with anxiety disorders. *Journal of Consulting and Clinical Psychology, 56,* 137–141.

Strauss, C. C., & Last, C. G. (1991). *Phobic disorders in childhood and adolescence.* Manuscript submitted for publication.

Strauss, C. C., Last, C. G., Hersen, M., & Kazdin, A. E. (1988). Association between anxiety and depression in children and adolescents with anxiety disorders. *Journal of Abnormal Child Psychology, 15,* 57–68.

Strauss, C. C., Lease, C. A., Last, C. G., & Francis, G. (1988). Overanxious disorder: An examination of developmental differences. *Journal of Abnormal Children Psychology, 16,* 433–443.

Tyrer, P., & Tyrer, S. (1974). School refusal, truancy, and adult neurotic illness. *Psychological Medicine, 4,* 416–421.

CHAPTER 5

Aspects of School Phobia

Ian Berg

It would be an important omission in a book such as this one not to include something on the subject of school phobia (called school refusal in Great Britain), which, at the very least, denotes manifest anxiety with reluctance or complete refusal to go to school. It also often refers to a syndrome that includes staying home excessively, limited social functioning, and an avoidance of situations from which escape is difficult, where there are crowds of people, and where demands are made, particularly the place that includes all these things, namely school. Typically anxiety symptoms in school phobia include physical complaints such as nausea, anorexia, vomiting, headache, pallor, abdominal pain, malaise, frequency of micturition and diarrhea. For more than half a century child psychiatrists and psychologists have written about this syndrome. It is characterized by the child remaining at home and refusing to go to school despite reasonable efforts on the part of parents to bring about regular attendance, and where there is little evidence of antisocial tendencies on the part of the child that might suggest deliberate avoidance of school. Descriptions of children affected in this way have provided some of the best accounts of anxiety disorders of various kinds, which occur during the school years (Berg, 1990; Broadwin, 1932; Hersov, 1960; Hersov, & Berg, 1980; Johnson, Falstein, Szureck, & Svendsen, Partridge, 1939).

Mysteriously, in recent years some of the best books on childhood disorders (e.g., Quay & Werry, 1986; Tonge, Burrows, & Werry, 1990) have given school phobia scant attention, and the two important systems of classification for psychiatric disorders—DSM-III-R and ICD 10—fail to provide a category for it. This neglect of school phobia in current thinking after so many years of popularity must be deliberate. It would seem to be due to the fact that because several sorts of psychiatric disorders can occur in association with school phobia, the focus has moved from that to the accompanying disorders of anxiety and mood disturbance. It would be preferable to keep the syndrome of school phobia as a classifiable condition even though it would increase comorbidity and add yet another category to the list of disturbances shown by the child. There is an argument for keeping school phobia as a psychiatric disorder, which has many features of agoraphobia affecting adults but that is sufficiently distinctive, because of developmental considerations, to categorize it separately.

There are two main types of school phobia: those that come on acutely in a child who has functioned reasonably normally before onset, and those that arise in a child who has had similar problems from the preschool years and has never developed the social skills that would permit normal functioning (Berg, Nichols, & Pritchard, 1969; Coolidge, Hahn, & Peck, 1957). There are two ways in which the chronic type may be conceptualized as a developmental problem: first, the fact that the child remains overdependent (Berg & McGuire, 1971) and fails to develop the social skills required to travel freely away from home, be self-reliant, and mix normally with other children makes the disorder similar to other situations in which a normal skill fails to develop satisfactorily; and second, the fact that the features of the disorder include behaviors that are more appropriate in preschool children including clinging to parents and seeking the security of home when any threat is perceived.

Both DSM-III-R and ICD 10 classifications give school refusal as a feature of separation anxiety disorder and ICD 10 also specifies onset before age 6 as a criterion for separation anxiety disorder. Although it is true that most children with school phobia have marked separation anxiety, in one study 85% of cases irrespective of age (Gittleman-Klein & Klein, 1980), this is by no means always the case (Smith, 1970), and other diagnostic categories in these classifications have to be used (see chapter 8). Only a minority of cases of school phobia clearly begin in early childhood (Berg, Nichols, & Pritchard, 1969), and when there is severe separation anxiety it often comes on, inappropriately from a developmental viewpoint, in the early teenage years (Gittleman-Klein & Klein, 1980).

An interesting variant of school phobia is the masquerade syndrome (Waller & Eisenberg, 1980) in which school phobia can for a time masquerade as physical illness that appears to justify absence from school. It may be superimposed on actual physical illness in the situation in which so much time off school would not be appropriate. Characteristically, when negative physical investigations suggest that the child is not ill enough to be kept away from school and the family is informed, the problem becomes transformed into more typical school phobia. It should not be assumed that school phobia is always accompanied by a definite psychiatric disorder (Bools, Foster, Brown, & Berg, 1990). Sometimes the emotional upset on school mornings accompanying refusal to go to school is insufficient to justify the existence of a DSM-III-R or an ICD 10 diagnosis. School phobia is a condition that affects boys and girls equally, has no particular social class distribution, is unrelated to intelligence or educational ability, and characteristically occurs in the early teenage years (Berg, 1984; Hersov, 1985).

Neither DSM-III-R nor ICD 10 have been available long enough for empirical studies to have been reported on the psychiatric disorders accompanying school phobia. So much comorbidity was found with DSM III that it seems likely that several anxiety disorders and also depression will be appropriately diagnosed using these newer classifications (Bernstein & Garfinkel, 1986; Hoshino et al., 1987; Kolvin, Berney, & Bhate, 1984).

CLASSIFICATION OF ANXIETY DISORDERS IN SCHOOL PHOBIA

In DSM-III-R there are three categories in the group of anxiety disorders first evident in infancy—childhood or adolescence. Separation anxiety is one of them. Children who suffer from this have excessive anxiety about being separated from those to whom they are attached. There are nine criteria and at least three of them must be present to make the diagnosis. In essence, the criteria require that an affected child is concerned about an attachment figure coming to harm or going away, is worried about harm befalling themselves leading to separation from an attachment figure, shows reluctance or refusal to go to school, has clinging behavior, suffers from nightmares with a theme of separation, manifests physical symptoms on school days, has excessive distress in anticipation of separation, or shows distress away from home wanting to return there. Although many cases of school phobia (Eisenberg, 1958) will fall into this category, it is evident that separation anxiety disorder can occur without school refusal. The two other disorders in the same section of DSM-III-R are avoidant disorder, which is characterized by wariness of strangers, and overanxious disorder, reflecting a variety of worries and also physical symptoms of anxiety. Both of these disorders would appear to be featured in reported cases of school phobia, at least to a small extent (Smith, 1970). Various "adult" disorders also affect children and may be associated with school phobia.

Panic disorder is characterized by severe anxiety attacks (Gelder, 1986). Some of the symptoms are due to overbreathing. It can lead to a phobic avoidance of situations in which the anxiety attacks occur. The two relevant DSM-III-R disorders are panic disorders with agoraphobia and panic disorder without agoraphobia. Both occur from the middle teenage years and may be associated with school phobia (Kolvin et al., 1984), although, uncommonly, in this author's experience. Agoraphobia may be defined as the avoidance of situations difficult to escape from, such as dense crowds of people or railway trains, as well as places where help from a familiar person is not at hand if anxiety occurs. As discussed previously it would seem that agoraphobia without a history of panic disorder is a DSM-III-R category relevant to school phobia, particularly for those in their teens (Berg & Jackson, 1985). About 10% to 15% of agoraphobic adults began to suffer from this condition before school leaving age (Marks, 1970; Roth, 1959), and it is easy to understand how it could interfere with school attendance.

Social phobia is essentially a fear of performing in public, and anxiety about possible criticism and humiliation. Fears of speaking or eating in public are examples. Occasionally school phobia is clearly related to some circumstances at school or on the way to school, which amounts to a social phobia (Eysenek & Rachman, 1965). For example, fears of showers, games, playground activities, or answering of questions in class may be considered to be a social phobia on DSM-III-R.

Simple phobia is also a circumscribed fear but not of a social situation. An obvious example concerns a 12-year-old boy chased and bitten by a dog while playing football who was referred to the author. A subsequent severe and debilitating fear of dogs developed that prevented the child from going out except when taken in the car and picked up. He was only able to attend school when transported. At first sight, the problem that seemed to be school phobia of the sort which is usually found turned out instead to be a simple phobia. Other DSM-III-R disorders that may be associated with school phobia (J. Werry, personal communication) are OCD, PTSD, GAD, adjustment disorder with anxious mood, and hypochondriasis.

ICD 10 classifies separately some disorders that are conceptualized as reflecting an exaggeration of behavior that occurs in the normal course of development. There are three in the group of emotional disorders with onset specific to childhood that are relevant to school phobia. The category of separation anxiety disorder of childhood, already referred to, has fear of separation from family and home, refusal to go to school, and onset under age 6 among criteria for inclusion. Social anxiety disorder of childhood has social anxiety of the sort that normally affects preschool children such as wariness of strangers and onset before age 6 among the criteria for inclusion. Phobic anxiety disorder of childhood is not limited to onset in preschool children but reflects some developmentally appropriate fear that is exaggerated and associated with social impairment. Cases of school phobia that are clearly related to some aspect of the school situation may be appropriately classified using this category. When developmental aspects are not evident, ICD 10 mood and neurotic disorders will often be the categories to be used in cases of school phobia. Thus agoraphobia, a subcategory of phobic anxiety disorder, is likely to be chosen when there are fears of travel away from home or alone, crowds, and public places that lead to avoidance of these circumstances. There are two sorts of agoraphobia, with or without panic disorder. Depressive episode may also be relevant in some cases of school phobia.

DEPENDENCY

Dependency is a term used to describe a child's attachment to (person orientated) and reliance on (task orientated) other people (Bandura & Walters, 1963). Its manifestations are influenced by the way in which the child is reared (Whiting & Child, 1953), and its features change with the age of the child. Toddlers stay close to their mothers, display affection, and often rush toward them when anything occurs to cause alarm. Clinging is characteristic of the preschool child. Any physical separation causes obvious emotional upset. By contrast, in older children there is less close physical contact and only occasional displays of affection, although children like to know where their mothers are and to keep in touch with them. Separation for short periods is much less upsetting (Heathers, 1960).

There are obvious similarities between separation anxiety and dependency so it is hardly surprising that children who suffer from school phobia have been considered to be overdependent on and also overprotected by their parents, particularly their mothers (Kahn & Nursten, 1962). A Self-Administered Dependency Questionnaire (SADQ) for completion by mothers was developed and standardized on a sample of 8- to 15-year-old children from the general population. Using the statistical method of principle component analysis there appeared to be four independent varieties of dependency. They were *affection, communication, assistance,* and *ability to travel alone,* respectively. The scale was completed by 42 mothers of young teenage school children with school phobia severe enough for them to be admitted to a psychiatric hospital inpatient unit (Berg, 1974). Compared with general population controls, school phobic children required more assistance from their mothers for dressing, washing, and so on, and the school phobic girls had more problems traveling on their own. Other psychiatric patients in the unit did not show any excessive dependency. These findings suggested that, rather than undue emotional attachment, the school phobic children had difficulty coping (Murphy, 1962), and in consequence were excessively reliant on their mothers for help in carrying out routine domestic activities, and school phobic girls were less venturesome than they otherwise would be.

In an investigation of 63 school phobic youngsters, it was found that there were more children who were youngest in their family than would otherwise be expected (Smith, 1970). An excess of youngest children was also found in boys who disliked school who came from a random sample of 6,000 children from the normal school population in Britain (Mitchell & Shepherd, 1967). Slater's Index (Slater, 1962) can be used to measure birth order. It is a statistic derived from the fraction $(m-1)/(n-1)$ where m is the ordinal position in the sibship, and n is the family size. It ranges from 0 to 1. The mean normally tends toward 0.5. When Slater's Index was used to investigate 100 school phobic teenagers, compared with 91 psychiatric and 127 normal controls, it was found that the mean value was 0.59 in the school phobics, indicating that they tended to come late in birth order, but this was only when there were more than two children in the family (Berg & McGuire, 1971) In this study, there was no excess of only children in the families of the school phobics. The size of family (mean = 2.19) was similar to that of the normal controls (mean = 2.60). In keeping with the excess of younger children in the family, mothers of the school phobic children tended to be older than those of the normal controls. It is a plausible explanation for separation problems and undue dependency that it reflects at least to some extent the influence of parents who are older than they otherwise would be.

Some evidence for overprotective attitudes on the part of the mothers of school phobic children was provided by the SADQ using preference ratings rather than measures of actual behavior (Berg, & McGuire, 1971). It was found that these mothers appeared to encourage affection and communication to an undue extent. A study of family life variables was carried out to see if the parents of school phobic children lived their lives in a way that might be considered to encourage overprotection and foster undue dependency (Berg, Butler, Fairburn, & McGuire, 1981). Nineteen families who were investigated included a school phobic teenager, 29 families included a young adolescent with a psychiatric disorder other than school phobia, and there were 12 comparable families from the general population. No evidence emerged to suggest that parents of school phobic children participate in, or make decisions about, family-life activities, such as management of domestic affairs, patterns of work, leisure activities, or contact with relatives and friends in any way different from parents of other cases or controls.

OUTCOME

Continuities between school phobia and conditions characterized by anxiety and depression in adult life have been investigated by follow-back studies (see also chapter 8). In one of these, nearly 800 women who belonged to a nationwide correspondence club for people with agoraphobia filled in a questionnaire that asked about school phobia occurring when they were of school age (Berg, Marks, McGuire, & Lipsedge, 1974). About 60 nonagoraphobic psychiatric outpatients acted as controls. A fifth of the agoraphobic women admitted that they had stayed away from school for at least 2 weeks, only going back there with great reluctance or fear. Most of them had had this difficulty in their teenage years. Positive responses to this question appeared to be a valid criterion of school phobia because they correlated with scores on other questions asking about fears of school, worries about separating from parents, and tendencies to remain at home excessively. Also a doctor had been consulted about the problem attending school in about a third. When school phobia had occurred, the adult agoraphobia came on earlier and more severely. Previous school phobia was found to a similar extent in the other psychiatric cases so that any continuity appeared to be with anxiety and depression in adult life rather than just agoraphobia. In another follow-back study, adults with anxiety and depression, with and without associated agoraphobia, and normal controls were investigated (Tyrer & Tyrer, 1974). It was found that 9% of cases appeared to have had school phobia in the past compared with only 2% of the controls. This was a significant finding. Again, it was anxiety and depression, not just agoraphobia, that was associated with previous school phobia.

Several follow-up studies of school phobic children have been carried out (Coolidge, Brodie, & Feeney, 1964; Hersov, 1960; Rodriguez, Rodriguez, & Eisenberg, 1959; Waldron, 1976; Weiss & Cain, 1964), but the number of cases investigated has usually been quite small, and the period of follow-up has often been short. Methods of assessment employed have also sometimes been difficult to interpret. Nevertheless, some suggestive findings linking school phobia and adult anxiety and depression, including phobic conditions, have emerged. Thus, in a later review of 16 school phobic adolescents who were assessed 6 or more years after discharge from a hospital psychiatric inpatient unit (Warren, 1960, 1965), it was found that on review four were seriously impaired socially by phobias, three had minor phobic difficulties, three had other neurotic problems, and only six were well. In a 15- to 20-year follow-up of 35 school phobic children aged 7 to 12 carried out in Sweden using health records (Flakierska, Lindstrom, & Gillberg, 1988), it was found that about a third had received psychiatric treatment as adults compared with only a tenth of controls. This was a significant difference. It also appeared that previous school phobics had more limited social relationships later on than the controls.

An attempt to follow up a group of 168 teenage school phobic children, an average of 10 years after inpatient hospital treatment, in which the author participated, will be outlined in more detail later (Berg & Jackson, 1985). On review the mean age of the group was about 24 years.

Several sources of information were used: interviews with parents, interviews with the previous school phobic cases, questionnaires completed by family doctors, and standard scales filled in by the ex-school phobics. The sample studied consisted of any child admitted to a psychiatric hospital inpatient unit over 1 decade who were considered at the time to be suffering from school phobia unless there was an associated psychosis. In fact, on this criterion only one case had to be excluded. One hundred sixty-eight school phobics were identified in this manner. Despite considerable efforts 16 families could not be traced, and information on another 9 was not found to be of any use. Two social workers attempted to carry out a home visit to see parents and ex-school phobics, if this was possible. Thirty of the young people were actually seen with their parents, and 18 of the parents were interviewed on their own. An attempt was then made to trace the young people not living at home. Twenty-five of them were interviewed. Another 23 refused to be seen, but agreed to complete a questionnaire and returned it through the mail. Fifty-five ex-school phobics either refused all contact or just failed to reply to letters. Family medical practitioners were written to and asked to fill in a questionnaire regarding any treatment for psychiatric disorders since discharge from the adolescent psychiatric inpatient unit. One hundred nineteen of them did so. Soon after the follow-up study began it was decided that the ex-patients should be requested to complete a Leeds Scale, which is a self-administered questionnaire for the measurement of anxiety and depression (Snaith, Bridge, & Hamilton, 1976). Sixty-five of these were completed. The interview carried out and the questionnaire sent by mail to those who did not wish to be interviewed contained a standard set of questions asking about symptoms of minor psychiatric illness, social impairment, and treatment for psychiatric problems. An attempt was made by the interviewers to build up a picture of the ex-school phobic's clinical state throughout the follow-up period. This had been done, apparently successfully, when a shorter follow-up study on a smaller scale had been carried out (Berg, Butler, & Hall, 1976).

An estimation was made of the proportion of the period of review during which the ex-patients were considered to be *ill* (incapacitating symptoms with marked social impairment), *slightly improved* (mild or moderate symptoms with minimal social impairment), and *well* (absence of symptoms and normal social adjustment). Comparing the results with an independent categorization carried out by a psychiatrist indicated that the ratings were reliable ($r = 0.9$).

Proportions of time spent in the improvement categories were combined to form three positively correlated variables: (a) *well* scores, (b) *well* and *much improved* scores, and (c) *well* and *much improved* and *slightly improved* scores. A principal components analysis was carried out. This produced a general component accounting for 60% of variance, which was used as a measure of improvement. Age, sex, IQ, and social class, the various features known at the time of discharge, were used as predictors, and the general component was made the criterion, in a multiple regression analysis. Six scales were derived from the interview data by a child psychiatrist that appeared to measure depression, situational anxiety, general anxiety, work type, work stability, and social relationships, respectively. They were looked at in relation to various features of the group using analyses of variance.

Comparisons of the features of the various subgroups studied in different ways did not reveal any important differences between them that might have biased the results. About a third of the ex-patients (64 out of 143: 31%) had been treated for psychiatric illness by a family doctor or a psychiatrist on at least one occasion in the decade after discharge—twice as many women as men. One in seven had seen a psychiatrist at least once (20 out of 143: 14%). One in 20 had received inpatient psychiatric treatment (7 out of 143: 5%). These are the 10-year *inception rates* for psychiatric treatment. Inpatient treatment was for affective disorders. Those who had been treated had higher scores on various measures of psychiatric disturbance and social impairment on follow-up including higher ratings on poor social relationships, unemployment, and depressive tendencies.

A third of the ex-patients was found to have pathologically high scores on the Leeds Scales (20 out of 63: 31%) on review, that is, a score of 7 or more on either the A (anxiety) or D (depression) subscales; nine were high scores on both subscales. Clinical ratings of interview data showed that high scores were more likely to have both excessive situational and general anxiety.

Concerning outcome categories of those who were interviewed, ex-school phobics were ill or only slightly improved for about a quarter of the follow-up period. Conversely, one in two of them (24 out of 55: 44%) were well or much improved throughout the follow-up period. There was a tendency for improvement to occur in time over the decade. It was found that IQ and, to a lesser extent, age significantly predicted outcome measured in this way. Brighter school phobics under the age of 14 when they were first treated did best.

Comments

Nothing emerged from the study to suggest that any of the various samples investigated in various ways were not reasonably representative of the whole group of 168. It was considered that the methods of measuring outcome both during the period of follow-up and at the time of review were reliable and valid. It thus appeared that the point prevalence rate for minor psychiatric disorder of 30% on follow-up could be relied on and represented a level of disorder in excess of what would otherwise be expected. There is good evidence that the Leeds Scales measures disturbance in a similar fashion (Forrest & Berg, 1982) to the General Health Questionnaire (GHQ). A large-scale survey in Australia using the 60-item GHQ showed that about 16% of young adults on any particular day would be likely to get a score of 12 or more on that questionnaire (Finlay-Jones & Burvill, 1978).

Regarding inpatient psychiatric treatment during the period of follow-up, the extent of it was compared with the *decennial inception rate* for a large area around the unit where the school phobic children were originally treated. The area covered an average number of half a million 15- to 29-year-olds. Admission rates were under 2%. The school refusers had 2½ to 3 times the likelihood of being admitted for psychiatric illness (5.6%). Similar findings emerged from comparisons with national figures (Wadsworth, 1979) based on a group of 4,600 individuals aged 26 in 1972. It is interesting that only 1% of this countrywide group had received outpatient psychiatric treatment by age 26. This may be contrasted with the 14% rate of outpatient treatment of the school phobics for conditions not connected with the school phobia. This figure reflects a substantial prevalence of symptoms of anxiety and depression as well as considerable social impairment.

PREVALENCE OF SCHOOL PHOBIA IN NONCLINICAL POPULATIONS WITH SEVERE SCHOOL ATTENDANCE PROBLEMS

Because school phobia has been widely recognized for so many years, it might be supposed that children suffering from this problem would be referred to psychological and psychiatric services for treatment. A study of children taken to juvenile court for severe and persistent failure to attend school in Leeds, England (Berg et al., 1985), showed that about a fifth were in fact school phobics. A survey of poor attenders at school in another northern British city, Sheffield, also found children with school phobia who had not been referred for treatment (Galloway, 1985). A further investigation in Leeds of children taken to a disciplinary school attendance committee (Bools et al., 1990), which was the procedure adopted shortly before a court summons is issued in that city, will be outlined in more detail later.

At the school attendance committee, parents of the children were in-

terviewed by education welfare officers who filled in a simple questionnaire asking about the features of the school attendance problem shown by
their child. Permission was sought for a more searching interview to be
carried out by child psychiatrists at their home. For this, a semistructured
interview schedule was employed covering the family circumstances, evidence of any childhood psychiatric disturbance, and features of the school
attendance problem. The psychiatrists decided what school attendance
problem appeared to exist and what psychiatric disorder was present, if
any, using the ICD 9 classification (World Health Organization, 1980). In
summary, the definition of school phobia used was (a) emotional upset at
the prospect of having to go to school or complaints of physical illness
thought to have an emotional basis, (b) at home with parents, and (c) no
conduct disorder. One hundred families were interviewed. Interrater
reliability between the two psychiatrists, either present together at the
interviews ($n = 18$), or rating each other's completed schedules ($n = 82$)
was high ($r = .9$). ICD 9 diagnoses were made by the two psychiatrists after
seeing the 18 families jointly, and the agreement between them on presence and absence of both school phobia and a neurotic disorder was high
using the random coefficient of agreement (Maxwell, 1977).

Eighteen items on the interview schedule that occurred in more than
15% and less than 85% of the group were subjected to a principle component analysis. This produced three factors accounting for about half the
variance that appeared to be measuring general neurotic disturbance,
emotional symptoms on school mornings, and antisocial behavior, respectively. A cluster analysis (Everitt & Dunn, 1983) was carried out on these
three factors using Ward's method, and it produced a meaningful three-
cluster solution. The information available—(a) type of school attendance
problem irrespective of any disorder; (b) ICD 9 psychiatric disorder, if any;
and (c) membership in one of the three clusters—was then analyzed using
log-linear methods (Cox & Snell, 1981) suitable for categorical data in
multiple contingency tables.

There were 41 girls and 59 boys in the sample studied with a mean age of
14 (SD = 1.3) years. Only half the children were living with both natural
parents. Most of the families were in manual work, skilled, or unskilled
categories. Slater's Index for birth order was 0.57. Average family size was
4.1. Significantly more parents of children with school phobia had received
psychiatric treatment than those of other children, mostly for anxiety,
depression, or agoraphobia.

Twenty-four school phobic children were in the sample. Twelve of them
(10 girls and 2 boys) had ICD 9 emotional disorders, and 3 had mixed
disorders of emotions and conduct. Another nine children had both school
phobia and truancy at different times; two of these had an ICD 9 emotional
disorder, and three had an ICD 9 mixed disorder of emotions and conduct.

Physical symptoms considered to reflect emotional upset were the main complaints in 8 of the school phobic children. Most school phobics were in one of the clusters emerging in the cluster analysis. This contained 21 children, 17 of whom (four fifths) were school phobic, and four (one fifth) experienced mixed school phobia and truancy. Half of the children in this cluster had an ICD 9 emotional disorder, and between one quarter and one third of them had a mixed disorder of conduct and emotions. The general neurotic disturbance component and the morning symptoms component that came out of the principle component analysis scored significantly higher using analysis of variance in this cluster than either of the other two. Using log-linear analysis, it emerged that girls predominated significantly among the school phobic children.

Comments

Some have suggested previously that children treated as disciplinary problems and presumed to be "truants" were sometimes actually suffering from school phobia. Thus 65 boys sent to a remand center by juvenile courts because of failure to attend school satisfactorily were studied, and eight of them were found to have features in keeping with school phobia (Tennent, 1969). In a survey of children who were absent from school more than half the time a group of school phobics were identified who had not been referred for treatment (Galloway, 1985). In the work outlined earlier, the 24 school phobics had seldom had any contact with treatment services. It is interesting that these cases of school phobia had disorders characterized by anxiety rather than depression. It is also interesting that about one third of the school phobics had a problem limited to anxiety symptoms on school mornings. The fact that there were two main groups of school phobics, one with a circumscribed adjustment reaction and a group with a more general neurotic disorder is reminiscent of previous classifications of school phobics (Coolidge, Hahn, & Peck, 1957; Kennedy, 1965). In a previous study of school phobic children admitted to an inpatient psychiatric unit (Berg, Nichols, & Pritchard, 1969), cases were categorized into "acute" and "chronic." It was found that the chronic subgroup had significantly higher neurotic scores on the Junior Eysenek Personality Inventory and were more maladjusted on the Bristol Social Adjustment Guides than was the acute subgroup. In a study of school phobia actually defined as poor school attendance accompanied by a neurotic disorder (Kolvin et al., 1984), somewhat transitory depression affected about half the cases. The definition employed probably limited the cases investigated to severer examples of school phobia and probably excluded children with anxiety confined to school mornings. The study summarized previously was also unusual (Leventhal & Sills, 1964) in so far as there was a preponderence of girls. This could be explained by their being a group of girls whose symptoms were mainly those of physical illness, possibly in the form of the masquerade syndrome (Waller & Eisenberg, 1980).

CONCLUSION

It is hoped that in future reviews of ICD and DSM classifications the arguments for including a diagnostic category for school phobia will be looked at again in a favorable light. In another vein, it is clearly important for physicians and surgeons to be constantly aware of the possibility that physical symptoms without obvious cause that lead to absence from school may represent school phobia in disguise, and for education authorities and their associated welfare agencies to be aware of the likelihood that a high proportion of children with severe attendance problems and often from poor families has school phobia. Possible links between child and adult psychiatric disorders involving school phobia on the one hand and agoraphobia on the other need to be kept in mind for future research (see chapter 8). So far, the distinction between chronic cases of school phobia, in which developmental aspects are particularly relevant, and the more acute cases, in which they are not, has failed to have much impact on research into the problem. It may be that this will change as a result of the distinctions made in DSM-III-R and ICD 10 between the two varieties of school phobia. The close relationship between school phobia and anxiety disorders should continue to provide a stimulus for research and produce further information concerning the developmental aspects of school phobia.

REFERENCES

American Psychiatric Association. (1987). *Diagnostic and statistical manual of mental disorders* (3rd ed., rev.), Washington, DC: Author.

Bandura, A., & Walters, R. H. (1963). *Social learning and personality development.* New York: Holt, Reinhart & Winston.

Berg, I. (1974). A self-administered dependency questionnaire (SADQ) for use with mothers of school children. *British Journal of Psychiatry, 124,* 1–9.

Berg, I. (1984). School refusal. *British Journal of Hospital Medicine,* January 31, 59–62.

Berg, I. (1990). School avoidance, school phobia and truancy. In M. Lewis (Ed.), *Child and adolescent psychiatry—a comprehensive textbook.* Baltimore: Williams & Wilkins.

Berg, I., & McGuire, R. (1971). Are school phobic adolescents overdependent? *British Journal of Psychiatry, 119,* 167–168.

Berg, I., Butler, A., Fairburn, I., & McGuire, R. (1981). The parents of school phobic adolescents—a preliminary investigation of family life variables. *Psychological Medicine, 11,* 79–84.

Berg, I., Butler, A., & Hall, G. (1976). The outcome of adolescent school phobia. *British Journal of Psychiatry, 128,* 80–85.

Berg, I., Butler, A., & McGuire, R. (1972). Birth order and family size of school phobic adolescents. *British Journal of Psychiatry, 121,* 509–514.

Berg, I., Casswell, G., Goodwin, A., Hullin, R., McGuire, R., & Tagg, G. (1985). Classification of severe school attendance problems. *Psychological Medicine, 15,* 157–165.

Berg, I., & Jackson, A. (1985). Teenage school refusers grow up: A follow up study of 168 ten years on average after inpatient treatment. *British Journal of Psychiatry, 147,* 366–370.

Berg, I., Marks, I., McGuire, R., & Lipsedge, M. (1974). School phobia and agoraphobia. *Psychological Medicine, 4,* 428–434.

Berg, I., Nichols, K., & Pritchard, C. (1969). School phobia—its classification and relationship to dependency. *Journal of Child Psychology and Psychiatry, 10,* 123–141.

Bernstein, G. A., & Garfinkel, B. D. (1986). School phobia: the overlap of affective and anxiety disorders. *Journal of the American Academy of Child Psychiatry, 25,* 235–241.

Bools, C., Foster, J., Brown, I., & Berg, I. (1990). The identification of psychiatric disorders in children who fail to attend school: A cluster analysis of a non-clinical population. *Psychological Medicine, 20,* 171–181.

Broadwin, I. T. (1932). A contribution to the study of truancy. *American Journal of Orthopsychiatry, 2,* 253–259.

Coolidge, J. C., Brodie, R. D., & Feeney, B. (1964). A ten year follow up of sixty school phobic children. *American Journal of Orthopsychiatry, 34,* 675–684.

Coolidge, J. C., Hahn, P. B., & Peck, A. L. (1957). School phobia: Neurotic crisis or way of life. *American Journal of Orthopsychiatry, 27,* 296–306.

Cox, D. R., & Snell, E. J. (1981). *Applied statistics—principles and examples.* London: Chapman & Hall.

Eisenberg, L. (1958). School phobia: A study in the communication of anxiety. *American Journal of Psychiatry, 114,* 712–718.

Everitt, B. S., & Dunn, G. (1983). *Advanced methods of data, exploration and modelling.* London: Heinemann Educational Books.

Eysenek, H. J., & Rackman, S. J. (1965). The application of learning theory to child psychiatry. In J. Howells (Ed.), *Modern perspectives in child psychiatry.* Edinburgh: Oliver & Boyd.

Finlay-Jones, R. A., & Burvill, P. W. (1978). Contrasting demographic patterns of minor psychiatric morbidity in general practice and the community. *Psychological Medicine, 8,* 455–466.

Flakierska, N., Lindstrom, M., & Gillberg, C. (1988). School refusal: A 15–20 year follow up study of 35 Swedish urban children. *British Journal of Psychiatry, 152,* 834–837.

Forrest, G., & Berg, I. (1982). Correspondence: Leeds Scales and the GHQ in women who had recently lost a baby. *British Journal of Psychiatry, 141,* 429–430.

Galloway, D. (1985). *Schools and persistent absentees.* Oxford: Pergammon Press.

Gelder, M. (1986). Panic attacks: New approaches to an old problem *British Journal of Psychiatry, 149,* 346–352.

Gittleman-Klein, R., & Klein, D. (1980). Separation anxiety in school refusal. In L. Hersov & I. Berg (Eds.), *Out of school.* New York: Wiley.

Heathers, L. A. (1960). Persistent non-attendance at school. *Journal of Child Psychology and Psychiatry, 1,* 130–136.

Hersov, L. A. (1960). Refusal to go to school. *Journal of Child Psychology and Psychiatry, 1,* 137–145.

Hersov, L. A. (1985). School refusal. In M. Rutter & L. Hersov (Eds.), *Child and adolescent psychiatry: Modern approaches* (2nd ed.). Oxford: Blackwell Scientific.

Hersov, L., & Berg, I. (Eds.). (1980). *Out of school.* New York: Wiley.

Hoshino, Y., Nikkuni, S., Kaneko, M., Endo, M., Yashima, Y., & Kumashiro, H. (1987). The application of DSM III diagnostic criteria to school refusal. *The Japanese Journal of Psychiatry and Neurology, 41,* 1–7.

Johnson, A. M., Falstein, E. I., Szureck, S. A., & Svendsen, M. (1941). School phobia. *American Journal of Orthopsychiatry, 11,* 702–711.

Jung, C. G. (1961). A case of neurosis in a child. In *The Collected Works of C G Jung* (Vol. 4). New York: Basic Books. (Original work published 1913)

Kahn, J. H., & Nursten, J. P. (1962). School refusal: A comprehensive view of school phobia and other failures of school attendance. *American Journal of Orthopsychiatry, 32,* 707–718.

Kennedy, W. A. (1965). School phobia: Rapid treatment of fifty cases. *Journal of Abnormal Psychology, 70,* 285–289.

Kerr, T. A., Roth, M., Schapera, K., & Gurney, C. (1972). The assessment and prediction of outcome in affective disorders. *British Journal of Psychiatry, 121,* 167–174.

Kolvin, I., Berney, T., & Bhate, S. (1984). Classification and diagnosis of depression in school phobia. *British Journal of Psychiatry, 145,* 347–357.

Leventhal, T., & Sills, M. (1964). Self image in school phobia. *American Journal of Orthopsychiatry, 37,* 64–70.

Marks, I. (1970). Agoraphobia syndrome (phobic anxiety state). *Archives of General Psychiatry, 23,* 538–553.

Maxwell, A. E. (1977). Coefficients of agreement of between two observers and their interpretation. *British Journal of Psychiatry, 130,* 79–83.

Mitchell, S., & Shepherd, M. (1967). The child who dislikes going to school. *British Journal of Educational Psychology, 37,* 32–40.

Murphy, L. B. (1962). *The Widening World of Childhood.* New York: Basic Books.

Partridge, J. M. (1939). Truancy. *Journal of Mental Science, 85,* 45–81.

Quay, H. C., & Werry, J. S. (1986). *Psychopathological disorders of childhood* (3rd ed.). New York: Wiley.

Rodriguez, A., Rodriguez, M., & Eisenberg, L. (1959). The outcome of school phobia. *American Journal of Psychiatry, 116,* 540–544.

Roth, M. (1959). The phobic-anxiety depersonalization syndrome. *Proceedings of the Royal Society of Medicine, 52,* 587–595.

Slater, E. (1962). Birth order and maternal age of homosexuals *Lancet, 1,* 69–71.

Smith, S. L. (1970). School refusal with anxiety: A review of sixty three cases. *Canadian Psychiatric Association Journal, 15,* 257–264.

Snaith, R., Bridge, G. W. K., & Hamilton, M. (1976). The Leeds Scales for the self assessment of anxiety and depression. *British Journal of Psychiatry, 128,* 156–165.

Tennent, T. G. (1969). *School Non-attendance and Delinquency.* MD thesis, University of Oxford.

Tonge, B. J., Burrows, G. D., & Werry, J. (1990). *Handbook of studies on child psychiatry.* Amsterdam: Elsevier.

Tyrer, P., & Tyrer, S. (1974). School refusal, truancy and adult neurotic illness. *Psychological Medicine, 4,* 416–421.

Wadsworth, M. (1979). *Roots of delinquency*: Infancy, adolescence, and crime. Martin Robertson, Oxford.

Waldron, S. (1976). The significance of childhood neuroses for adult mental health: A follow up study. *American Journal of Psychiatry, 133,* 532–538.

Waller, D., & Eisenberg, L. (1980). School refusal in childhood—a psychiatric-pediatric perspective. In L. Hersov & I. Berg (Eds.), *Out of school* New York: Wiley.

Warren, W. (1960). Some relationships between the psychiatry of children and of adults. *Journal of Mental Science, 106,* 815–826.

Warren, W. (1965). A study of adolescent psychiatric inpatients and the outcomes six or more years later. *Journal of Child Psychology and Psychiatry, 6,* 1–17 and 141–160.

Weiss, M., & Cain, B. (1964). The residential treatment of children and adolescents with school phobia. *American Journal of Orthopsychiatry, 34,* 103–112.

World Health Organization. (1980). *The International Classification of Diseases* (9th rev.). Geneva: Author.

Whiting, J. W., & Child, I. L. (1953). *Child training and personality—a cross-cultural study.* New Haven: Yale University Press.

CHAPTER 6

Relationship Between Familial and Childhood Anxiety Disorders

Cynthia G. Last

Family studies generally are considered to be important means for establishing the validity of a diagnostic category. This type of study allows one to assess whether an increased prevalence of the same disorder exists among the close relatives of index cases. Such findings strongly suggest that one is dealing with a valid entity, independent of the question of etiology, that is, heredity or environmental causes (Feighner et al., 1972; Guze, 1967). It should be noted, however, that although most psychiatric illnesses have been shown to run in families, the absence of an increased family prevalence does not necessarily negate the validity of a diagnostic category, because not all illnesses show familial aggregation (Guze, 1967).

The investigation of familial aggregation of psychiatric disorders also provides important information regarding risk factors, which may be useful for early detection and intervention, and, ultimately, prevention. Of course, the fact that specific types of psychiatric illnesses run in families does not in and of itself address the issue of genetic versus environmental mode of transmission. Information obtained from family studies are an important *first step,* however, to understanding whether familial genetic or environmental factors may play a role in the development of psychiatric disorders.

Information concerning familial prevalence of psychiatric disorders may be obtained by either the *family history* method or the *family study* method (Andreasen, Endicott, Spitzer, & Winokur, 1977; Mendlewicz, Fleiss, Cataldo, & Rainer, 1975; Thompson, Orvaschel, & Kidd, 1982). The family history method essentially consists of obtaining information from the patient or other relatives about all family members. The family study method, conversely, involves direct interviewing of all available relatives concerning their own present and past psychiatric illnesses and symptomatology.

The family study method has been noted to be the preferred technique for studying familial prevalence, because this method yields data that are more precise and accurate than that obtained through use of the family history method. The family history method remains widely used, however, because it is often difficult, or impossible, to interview relatives directly. This especially is true in family research that examines close relatives of adult probands. In these cases, relatives of adult probands often are inaccessible because of geographical location or death. These factors usually do not constitute major problems for family studies of child probands. This particularly is relevant for first-degree relatives, that is, the parents and siblings of child probands, who usually will be residing in the same household as the proband. In addition, because of the younger age of child and adolescent probands, one may anticipate that a higher percentage of first-degree relatives will still be living and available for interview.

Unlike family studies with adult probands, the first-degree relatives of child and adolescent probands include parents and siblings only, because most of these youngsters do not yet have offspring of their own. When using the family study method with these family members, as well as second-degree relatives, the goal usually is to assess lifetime psychiatric illness (as opposed to current psychopathology only). Lifetime diagnoses are based on information obtained through unstructured (clinical) or structured psychiatric interviews and application of diagnostic criteria (e.g., DSM-III-R, RDC, etc.). Structured psychiatric interviews generally are the preferred means for collecting information on psychatric history because they yield more reliable information than unstructured interviews.

There are several interview schedules available that are appropriate for use with adult relatives. One of the most commonly used instruments in familial research is the *Schedule for Affective Disorders and Schizophrenia—Lifetime Version* (SADS-L) (Endicott & Spitzer, 1978). The SADS-L particularly is well suited for a family study because (a) the interview schedule is one of the few available that specifically is designed to obtain information relevant to psychiatric disorders over an entire lifespan, (b) information obtained from the SADS-L can be used readily to formulate DSM-III diagnoses, and (c) available data indicate that diagnostic reliability is high for this instrument (Andreasen et al., 1981; Mazure & Gershon, 1979).

Another instrument has been developed that offers certain advantages for use in familial research. The *Structured Clinical Interview for DSM-III-R* (SCID) (Spitzer, Williams, & Gibbon, 1986) is a DSM-III-R—based structured interview that incorporates diagnostic criteria from the major DSM-III-R disorders. The interview is easy to learn and administer, and requires only 45 minutes to 1 hour. It can be used to formulate both current and past diagnoses. The instrument appears to have good face validity; diagnostic reliability currently is being assessed by the authors (Dr. Janet Williams, personal communication), as well as other independent investigators (e.g., Last, Hersen, Kazdin, Francis, & Grubb, 1987).

Although both of these instruments adequately tap adult diagnoses, they do not explore in detail certain psychiatric disorders that are specific to childhood. When conducting a family study with child probands, one may be interested to see whether relatives have a history of the same disorder that the identified patient currently presents. For example, in investigating psychiatric illness in family members of children with separation anxiety disorder, it would be of interest to know whether the mothers (or other relatives) of these children had separation anxiety disorder when they, themselves, were youngsters. (Of course, it also would be of interest to examine the prevalence of adult anxiety disorders, such as agoraphobia).

To obtain information needed to determine diagnoses specifically applicable to children and adolescents, it may be necessary to administer sections of other interview schedules that have been designed for children and adolescents. Some DSM-III-R–oriented instruments that have been shown useful include the Schedule for Affective Disorders and Schizophrenia for School-Age Children (Chambers, Puig-Antich, & Tabrizi, 1978), the CAS (Hodges, Stern, Cytryn, & McKnew, 1982), the Interview Schedule for Children (Kovacs, 1983), and the NIMH Diagnostic Interview Schedule for Children (Costello, Edelbrock, Dulcan, Kalas, & Klaric, 1984). Specific sections of these interviews may be administered to evaluate whether adult relatives have shown certain psychiatric disorders that are specific to childhood or adolescence (e.g., separation anxiety disorder, attention deficit hyperactivity disorder, conduct disorder, etc.).

Unlike family studies with adult probands, the siblings of child probands usually are under 18 years of age. Thus, it is necessary to use diagnostic interview schedules for children with these family members. The interviews mentioned earlier can be used for this purpose.

REVIEW OF LITERATURE

Whether there is a familial factor involved in the development of childhood anxiety disorders has been addressed by several investigations. One approach for studying this question has been referred to as the "top-down" method, in which the children of adult patients diagnosed as having an anxiety disorder are studied. The second approach has been referred to as the "bottom-up" method, in which parents and other relatives of children diagnosed as having anxiety disorders are studied. Investigations using both of these methods and their results are described subsequently.

"Top-Down" Studies

Four studies have used the top-down method to assess anxiety disorders in children. Berg (1976) investigated the prevalence of school phobia in the children of agoraphobic women via a questionnaire survey. School phobia was assumed to have been present when mothers answered "yes" to this question: "Has the child ever completely refused to go to school for longer than one or two days since starting Junior school at 7?" (p. 86). Results for children aged 7 to 15 years showed a prevalence rate of 7%. When children of secondary school age (11 to 15 years) were considered separately, however, the prevalence rate rose to 14%. Berg states that these rates (particularly for children 11 to 15 years) are higher than what would be expected in the general population.

Interpretation of findings for this study are hampered by several methodological problems: (a) the criterion for identifying cases of school phobia is overinclusive, as cases of depression, medical illness, and truancy may meet the criteria and result in misclassification as "school phobia," (b) lack of a psychopathological control group renders one unable to determine whether the rates of school phobia observed are due to psychopathology per se rather than agoraphobia specifically; and (c) lack of a matched normal control group precludes comparison of obtained rates with "base rates" for the general population.

In a similar but smaller study, Buglass, Clarke, Henderson, Kreitman, and Presley (1977) compared the offspring of 20 agoraphobic women with the offspring of 30 matched nonpsychiatrically disturbed women. Information on the children was obtained through interviewing of the mothers and a symptom checklist. Results indicate that the two groups did not differ in the rate of psychiatric illness in general or school phobia in particular. In fact, contrary to expectation, none of the agoraphobics' children showed agoraphobia or school refusal.

Unfortunately, the investigation did not report the number of offspring in different age brackets. Because school phobia has been shown to yield a higher prevalence rate in preadolescence and adolescence, rather than early or middle childhood (e.g., Berg, 1976; Last, Francis, Hersen, Kazdin, & Strauss, 1987), such information is of importance. As noted by Gittelman (1986), it is possible for no case of school phobia to occur in a very small sample if the expected rate is relatively low (e.g., 10% to 15%) (p. 114). Moreover, the use of the family history method, in which the children themselves were not interviewed directly, most probably resulted in an underestimate of psychiatric illness in this study.

Weissman, Leckman, Merikangas, Gammon, and Prusoff (1984) compared children of women with major depression with or without a history of anxiety disorder and a group of matched control subjects. The family history method was used, in which information on the children's psychiatric status was obtained from the proband, spouse, and other adult first-degree relatives. The depressed probands with concurrent anxiety disorders were divided into three groups: (a) depression and agoraphobia, (b) depression and panic disorder, and (c) depression and generalized anxiety disorder. The anxiety groups then were compared with women who had depression but no anxiety disorder and with normals.

Results are summarized in Table 6.1. As can be observed, an increased risk of anxiety disorders, specifically, SAD, was present in the children of women with depression and panic disorder, with 11 of 19 (36.8%) offspring meeting DSM-III criteria for the diagnosis. None of the offspring of normal or depressed-only probands met criteria for SAD. In the other two depression plus anxiety disorder groups, relatively low rates were obtained for SAD, with 2 of 18 (11.1%) children of agoraphobic probands and 2 of 32 (6.3%) children of generalized anxiety disorder women meeting diagnostic criteria. When the offspring of agoraphobic and panic disorder women are combined, the risk of SAD decreased to 24.3%, a rate still greater than in the other groups.

Although these data are important, it should be noted that use of the family history method, in which the offspring have not been interviewed directly, most probably resulted in an underestimation of the rate of psychopathology. Therefore, the study addreses the *relative* rate of SAD in the children of the groups studied but not the expected rates. The possible effect of comorbid major depression in the mothers cannot be evaluated because the children of patients with anxiety disorders only were not included in the study (such studies are ongoing in several centers). It should be emphasized that an increased rate of anxiety disorders *only* was

TABLE 6.1 Anxiety Disorders in Offspring of Normal, Depressed-Only, and Depressed and Anxious Probands

Proband group	No. of children at risk	Any Anxiety disorder		SAD	
		%	n	%	n
Normal	87	2.3	2	0.0	0
Depression, no anxiety disorder	38	0.0	0	0.0	0
Depression plus agoraphobia	18	11.1	2	11.1	2
Depression plus panic	19	36.8	7	36.8	7
Depression plus GAD	32	6.3	2	6.3	2
Depression plus agoraphobia/panic	37	24.3	9	24.3	9

Note. Adopted from Weisman, M. M., Leckman, J. F., Merikangas, K. R., Gammon, G. D., & Prusoff, B. A. (1984). Depression and anxiety disorders in parents and children. *Archives of General Psychiatry, 41,* 847–849.

obtained in the children of patients with panic disorder. Agoraphobia and generalized anxiety disorder did not result in a higher morbid risk for offspring. The reason for this is unclear, at least for agoraphobia, given previous research findings supporting a relationship between panic disorder and agoraphobia. Indeed, the DSM-III-R considers the two illnesses to be variants of the same disorder (American Psychiatric Association, 1987). The number of mothers with agoraphobia was small, however, and was probably insufficient to yield firm results.

Turner, Beidel, and Costello (1987) directly assessed children of anxiety-disordered patients. These children were compared with children of patients with dysthymic disorder, children of normal parents, and normal school children. All children were assessed with a semistructured interview schedule and diagnosed according to DSM-III. Results indicated that of 16 children of anxiety disorder probands, 6 (38%) received a diagnosis of an anxiety disorder. Four of the children met criteria for SAD, and two met criteria for overanxious disorder. By comparison, 3 of the 14 offspring (21%) of dysthymic disorder patients met diagnostic criteria for an anxiety disorder including one child with SAD, one with overanxious disorder, and one with social phobia. Only one child of the normal parents and none of the normal school children met criteria for an anxiety disorder diagnosis. Statistical analysis of the data indicated that the anxiety disorders group significantly differed from both normal control groups but not from the dysthymic disorder group.

The preceding results were obtained by the inclusion of multiple offspring of the same parents. Turner et al. (1987) reanalyzed their data with a reduced sample, randomly selecting only one child from each of the families with multiple children. Reanalysis with the reduced sample replicated the full sample results, with 6 of 13 offspring (46%) in the anxiety disorders group meeting criteria for an anxiety disorder (4 with separation anxiety and 2 with overanxious disorder), 3 of 11 dysthymic offspring (27%) meeting diagnostic criteria for an anxiety disorder (1 with overanxious disorder, 1 with separation anxiety disorder, and 1 with social phobia), and no children in the solicited normal or school normal groups meeting diagnostic criteria.

Although Turner et al. (1987) were able to demonstrate an increased risk of anxiety disorders in the children of anxiety-disordered patients compared with the two nonpatient groups, they were not able to demonstrate differences between the two patient groups. The selection of dysthymic disorder probands as the psychopathological control group for the study may be problematic, in that a relationship between affective and anxiety disorders has been suggested by previous research. Therefore, studies with more power (i.e., larger samples) are necessary to investigate the issue.

Bottom-Up Studies

Several bottom-up studies have been conducted, in which the relatives of child patients with anxiety disorders have been evaluated, Berg, Butler, and Pritchard (1974) evaluated maternal psychiatric illness in school phobic adolescents admitted to an inpatient psychiatric unit. Maternal psychiatric histories of 100 school phobic youngsters were compared with maternal histories of 113 hospitalized non–school phobic patients. Maternal psychiatric illness was evaluated by examining hospital and medical records. One fifth of the mothers in both groups had a history of some type of psychiatric disturbance. Of these approximately one-half were diagnosed as having an affective disorder, which was defined in this study as anxiety, depression, or phobias. Thus, maternal psychiatric illness in the two patient groups did not significantly differ. Obviously, the use of record review as opposed to direct interviews severely hampers conclusions that can be drawn from this investigation. Moreover, the lumping together of affective and anxiety disorders under the category of "affective disorders" limits interpretation of findings.

Gittelman-Klein (1975) interviewed the parents of 41 school phobic and 42 hyperactive children to determine their psychiatric histories. Results were analyzed for three specific diagnostic categories: major depression, specific phobias, and SAD. No differences appeared between the two groups of parents for major depression or specific phobias. The parents of school phobic youngsters were found to have a significantly higher rate of SAD, however, than parents of hyperactive children (19% versus 2%, respectively).

In addition to the preceding, parents reported on siblings' histories of psychiatric illness, particularly school phobia. Among 67 siblings of the school phobic children, 11 (16%) had a clear-cut history of school phobia. By contrast, none of 66 siblings of hyperactive probands were reported to have a history of school phobia. These differences between the two groups were statistically significant. Interestingly, when the relationship between parental separation anxiety disorder and school phobia in siblings was examined, it was found that separation anxiety in the parents was not correlated with the presence of school phobia in the siblings. Interpretation of findings from this investigation is hampered by several ambiguities. First, diagnostic criteria for school phobia and SAD are not reported. Second, a related question concerns why SAD was examined in the parents, whereas school phobia was examined in the siblings. Finally, although interviewers were unaware of the questions investigated, they were not blind to the children's diagnostic status, which potentially could seriously bias results.

Last, Phillips, and Statfeld (1987) examined the prevalence of two childhood anxiety disorders, separation anxiety and overanxious disorders, in the mothers of children diagnosed as having one or both of these disorders, and a control group of mothers who were psychiatrically disturbed but did not have an anxiety or affective disorder. DSM-III diagnostic criteria were used to diagnose both the children and their mothers, and the diagnosis of the mothers' childhood disorders were conducted blindly through the use of a structured diagnostic questionnaire (Childhood History Questionnaire) by raters who were unaware of the children's disorders. The study was designed to determine whether there is a relationship between mothers and their children for childhood anxiety disorders, and whether the nature of this relationship is general or specific. It was hypothesized that a specific relationship would exist, that is: (1) mothers of children with SAD had SAD as children, and (b) mothers of overanxious children had overanxious disorder as children.

Results indicate that only one of the two hypotheses was supported. For SAD, no differences were found in the rates for the three groups of mothers. By contrast, the rate of overanxious disorder was significantly higher in mothers of overanxious children than in mothers of either separation anxious children or control children. More specifically, in the overanxious disorder group, 18 of 43 mothers (42%) reported a childhood history of overanxious disorder compared with 2 of 21 mothers (9.5%) in the SAD group and 5 of 33 mothers (15%) in the control group.

Although data from this study support a specific relationship between overanxious disorder in mothers and their children, such a relationship was not shown for SAD. These findings are in contrast to those reported previously from Gittelman-Klein (1975). It is possible that the method of assessment used in the Last et al. study obscured a relationship for SAD. SAD symptoms, as compared with those present in overanxious disorder, generally are more specific and of a shorter duration, with DSM-III requiring only a 2-week duration for the diagnosis. Direct interviews with the mothers, rather than a symptom checklist, might have helped to probe for the more specific and relatively transient symptoms of SAD.

In a bottom-up study conducted by Livingston, Nugent, Rader, and Smith (1985), the relatives of 12 anxious and 11 depressed children were examined using the family history method. Relatives primarily included mothers, fathers, and grandparents, yielding a sample size of 69 in the anxiety disorder group and 58 in the depressed group. Results indicated that in most respects the family histories of the two groups did not differ. Strikingly, only one relative in each of the groups was diagnosed as having an anxiety disorder.

As the investigators themselves note, their study must be considered in light of methodological limitations including the small number of probands included and use of the family history method to diagnose psychiatric illness. In concluding their article, they state that large-scale family studies are needed with instruments used that are sensitive to detecting anxiety disorders.

Another small study (Bernstein & Garfinkel, 1988) examined psychopathology in the first-degree relatives of six chidren with school phobia using the family study method. Familial psychopathology in the school phobic families was compared with rates obtained in five families of children with other psychiatric disorders. Results indicated that 7 of 12 (58%) parents of school phobic children showed an anxiety disorder as compared with 3 of 10 (30%) parents of psychiatric controls. For siblings, 5 of 10 (50%) met criteria for an anxiety disorder in the school phobic group compared with none of 5 (0%) siblings in the control group. Unfortunately, the findings from this study may be regarded only as preliminary given the small number of probands included in the school phobic and control groups (six and five, respectively).

Last, Hersen, Kazdin, Francis, and Grubb (1987) used the family study method to compare maternal psychiatric illness for children with SAD and overanxious disorder ($n = 58$), and for children who were psychiatrically disturbed but did not manifest an anxiety or affective disorder ($n = 15$). Mothers were interviewed directly about lifetime psychiatric illness with a semistructured diagnostic interview and diagnosed according to DSM-III criteria. Interviewers were blind to children's diagnoses, and diagnostic agreement was evaluated by having a second clinician, also blind to children's diagnoses, independently score audiotapes of the interviews. Children in the control group were diagnosed as having behavior disorders including conduct disorder, attention deficit disorder, or oppositional disorder.

Results indicated that mothers of children with anxiety disorders had a significantly higher lifetime rate of anxiety disorders than mothers of control children (83% vs. 40%, respectively). Moreover, when current rates of anxiety disorders were examined, the mothers of anxiety-disordered children once again showed a significantly higher rate than the mothers of control children (57% vs. 20%, respectively).

Findings from the study are striking in that most mothers of this clinic sample of anxiety-disordered children showed a lifetime history of anxiety disorder. Moreover, approximately one half of these mothers presented with an anxiety disorder at the same time at which their children were seen for similar problems. Because mothers alone were interviewed, however, it is unclear whether the relationship for anxiety disorders is specific to the mother-child dyad or is indicative of a more general pattern of familial aggregation. The authors call for large-scale family studies of this population to address this question.

Recently, Last, Hersen, Kazdin, Orvaschel, and Perrin (in press) completed a large-scale family study of childhood anxiety disorders. Lifetime psychiatric illness was assessed in the first- and second-degree relatives of child probands diagnosed as having an anxiety disorder. The study will be described in detail subsequently.

Probands included 94 children with an anxiety disorder, a psychopathological control group of 58 children with ADHD, and a normal control group of 87 children who had never been psychiatrically ill. All probands were required to be currently residing with at least one biological parent. In addition, inclusion criteria for anxiety disorder probands required a current DSM-III-R diagnosis of an anxiety disorder and no history of ADHD. ADHD probands were required to receive a current DSM-III-R diagnosis of ADHD, and no history of an anxiety or affective disorder. Finally never psychiatrically ill probands, recruited from the community, were required to have no current or past psychiatric disorder, as well as no history of mental health contact.

All children in the study were administered a modified version (Last, 1986) of the Schedule for Affective Disorders and Schizophrenia for School-age Children (present episode (K-SADS-P; Chambers et al., 1978). This version of the K-SADS-P was modified to include comprehensive sections on all DSM-III-R anxiety disorders. In addition, the modified interview schedule uses rating scales based on DSM-III-R criteria and covers past as well as current psychopathology. The modified interview was administered to parents and their children by a child clinical psychologist. Interrater diagnostic agreement was obtained for 156 of the 239 probands (65%) by having a second interviewer score audiotapes of the interviews. Kappa coefficients of agreement for any anxiety disorder, ADHD, and no psychiatric disorder were 1.00, .98, and 1.00, respectively. Kappa coefficients for specific anxiety disorder diagnoses for anxiety-disordered probands were as follows: SAD = .94, overanxious disorder = .93, avoidant disorder = .74, panic disorder = .88, social phobia = .94, simple phobia = .71, OCD = .78, PTSD = 1.00. In the few instances in which the two interviewers disagreed regarding specific diagnosis(es), the diagnosis(es) of the "live" interviewer was used.

First-degree relatives (mothers, fathers, and full siblings, 5 years of age or older) were interviewed directly using the family study method. Adult first-degree relatives (18 years of age or older) were interviewed for current and past psychiatric illness with the SCID (Spitzer, Williams, & Gibbon, 1986). Childhood disorders not contained in the SCID (i.e., separation anxiety disorder, overanxious disorder, avoidant disorder, and ADHD) also were administered to the adult relatives using sections from the modified K-SADS-P. Child and adolescent siblings of the probands were interviewed for current and past psychiatric illness with the modifified K-SADS-P. Information on second-degree relatives (maternal and paternal grandparents, aunts, and uncles) was obtained from the parents using the family history method.

The number of first-degree relatives included in the study were as follows: 274 in the anxiety disorder group, 152 in the ADHD group, and 240 in the never psychiatrically ill group. Second-degree relatives included 812 in the anxiety disorder group, 484 in the ADHD group, and 718 in the never psychiatrically ill group.

All family interviews were conducted blindly. Interrater diagnostic agreement was obtained by having a second clinician independently score audiotapes from 95 (40%) complete families and assign DSM-III-R diagnoses. The Kappa coefficient of agreement between the two clinicians for any anxiety disorder was .95. Kappa coefficients for specific anxiety disorders were as follows: generalized anxiety disorder = 1.00, panic disorder = .86, simple phobia = .95, social phobia = .96, OCD = .86, PTSD = .96, separation anxiety disorder = .91, avoidant disorder = .89, overanxious disorder = .93.

Rates of anxiety disorders for first-degree relatives by relationship and sex are presented in Table 6.2. An increased rate of anxiety disorders was found in first-degree relatives of anxiety-disordered probands compared with first-degree relatives of both ADHD and NPI probands. Looking at the relationship and sex of relative, the data suggest that significant differences obtained for rates of anxiety disorders for parents and siblings of anxiety-disordered probands were due, primarily, to differences among male, as

TABLE 6.2 Rates of Anxiety Disorders in First-Degree Relatives of Anxiety Disordered (N = 94), ADHD (N = 58), and Never Psychiatrically Ill (N = 87) Children

	Proband diagnosis		
	Anxiety	ADHD	NPI
All first degree	34.6[a,b]	23.5	16.3
Parents	40.4[a,b]	28.3[c]	18.5
Siblings	21.7[d]	8.3	10.8
First-degree males	23.9[a,e]	10.5	8.0
First-degree females	45.5[e]	37.0[c]	24.2

Note. Probabilities based on chi-square tests with Yates correction for continuity or Fisher's exact tests. Rates are unadjusted. Sample sizes for first-degree relatives for each of the proband groups were as follows: all first degree—anxiety = 274, ADHD = 152, NPI = 240; parents—anxiety = 188, ADHD = 116, NPI = 173; siblings—anxiety = 86, ADHD = 36, NPI = 67; first-degree males—anxiety = 141, ADHD = 79, NPI = 120; first-degree females—anxiety = 133, ADHD = 73, NPI = 120.
[a] vs. ADHD, $p < .05$. [b] vs. NPI, $p < .00001$. [c] vs. NPI, $p < .10$. [d] vs. ADHD, $p < .10$. [e] vs. NPI, $p < .001$.

opposed to female, relatives. Comparison of second-degree relatives did not show differences between the anxiety (11.5%) and ADHD (11.0%) groups, but both of these patient groups differed significantly from the (NPI) (7.3%) group (anxiety versus never psychiatrically-ill, $p < .01$; ADHD versus NPI, $p < .05$).

Although prevalence rates provide useful information, they give little indication about how anxiety disorders may aggregate within families. To examine this, we used individual families as the unit of analysis and compared the three groups on the following (a) number (percentage) of families containing a first-degree relative with an anxiety disorder, (b) number (percentage) of families containing a parent with an anxiety disorder, and (c) number (percentage) of families containing a sibling with an anxiety disorder. The percentage of families having at least one first-degree relative with an anxiety disorder was as follows: anxiety = 69.9%, ADHD = 50.0%, and NPI = 40.5%; differences between the anxiety and ADHD groups, and the anxiety and NPI groups were statistically significant ($p < .05$ and $p < .0005$, respectively). The percentage of families having at least one parent with an anxiety disorder was as follows: anxiety = 65.6%, ADHD = 50.0%, and NPI = 35.7%; comparison of the anxiety and NPI group yielded a significant difference ($p < .0001$), whereas comparison of the anxiety and ADHD groups showed a trend toward statistical significance ($p < .10$). The pattern of results for siblings was in the expected direction, but nonsignificant: anxiety = 26.3%, ADHD = 10.7%, and NPI = 13.6%.

Prevalence rates for specific anxiety disorders in the first-degree relatives of probands in each of the three groups are presented in Table 6.3. As indicated, simple phobia and overanxious disorder were the two specific anxiety disorders that were most frequent among the relatives of anxiety-disordered probands; these rates were significantly higher than rates obtained for the two disorders for both the ADHD and NPI relatives. Panic disorder (with or without agoraphobia), social phobia, OCD, and avoidant disorder were more prevalent among the first-degree relatives of anxiety-disordered probands than NPI probands, but no differences emerged between the two patient groups for any of these disorders. A trend toward statistical significance emerged when comparing the anxiety and control groups for the prevalence of separation anxiety disorder. There were no differences among the three groups of relatives for generalized anxiety disorder. For ADHD relatives, rates of OCD, PTSD, and avoidant disorder showed trends toward statistical significance when compared with rates obtained for the relatives of NPI probands, but no differences emerged between the two patient groups for any of these disorders.

Rates for specific anxiety disorders also were compared, separately, for first-degree male and female relatives of probands in the three groups. For first-degree male relatives, simple phobia (anxiety = 7.6%, ADHD = 1.3%,

TABLE 6.3 Rates of Specific Anxiety Disorders in First-Degree Relatives of Anxiety-Disordered *(N = 94)*, ADHD *(N = 58)*, and Never Psychiatrically Ill *(N = 87)* Children

	Proband diagnosis		
	Anxiety	ADHD	NPI
Panic disorder (with or without agoraphobia)	4.9[a]	2.0	0.4
Social phobia	8.7[b]	7.4	3.4
Simple phobia	11.7[a,c]	4.7	4.3
OCD	2.3[b]	2.0[d]	0.0
GAD	2.7	2.0	0.9
PTSD	5.0	7.4[d]	3.1
SAD	9.2[d]	5.6	4.3
Overanxious disorder	18.9[c,e]	10.3	8.1
Avoidant disorder	5.9[a]	4.0[d]	1.5

Note. Probabilities based on chi-square tests with Yates correction for continuity or Fisher's exact tests. Rates are unadjusted. Sample sizes for first-degree relatives for each of the proband groups were as follows: anxiety = 274, ADHD = 152, NPI = 240. [a] vs. NPI, $p < .005$. [b] vs. NPI, $p < .05$. [c] vs. ADHD, $p < .05$. [d] vs. NPI, $p < .10$. [e] vs. NPI, $p < .001$.

NPI $= 0.9\%$); separation anxiety disorder (anxiety $= 8.4\%$, ADHD $= 1.9\%$, NPI $= 1.1\%$); and overanxious disorder (anxiety $= 14.7\%$, ADHD $= 1.9\%$, NPI $= 5.4\%$) were more prevalent in relatives of anxiety-disordered probands than relatives in both of the other two groups (simple phobia: anxiety versus ADHD, $p < .05$, anxiety versus NPI, $p < .01$; separation anxiety disorder: anxiety versus ADHD, $p < .10$, anxiety versus NPI, $p < .05$; overanxious disorder: anxiety versus ADHD, $p < .001$, anxiety versus NPI, $p < .05$). No other differences emerged among the groups.

By contrast, for first-degree female relatives, there were no differences between the anxiety and ADHD groups for any of the specific anxiety disorders. Each of the anxiety disorders, with the exception of generalized anxiety disorder, PTSD, and SAD, was more prevalent among the female first-degree relatives of anxiety disordered probands than among the female first-degree relatives of NPI probands (panic disorder $= p < .005$, social phobia $= p < .05$, simple phobia $= p < .10$, OCD $= p < .05$, overanxious disorder $= p < .05$, avoidant disorder $= p < .001$). The relatives of ADHD probands showed higher rates of PTSD ($p < .05$) and avoidant disorder ($p < .01$) than relatives of NPI probands.

A priori we had hypothesized that specific anxiety disorders in our child probands would be associated with specific anxiety disorders in the children's relatives. More specifically, we had hypothesized that the rates of separation anxiety disorder and panic disorder would be highest for the relatives of SAD probands, and that overanxious disorder and generalized anxiety disorder would be more prevalent among the relatives of probands with OAD. To examine these issues, we compared the first-degree relatives of three groups of anxiety-disordered children—those with SAD but not overanxious disorder, those with overanxious disorder but not SAD, and those with an anxiety disorder other than separation anxiety or over-anxious disorder (anxiety controls) for rates of separation anxiety, panic, overanxious, and generalized anxiety disorders.

As indicated in Table 6.4, contrary to expectation, SAD was more preva-lent among the relatives of *both* SAD and OAD probands (compared with the relatives of probands with other anxiety disorders), and panic disorder was highest in OAD relatives (compared with relatives in each of the other two groups). Again, contrary to expectation, overanxious disorder was more prevalent among the relatives of *both* SAD and OAD probands (com-pared with relatives of probands with other anxiety disorders), and no differences emerged among any of the three groups of relatives for general-ized anxiety disorder.

We also investigated the relationship between other specific anxiety disorders in children and their relatives. OCD and panic disorder were the only two anxiety disorders that showed a suggestion of a specific relation-ship in children and their relatives. The rate of OCD in the first-degree relatives ($n = 47$) of children with OCD ($n = 14$) was somewhat higher than

TABLE 6.4 Rates of Specific Anxiety Disorders in First-Degree Relatives of Probands with Separation Anxiety *(N = 28)*, Overanxious *(N = 17)*, and Other Anxiety Disorders *(N = 43)*

	Proband diagnosis		
	SAD	OAD	Other
Any anxiety disorder	31.5	50.0[a,b]	27.0
SAD	10.3[c]	18.8[b]	3.4
Overanxious disorder	23.7[d]	29.8[e]	11.0
Panic disorder (with or without agoraphobia)	2.7	11.5[b,f]	0.0
GAD	4.2	3.8	0.8

Note. Probabilities based on chi-square tests with Yates correction for continuity or Fisher's exact tests. Rates are unadjusted. Sample sizes for first-degree relatives for each of the proband groups were as follows: SAD = 74, OAD = 54, other = 130. Six anxiety disordered probands with both separation anxiety and overanxious disor-ders have been excluded from those analyses. The relatives ($n = 35$) of 9 children with panic disorder were eliminated from the "other" group for this analysis.
[a] vs. SAD, $p < .10$. [b] vs. other, $p < .005$. [c] vs. other, $p < .10$. [d] vs. other, $p < .05$. [e] vs. other, $p < .01$. [f] vs. SAD, $p < .05$.

the rate obtained for relatives of anxiety-disordered probands without OCD (6.7% versus 1.4%, $p < .10$). Similar findings were obtained when comparing relatives ($n = 39$) of children with panic disorders ($n = 13$) with relatives of anxiety-disordered probands without panic disorder (10.8% versus 3.9%, $p < .10$).

In summary, findings from this family study showed significantly higher rates of anxiety disorders in the first-degree relatives of anxiety-disordered children compared with relatives of both ADHD and never psychiatrically ill controls. Differences for first-degree male relatives particularly were striking; male relatives of anxiety-disordered children had a rate of anxiety disorders more than twice that of the other two groups. Inspection of the specific types of anxiety disorders among male relatives showed elevated rates of separation anxiety disorder, overanxious disorder, and simple phobia. For first-degree female relatives, the anxiety group significantly differed in rates of anxiety disorder from the normal control group but not the psychopathological control group. Additional analyses with individual families as the unit of analysis also revealed that anxiety disorders were more likely to aggregate within families of anxiety-disordered children than families of both ADHD and NPI children.

Our prediction about the relationship between childhood separation anxiety disorder and adult onset panic disorder was not supported in the present study. Weissman, Leckman, Merikangas, Gammon, and Prusoff (1984) found an increased risk of separation anxiety disorder in the offspring of mothers with comorbid depressive and panic disorders. By contrast, we found an increased risk of panic disorder in the relatives of children with panic disorder or overanxious disorder but not children with separation anxiety disorder. Because our findings on the relationship for separation anxiety disorder and panic disorder were presented for all first-degree relatives, data were reanalyzed for mothers only (more akin to the Weissman analysis); we again failed to find a relationship between the two disorders.

Discrepancies in the findings from the two studies may be due to methodological differences. First, in the Weissman investigation all of the probands had concurrent depressive disorder. Second, their study observed illness in the offspring of disordered adults, whereas we observed illness in relatives of disordered children. Finally, the Weissman investigation used the family history method, rather than the family study method, to diagnose offspring. It should be noted that when the offspring from the initial study later were subjected to direct interviews, original findings for SAD were not substantiated; in other words, results from the direct interviews did not support a relationship between panic disorder in the parent and SAD in the child (Mufson, Weissman, & Warner, 1991).

There also was a trend for panic disorder to be more frequent in the relatives of children who had panic disorder. The same pattern held true for OCD (a trend for OCD to be more frequent in the relatives of OCD children) but not so for the other specific anxiety disorders. This specific relationship for panic disorder and OCD supports previous genetic research (see chapter 7). Our findings for childhood OCD also are consistent with results from a recent uncontrolled family study of the disorder (Lenane, Swedo, Leonard, et al., 1990).

Genetic Versus Environmental Transmission

Obviously, the studies reviewed previously do not address the issue of mode of transmission, that is, environmental or genetic transmission. The top-down and bottom-up studies indicate that anxiety disorders tend to run in families, but only investigations using methodologies common to genetic research (twin studies, adoption studies) can assess whether a hereditary component is present. What family studies can accomplish, in this regard, is to generate "negative proof," that is, if a higher frequency of a disorder is not observed among biological relatives, then genetic factors cannot be involved.

In chapter 7, Torgersen concludes that panic disorder, phobic disorders, and OCD seem to be influenced by genetic factors. By contrast, generalized anxiety disorder and PTSD do not appear to be mediated through genetic transmission.

Two interesting questions emerge regarding the mode of transmission of childhood anxiety disorders. If transmission is genetic, what, specifically is inherited? Conversely, if transmission is environmental, how, specifically, is it accomplished?

From a hereditary perspective, individual differences in infants' temperaments (e.g., Kagan, 1988; Thomas, Chess, Birch, Hertzig, & Korn, 1963, and arousal level and habituation to stimuli (Johnson & Melamed, 1979) may be related to the acquisition of fear and anxiety disorders in childhood. This may be referred to as "anxiety proneness" or "vulnerability," but in either case denotes an inherited "disposition" toward developing anxiety disorders.

Such an inherited disposition may interact adversely with certain environmental events, such as stressful life events (see later) or family interaction patterns and child-rearing practices. In this regard, the mother-child relationship repeatedly has been implicated, on both theoretical and empirical grounds, as an etiological factor in the development of SAD and school phobia (e.g., Berg & McGuire, 1974; Eisenberg, 1958; Hersov, 1960). Generally, mothers are described as being overprotective, having separation anxiety issues of their own, and reinforcing dependency and lack of autonomy in their children.

The notion that maternal psychopathology plays a causal or maintenance role in children's anxiety disorders is of considerable importance
because inferences have been drawn regarding intervention (Eisenberg, 1958). Considerably more research is needed regarding the relative
roles (alone and in combination) of hereditary and family interaction
variables.

CONCLUSION

Available data from both top-down and bottom-up family studies suggest
that the offspring of anxiety-disordered parents are at increased risk to
develop anxiety disorders. Questions remain regarding the specificity of
this relationship in two reports. Two recent studies have failed to show
differences between anxiety disorder and psychopathological control
groups (Last et al., in press; Turner et al., 1987). In Turner's investigation of
the offspring of anxiety-disordered versus dysthymic parents, both groups
were equally likely to show anxiety disorder. Last found an increased
prevalence of anxiety disorders in the first-degree relatives of anxiety-
disordered children compared with the relatives of ADHD children; however, further inspection of the data showed these differences held true for
male relatives only—female first-degree relatives did not differ in rates of
anxiety disorders for the two groups.

The second "specificity" issue is whether children develop the same or
related types of anxiety disorders expressed by a parent, or whether the
relationship is more general (i.e., anxiety disorder as a general class of
disorder). Weissman's data indicated that there was a specific relationship
between panic disorder in the parent and separation anxiety in the child,
although this relationship was not replicated when the same subjects were
interviewed directly (Mufson et al., in press). Last did not find a specific
relationshp between SAD and panic disorder, nor did she find a relationship between overanxious disorder in the child and generalized anxiety
disorder in the parents, a relationship that has been hypothesized by
others in the field. In fact, Last's data showed specific relationships for only
two of the anxiety disorders: OCD and panic disorder. The first-degree
relatives of children with OCD tended to have higher rates of OCD than
relatives of children with other types of anxiety disorders. The same held
true for panic disorder.

It is interesting that OCD and panic disorder rather convincingly have
shown positive findings on genetic examination. As Torgersen discusses at
length in the next chapter, family studies cannot separate environmental
from heredity influences. Such questions must be addressed through genetic research and family interaction studies.

REFERENCES

Andreasen, N. C., Endicott, J., Spitzer, R. L., & Winokur, G. (1977). The family history method using diagnostic criteria. *Archives of General Psychiatry, 34,* 1229–1235.

Andreasen, N. C., Grove, W. M., Shapiro, R. W., Keller, M. B., Hirschfeld, R. M. A., & McDonald-Scott, P. (1981). Reliability of lifetime diagnosis. *Archives of General Psychiatry, 38,* 400–405.

Berg, I. (1976). School phobia in children of agoraphobic women. *British Journal of Psychiatry, 128,* 86–89.

Berg, I., Butler, A., & Pritchard, J. (1974). Psychiatric illness in the mothers of school-phobic adolescents. *British Journal of Psychiatry, 125,* 466–467.

Berg, I., & McGuire, R. (1974). Are mothers of school-phobic adolescents overprotective? *British Journal of Psychiatry, 124,* 10–13.

Bernstein, G. A., & Garfinkel, B. D. (1988). Pedigrees, functioning, and psychopathology in families of school phobic children. *American Journal of Psychiatry, 145,* 70–74.

Buglass, D., Clarke, J., Henderson, A. S., Kreitman, N., & Presley, A. S. (1977). A study of agoraphobic housewives. *Psychological Medicine, 7,* 73–86.

Chambers, W. J., Puig-Antich, J., & Tabrizi, N.A. (1978). The ongoing treatment of the Kiddie-SADS. Paper presented at the American Academy of Child Psychiatry Annual Meeting, San Diego.

Costello, A. J., Edelbrock, C., Dulcan, M., Kalas, R., & Klaric, S. H. (1984). Report on the NIMH Diagnostic Interview Schedule for Children (DISC). Unpublished manuscript.

Eisenberg, L. (1958). School phobia: A study in the communication of anxiety. *American Journal of Psychiatry, 114,* 712–718.

Endicott, J., & Spitzer, R. L. (1978). A diagnostic interview: The Schedule for Affective Disorders and Schizophrenia. *Archives of General Psychiatry, 35,* 837–844.

Feighner, J. P., Robins, E., Guze, S. B., Woodruff, R. A., Winokur, G., & Munoz, R. (1972). Diagnostic criteria for use in psychiatric research. *Archives of General Psychiatry, 26,* 57–63.

Gittelman, R. (1986). Childhood anxiety disorders: Correlates and outcomes. In R. Gittelman (Ed.), *Anxiety disorders of childhood.* New York: Guilford.

Gittelman-Klein, R. (1975). Psychiatric characteristics of the relatives of school phobic children. In D. V. S. Sankar (Ed.), *Mental health in children* (Vol. 1, pp. 325–334). Wesbury, NJ: PJD Publications.

Guze, S B. (1967). The diagnosis of hysteria: What are we trying to do? *American Journal of Psychiatry, 124,* 491–498.

Hersov, L. A. (1960). Persistent non-attendance at school. *Journal of Child Psychology and Psychiatry, 1,* 130–136.

Hodges, K., Stern, L., Cytryn, L., & McKnew, D. (1982). The development of a child assessment schedule for research and clinical use. *Journal of Abnormal Child Psychology, 10,* 173–189.

Johnson, S. B., & Melamed, B. G. (1979). Assessment and treatment of children's fears. In B. B. Lahey & A. E. Kazdin (Eds.), *Advances in clinical child psychology* (Vol. 2). New York: Plenum.

Kagan, J. (19880. Biological bases of childhood shyness. *Science, 240,* 167–171.

Kovacs, M. (1983). The Interview Schedule for Children (ISC): Form C, and the follow-up form. Unpublished manuscript.

Last, C. G. (1986). Modification of the K-SADS-P. Unpublished manuscript.

Last, C. G., Francis, G., Hersen, M., Kazdin, A. E., & Strauss, C. C. (1987). Separation anxiety and school phobia: A comparison using DSM-III criteria. *American Journal of Psychiatry, 144,* 653–657.

Last, C. G., Hersen, M., Kazdin, A. E., Francis, G., & Grubb, H. J. (1987). Psychiatric illness in the mothers of anxious children. *American Journal of Psychiatry, 144,* 1580–1583.

Last, C. G., Hersen, M., Kazdin, A. E., Orvaschel, H., & Perrin, S. (1991). Anxiety disorders in children and their families. *Archives of General Psychiatry, 48,* 928–934.

Last, C. G., Phillips, J. E., & Statfeld, A. (1987). Childhood anxiety disorders in mothers and their children. *Child Psychiatry and Human Development, 18,* 103–112.

Lenane, M. C., Swedo, S. E., Leonard, H., et al. (1990). Psychiatric disorders in first-degree relatives of children and adolescents with obsessive-compulsive disorder. *Journal of the American Academy of Child and Adolescent Psychiatry, 29,* 407–412.

Livingston, R., Nugent, H., Rader, L., Smith, G. R. (1985). Family histories of depressed and severely anxious children. *American Journal Psychiatry, 142,* 1497–1499.

Mazure, C., & Gerson, E. S. (1979). Blindness and reliability in lifetime diagnosis. *Archives of General Psychiatry, 36,* 521–525.

Mendlewicz, J., Fleiss, J. L., Cataldo, M., & Rainer, J. D. (1975). Accuracy of the family history method in affective illness. *Archives of General Psychiatry, 32,* 309–314.

Mufson, L., Weissman, M. M., & Warner, V. (in press). Depression and anxiety in parents and children: A direct interview study. *Journal of Anxiety Disorders.*

Spitzer, R. L., & Williams, J. B. W. (1984). *Structured clinical interview for DSM-III— Non-patient version* (SCID-NP 5/1/84). Unpublished manuscript.

Spitzer, R. L., Williams, J. B. W., & Gibbon, M. (1986). *Structured clinical interview for DSM-III-R (SCID).* Unpublished manuscript.

Thomas, A., Chess, S., Birch, H. G., Hertzig, M., & Korn, S. J. (1963). *Behavioral individuality in early childhood.* New York: University Press.

Thompson, W. D., Orvaschel, H., & Kidd, J. R. (1982). An evaluation of the family history method for ascertaining psychiatric disorders. *Archives of General Psychiatry, 39,* 53–58.

Turner, S. M., Beidel, D. C., & Costello, A. (1987). Psychopathology in the offspring of anxiety disorders patients. *Journal of Consulting and Clinical Psychology, 55,* 229–235.

Weissman, M. M., Leckman, J. F., Merikangas, K. R., Gammon, G. D., & Prusoff, B. A. (1984). Depression and anxiety disorders in parents and children: Results from the Yale Family Study. *Archives of General Psychiatry, 41,* 845–852.

CHAPTER 7

Relationship Between Adult and Childhood Anxiety Disorders: Genetic Hypothesis

Svenn Torgersen

One might think of two ways to study the relationship between childhood and adult anxiety. The more straightforward way would be to see whether there exists some continuity of anxiety within an individual from childhood to adulthood. A possible continuity might be revealed through retrospective or longitudinal studies. The latter would be better, but is difficult to accomplish because of the timespan needed and changing methods, diagnostic concepts, and research interests. The other more indirect method is to study relatives and look for some co-occurrence of anxiety in parents and children, as discussed in chapters 2 and 6. Symptoms in children and parents might be considered as different stages in a developmental process.

In cases in which there exists a continuity of anxiety from childhood to adult age and a co-occurrence of anxiety in children and parents the question arises: To what extent is the relationship between childhood and adult anxiety owing to environmental factors and to what extent genetically caused? One can easily imagine that anxiety development starts in childhood and continues into adulthood, both as a consequence of traumas, identification, imitation and learning, and owing to the effect of genetically monitored biological processes.

Family studies will not give a final answer. Aggregation of anxiety in families might as well be due to common experiences and learning as to common genes. Conversely, if there does not exist any co-occurrence of anxiety in families, then genetic factors cannot be involved. Hence, family studies can only disprove, not prove, the influence of genes on behavior.

There are three available methods to test a positive hypothesis about genetic factors causing any observed relationship between childhood and adult anxiety: twin studies, adoptive studies, and genetic linkage studies. Twin studies capitalize on the fact that monozygotic (MZ) twins have

identical genes, whereas dizygotic (DZ) twins are not more similar genetically that nontwin siblings. A higher concordance among MZ than among
DZ twins is usually then ascribed to identical genes and considered as
evidence of the influence of genes on behavior. However, the environment
is also more similar among MZ than among DZ twins (Torgersen, 1981),
and it also seems as if similarity in environment effects MZ twins differently
from DZ twins (Clifford, Hooper, Fulker, & Murray, 1984). Thus, the interpretation of twin studies are not so straightforward. A way to separate
the effect of environment and genes is to study adopted children. Adoption
of twins is relatively infrequent, however, the sample is selected, and the
children might have had important experiences with the mother before
adoption. It is also possible to combine the twin and adoption method by
looking at twins reared apart. However, it is, of course, rare not only to be a
twin, but also to be separated from the twin partner as a child, grow up in
separated homes, and, in addition, to have a clinically significant psychiatric disorder.

Recently, so–called genetic linkage studies have been developed. By
taking advantage of the phenomenon of recombination during the meiosis,
it is possible to calculate the likelihood of the existence of a locus of a gene
for a disorder on a certain chromosome (White & Lalouel, 1988). The
problem is to find enough genetic markers to be able to map the chromosome. The technique of restrictive fragment length polymorphism, however, has enlarged the number of possible sites of genetic markers considerably. It is necessary to have access to a sufficient sample of large families
with a number of children, and the disorder must occur frequently in the
family. Furthermore a single gene must be important, and it cannot rule out
heterogeneity and phenocopies, that some cases are not caused by the
gene under investigation.

A problem in investigating genetic factors in the development of anxiety
across the lifespan is to diagnose anxiety in children. Children do not
always have language for the experience of anxiety. Anxiety must be
disclosed in various alternative ways. It is sometimes diagnosed through
interview with the mother and thereby more of a measure of the mother's
perception of the child. It might also be based on observation of the child.
For small children more temperamental aspects have to be considered.
Various indications of anxiety in children and adults is dealt with in this
review, and evidence from twin, adoption, and linkage studies is discussed.

FEARFULNESS IN CHILDREN

Few twin studies have been conducted dealing with anxiety and fear in
childhood. Some studies have been published in which the Bayley Infant
Behavior Profile was applied (Freedman, 1965, 1974, 1976; Freedman &

Keller, 1963). These studies showed some evidence for a higher concordance for fearfulness in MZ twins compared with DZ. Goldsmith and Gottesman (1981) made another rating of behavior style in twin children, and observed a higher intrapair correlation at 7 years of a factor named "fearfulness" between MZ twins compared with DZ twins. Abe, Oda, and Hatta (1984) asked mothers of twins at 3 years about different kinds of fears. They found that MZ twins were statistically significantly more concordant on the following types of fear: marked fear of strangers in infancy, startled by sudden noises in infancy, unable to sleep alone without parent sitting nearby, and stranger anxiety during the test.

Another conceptualization of behavior in childhood is the New York Longitudinal Study temperamental evaluation (Thomas, Chess, & Birch, 1968). Of their nine temperamental characteristics, five constitute the "difficult child cluster" and are relevant to our review; irregularity of biological functions, negative withdrawal responses to new stimuli, nonadaptability or slow adaptability to change, and intense mood expressions that are frequently negative. The longitudinal study results indicated that this temperamental cluster is related to adjustment disorders in childhood and young adulthood (Thomas & Chess, 1984).

The temperament of a twin sample has been followed from birth to 15 years (A. M. Torgersen, 1981, 1987, 1989). The twins temperaments were evaluated at 2 and 9 months after birth, and at 6 and 15 years. The results showed that the intrapair correlations of MZ twins were higher than the correlations of DZ twins at all ages for intensity and mood, and higher at all measurement times, except 2 months, for adaptability and withdrawal (see Table 7.1). Irregularity was not measured at 15 years, so it is not included in the table. MZ twins were at all earlier measurement ages more similar than DZ twins, however. Even if this study does not measure anxiety or fear, it indicates that temperamental aspects possibly related to fearfulness are more similar between MZ than between DZ twins from the first year of life throughout childhood and adolescence. The merit of this study is also that it is longitidinal and not cross-sectional, showing that the higher similarity between MZ twins is stable through 15 years (A. M. Torgersen, 1989). It also showed that the correlations were moderately high between 6 years and 15 years, and most interesting, the correlation from 6 to 15 years was high in MZ pairs for withdrawal, adaptability, and intensity, and relatively lower in DZ pairs (see Table 7.2).

NEUROTICISM IN ADULTS

Perhaps the most widespread concept in studying anxiety in the common population is neuroticism. Although Eysenck's scale does not contain solely anxiety items, its correlation to clinical anxiety is fairly high

TABLE 7.1 Intrapair Correlations for Temperament in MZ and DZ Twins at Different Ages (1981, 1987, 1989)

Temperamental variables		Age			
		2 Months	9 Months	6 Years	15 Years
Withdrawal	MZ	.78	.87	.94	.93
	DZ	.86	.39	.45	.43
Nonadaptability	MZ	.81	.95	.81	.92
	DZ	.83	.53	.68	.35
Intensity	MZ	.82	.85	.95	.85
	DZ	.52	.02	.54	-.19
Mood	MZ	.84	.86	.37	.95
	DZ	.16	.32	-.06	.41

TABLE 7.2 Intra-pair Cross-Correlations for MZ and DZ Twins for Temperament

Temperamental variables		Cross-correlation
Withdrawal	MZ	.51
	DZ	.25
Nonadaptability	MZ	.50
	DZ	.06
Intensity	MZ	.53
	DZ	.28
Mood	MZ	.07
	DZ	.05

Note. From Torgersen, A. M. (1981, 1987, 1989).
Reprinted by permission.

(Eysenck, 1959). Most important, it has been studied applying many genetic methods, making securer conclusions possible.

The first twin study using the neuroticism concept was conducted by Eysenck and Prell (1951). They applied several personality tests to a sample of normal twins. A neuroticism factor was extracted, and they observed a correlation of .82 between MZ twins compared with .22 between DZ twin partners (see Table 7.3). Most interesting are the studies of twins reared apart. Shields (1962) studied normal twins having been reared apart from early childhood. He obtained a correlation of .53 between twins reared apart compared with a *lower* correlation of .38 between MZ twins reared together and .11 between DZ twins, mostly reared together. A recent Swedish study gives opposite results. They observed that the correlation between MZ twins reared apart was only .18 compared with .37 for MZ twins reared together, .01 for DZ twins reared apart, and .18 for DZ twins reared together (Pedersen, Friberg, Floderius-Myhrhed, McClearen, & Plomin, 1984). The results of a Finnish study of twins reared apart are somewhere in between. They observed a correlation of .25 for neuroticism of MZ twins reared apart, .32 for MZ twins reared together, .11 for DZ twins reared apart, and .10 for DZ twins reared together (Langinvaiono, Kaprio, Koskenvuo, & Lonngvist, 1984).

Finally, a study by Rose and Kaprio (1988) should be mentioned. They observed that the correlation between MZ twins declined the longer the twins had lived together in the family. Taken together the studies of twins reared apart show that some similarity in neuroticism might be observed

TABLE 7.3 Correlations for Neuroticism Between Relatives

Authors	Type of study	Correlations
Lienert and Reisse (1961)	Father–child	.13
	Mother–child	.31
Eysenck and Prell (1951)	MZ twins	.82
	DZ twins	.22
Shields (1962)	MZ twins reared apart	.53
	MZ twins reared together	.38
	DZ twins mostly reared together	.11
Pedersen et al.(1984)	MZ twins reared apart	.18
	MZ twins reared together	.37
	DZ twins reared apart	.01
	DZ twins reared together	.18
Langinvainio et al. (1984)	MZ twins reared apart	.25
	MZ twins reared together	.32
	DZ twins reared apart	.11
	DZ twins reared together	.10

in MZ pairs even if the twins have been reared apart. The magnitude of the correlations are not high, however, and at least some of the studies suggest that the correlation among MZ twins living together might be inflated by the common environment.

TWIN STUDIES OF FEARS IN ADULT AGE

Some twin studies of common fears and phobias in the normal population have been performed. Young, Fenton, and Lader (1971), gave the Middlesex Hospital Questionnaire (Crown & Crisp, 1966) to 17 MZ and 15 DZ twins. They observed a clearly higher intraclass correlation for MZ twin partners compared to DZ twins on the subtests: free-floating anxiety, phobic anxiety, and somatic concomitants of anxiety (see Table 7.4).

Torgersen (1979) administered a self-constructed fear questionnaire to 50 MZ and 47 DZ same-sex, predominantly unselected normal twin pairs. A factor analysis yielded five factors: agoraphobic, animal fears, blood injury, social, and one with mixed predominantly nature fears. The intraclass correlations were in all instances higher for MZ compared with DZ pairs and the heritabilities were generally high, higher when intraclass correlations were the basis for calculating the heritabilities compared with when the heritability was calculated based on intrapair variances (see Table 7.5).

The study also showed that MZ twins more often than DZ twins feared strongest the same kind of objects or situations. It was investigated whether twins who were together more as children also were more similar in phobic fears. That was not the case, however, so the higher environmental similarity of MZ twins did not seem to influence the results.

Rose and Ditto (1983) gave Geer's (1965) Fear Survey Schedule-II to 222 MZ and 132 DZ pairs of same twins between 14 and 34 years. Seven factors were extracted (see Table 7.5). The results show fairly high MZ intraclass correlations for all factors and relatively high heritability irrespective of whether it is calculated based on intraclass correlations or intrapair variance. Only fear of loved ones' misfortunes and deep water seem to yield

TABLE 7.4 Intraclass Correlations and Heritabilities for Middlesex Health Questionnaire Young et al., 1971

	'MZ	'DZ	h^2
Free-floating anxiety	.56	.12	.50
Phobic anxiety	.60	−.12	.64
Somatic concomitants of anxiety	.44	−.06	.47

TABLE 7.5 Intraclass Correlations and Heritabilities for Fear-Phobia Factors

	rMZ	rDZ	H[a]
Torgersen (1979)			
Nature	.55	.35	.53
Social	.88	.65	.40
Mutilation	.35	.20	.48
Animal	.48	.05	.47
Separation	.69	.39	.23
Rose and Ditto (1983)[a]			
Personal death	.52	.16	.50
Social responsibility	.54	.24	.50
Negative social interaction	.50	.28	.44
Small organisms	.53	.20	.41
Dangerous places	.43	.14	.32
Deep water	.52	.36	.32
Loved one's misfortunes	.52	.38	.23

[a]H is calculated from the intrapair variances W in Rose and Ditto (1983) according to the formula:$^wDZ - {}^wMZ/{}^wDZ$.

low heritability. They also looked at twins 19 years old or younger separately, and then they observed that there was no difference in intraclass correlations between MZ and DZ pairs for loved ones' misfortune and personal death. Rose and Ditto (1984) also included parents of the twins and found that the correlations between the twins and their parents were similar to the correlations between DZ twins.

Neale and Fulker (1984) extracted two factors from their study, fear of social criticism and fear of leadership, and included twins and their parents in the same bivariate path analysis of genetic and environmental influence on the development of the trait. They concluded that genetic and environmental factors contributed approximately half each to the development of the fears.

In an Australian study of 3,798 volunteer twin pairs 18 years and older, the Delusion-Symptoms-States Inventory was administered. It contains seven anxiety items (Jardine, Martin, & Henderson, 1984; Kendler, Heath, Martin, & Eaves, 1986). The genetic analysis suggested that 34% to 44% of the variance was due to additive genetic factors for four of the seven items. Furthermore, it seemed as if the same additive genetic variance was involved in the anxiety traits as in neuroticism, making our earlier discussion of twin studies of neuroticism relevant for the topic of the present chapter.

That the classical application of the twin data in disclosing genetic effect might be questioned is shown in an article by Clifford et al. (1984). They gave the Middlesex Hospital Questionnaire to 572 twin families including parents and sibs in addition to the twins. The results showed that if the twins only were analyzed in the classical way the estimate of heritability amounted to 50%. If the relatives also were considered, the estimate declined to 32%, and if the number of years since separation also was included in the model, the estimate of heritability was not higher than 19%.

The twin and twin-family studies thus seem to indicate that various kinds of fearfulness are influenced by genes. The classical analysis of twin data may lead to inflated heritability estimates, however, and the amount of variance in common fears and phobias explained by genetic factors may be modest.

TWIN STUDIES OF CLINICAL ANXIETY IN CHILDREN AND ADOLESCENTS

To our knowledge, only one study of clinical anxiety in twins has been published (Braconi, 1961). It is an Italian study of 20 MZ and 30 DZ pairs with neurosis. According to the characteristics of the twins, 8 MZ twins and 8 DZ twin pairs between the age of 6 and 14 years seem to contain an anxiety neurosis. All the MZ twin pairs appeared to be concordant for anxiety compared with only 1 of the 8 DZ pairs. Even if the basis for the diagnosis is a little unclear, the study preliminarily suggests a genetic influence of clinical anxiety in children. However, the possibility remains that the closeness between MZ twins, and hence imitation and identification, may have caused the concordance.

TWIN STUDIES OF CLINICAL ANXIETY IN ADULTS

Several anecdotal reports about adult twin pairs with clinical anxiety were published in the first half of this century. The first large study of anxiety state, broadly defined, was the Naudsley Hospital study (Shields & Slater, 1966). They reported a concordance of 42% among MZ twins compared with 4% among DZ twins (see Table 7.6).

The Norwegian study of 318 twin pairs, covering all official psychiatric treatment facilities in the country, yielded 28 MZ and 48 DZ pairs where at least one of the twins had an anxiety neurosis according to ICD 8–9 (Torgersen, 1985). The concordance for MZ pairs was 36% compared with 13% for DZ pairs (see Table 7.6).

TABLE 7.6 Twin Studies of Anxiety Neurosis

	Concordance	
Investigations	MZ	DZ
Shields & Slater (1966)	7/17 (42%)	1/28 (4%)
Torgersen (1985)	10/28 (36%)	6/48 (13%)

The twins were also diagnosed according to DSM-III, with fairly similar results, 34% concordance for MZ pairs and 17% for DZ, as Table 7.7 shows (S. Torgersen, 1983). If generalized anxiety disorder is treated separately, however, the concordance is similar for MZ and DZ, 17% and 20%, respectively. For the other anxiety disorders, panic disorder, phobias, and OCD, the concordance was 45% for MZ twin pairs and 15% for DZ. The amount of contact, identification and similar environment in childhood did not seem to influence the MZ/DZ concordance ratio. Anxiety disorders with panic attacks especially seem to have a high concordance among MZ twins and no concordance for panic attacks among DZ twins.

Thus, it appears that GAD solely is a product of environmental factors, whereas panic disorder is influenced by genes. This viewpoint is also strengthened by the same data relevant to the lifespan perspective. Patients with GAD have experienced much loss as children, whereas patients with panic disorder have not. Conversely, patients with panic disorder have more often been chronically anxious, even as children (S. Torgersen, 1986).

The Australian twin study also suggests that panic attacks may have a specific genetic etiology, apart from other anxiety reactions. Two of the anxiety items in their study, "heart pounding" and "feelings of panic," did

TABLE 7.7 DSM-III Anxiety Disorders in Probands cotwins

		Anxiety Disorders in cotwins	
Proband		n	(%)
GAD	MZ	2/12	(17)
	DZ	4/20	(20)
Other anxiety disorders	MZ	9/20	(45)
	DZ	5/33	(15)
All anxiety disorders	MZ	11/32	(34)
	DZ	9/53	(17)

Note. From Torgersen, S. (1983). Genetic factors in anxiety disorders. *Archives of General Psychiatry, 40,* 1085–1089. Reprinted by permission.

not fit an additive genetic model but rather a dominant genetic model, which means that a single gene may be partly responsible for the development of the symptom (Kendler et al., 1986; Martin, Jardine, Andrews, & Heath, 1988). Even if positive answers to such items do not imply that a clinical panic disorder exists, the results of the Australian twin study, in addition to results from the Norwegian twin study, point to a recently published genetic linkage study of panic disorder.

GENETIC LINKAGE STUDY OF PANIC DISORDER

The final test of whether genetic factors are involved in the development of a disorder will be to detect the genes themselves. Earlier, such a procedure for common neurotic disorders seemed near impossible. During the 1980s, however, the genetic technology developed rapidly, and a linkage study of panic disorder was published by the end of 1987 (Crowe, Noyes, Wilson, Elston, & Ward, 1987). Included in the study were 26 families where the proband had primary panic attacks with a probable or definite panic disorder, with or without agoraphobia. In all families, at least one other member of the family had panic attacks. Twenty-nine polymorphic marker systems over 10 chromosomes were studied applying electrophoresis and standard microplate techniques. The statistical analysis yielded a maximum lod score for alpha-haptoglobin of 2.27 at a recombination fraction of 0.0. Even though a lod score above 3.0 usually is required to state that a genetic linkage exists, the probability of getting the observed result by chance is only 1:186. The locus of the gene for alpha-haptoglobin is on chromosome 16. By means of a DNA probe for alpha-haptoglobin one might study the potentially more informative restriction fragment length polymorphism (White & Lalouel, 1988) and more certainly confirm the existence of a gene for panic attacks. Thus far, the Iowa linkage study is the best proof for a dominant genetic effect on the development of panic anxiety. It is interesting that panic with agoraphobia contributed most strongly to the lod score. Furthermore, the lod score did not increase if probands with panic, but without sufficient symptoms or frequency of panic attacks to receive the diagnosis of panic disorder, were excluded. Therefore, the study argues for a broader definition of panic disorder, more in accordance with DSM-III-R than DSM-III.

It is important to remember that such a linkage study does not preclude heterogeneity. Selecting families with at least two cases with anxiety favors detection of genetic etiology. Even if a linkage study can establish the locus of a gene for panic, a high percentage of cases might theoretically be outside the influence of genetic etiology.

GENETIC CONNECTION BETWEEN ANXIETY AND DEPRESSION

Some family studies have observed anxiety among children of parents with major depression (Merikangas, Prusoff, & Weissman, 1988; Weissman et al., 1984) and also depression among children of parents with anxiety (Merikangas et al., 1988) (see chapter 3). The frequent comorbidity of anxiety and depression in adults (Boyd et al., 1984) or children (Last et al., 1987) (see chapter 2), however, makes the interpretation of such studies difficult. It seems as if there are mixed probands with both anxiety and depression that have many relatives with both diagnoses (Coryell et al., 1988; Van Valkenburg, Akiskal, Puzantian, & Rosenthal, 1984). The crossing-over relationship—that pure depressives have relatives with pure anxiety and vice versa—is uncommon.

What do twin studies tell us? In the previously discussed Australian twin study a complicated factor analysis of polychoric correlations between the twin partners was applied (Kendler et al., 1987). The analysis of the seven anxiety and seven depressive items seemed to yield one "environmental" predominantly anxiety factor, one "environmental" predominantly depressive factor, and one "genetic" mixed anxiety-depression factor. They concluded that anxiety and depression had the same undifferentiated genetic basis, whereas specific environmental factors might result in some instances in either anxiety or depressive symptoms. As Carey (1987) suggests, however, all the three factors seem a little mixed. Furthermore, the statistical procedure is new and untested, and might favor the conclusions at which they arrive. Finally, as the authors themselves state, it may be unwarranted to draw firm conclusions about the relationship between clinical anxiety and depression based on a study of a few questionnaire items in a study of normal twins.

The Norwegian twin study divided the probands having an ICD 8–9 diagnosis of anxiety neurosis or neurotic depression into three groups by means of discriminant analysis (S. Torgersen, 1985). One consisted of "pure" anxiety neurosis, one of "mixed" anxiety-depression, and one of "pure" neurotic depression. The twin analysis showed that pure anxiety and pure depression seldom occurred in the same twin pair. Co-twins of pure cases more often had mixed anxiety-depression if they did not have the same disorder. Furthermore, for the pure anxiety probands, the concordance was clearly higher in MZ than in DZ pairs, pointing to a possible genetic influence. For the mixed cases and for the pure depressive cases, however, there was no difference in concordance between MZ and DZ pairs.

The sample was also analyzed according to DSM-III, and probands with pure major depression, major depression in combination with anxiety disorders (when the hierarchy was abolished), and pure anxiety disorders were compared (S. Torgersen, 1989). The results once again showed that pure depression and pure anxiety seldom occurred in the same twin pair. Furthermore, mixed cases and pure depression commonly occurred in the same pair, and there seemed to be stronger evidence for genetic influence in the mixed condition. If anxiety disorders with panic attacks only were considered, the results even more clearly suggested that the mixed cases were a genetically stronger variant of major depression, whereas pure anxiety disorder with panic was influenced by other genetic factors.

Looking at the family and twin studies together, it seems as if anxiety disorders and depression do not have the same genetic etiology. The mixed cases have created confusion, but they may preferably be seen as more genetically, and also clinically, severe variants of depression.

CONCLUSION

The genetic studies discussed in this chapter suggest that some anxious features manifested early in childhood might be more or less influenced by genetic factors. The same is true for fears and anxiety in adolescents and adults.

Children's clinical anxiety also seems to be genetically affected. As to clinical anxiety among adults, generalized anxiety disorder does not seem to be influenced by genetic factors, clinical phobias and obsessions might, whereas anxiety disorders with panic attacks seem rather definitely to be caused by possibly dominant genetic factors.

The genetic relationship between anxiety and depression is uncertain. Spurious relations can be caused by lack of reliability and validity, especially when children are studied. As for adults, major depression with anxiety seems to be a severe variant of major depression, whereas pure anxiety disorders, as well as major depression, are genetically unrelated to mixed cases.

It is thus reasonable to suggest that any relationship between adult and childhood anxiety at least partly might be due to the effect of genes. Even if genetic factors are involved in the development of anxiety disorders, however, environmental factors are important. Twin and linkage studies have the tendency to exaggerate the influence of genetic factors. More statistically advanced studies also considering other relatives, and environmental variation, show a reduced genetic influence, perhaps bordering to the negligible when panic disorders are excepted. It is important to conduct studies in which environmental as well as genetic factors are allowed to influence the results, preferably in a longitudinal perspective where the lifespan can be considered.

REFERENCES

Abe, K., Oda, N., & Hatta, H. (1984). Behavioral genetics of early childhood: Fears, restlessness, motion sickness and enuresis. *Acta Geneticae Medicae et Gemellologiae, 33,* 303–306.

Bedford, A., Foulds, G., & Sheffield, B. (1976). A new personal disturbance scale (DDSI/SAD). *British Journal of Social and Clinical Psychiatry, 15,* 387–394.

Boyd, J. H., Burke, J. D., Gruenberg, E., Holzer III, E. E., Rae, D. S., George, L. K., Karno, M., Stolzman, R., McEvoy, L., & Nestadt, G. (1984). Exclusion criteria of DSM-III: A study of co-occurrence of hierarchy-free syndromes. *Archives of General Psychiatry, 41,* 983–989.

Braconi, L. (1961). Le psiconevrosi e le psicosi nei gemelli. *Acta Geneticae et Medicae Gemellologiae, 10,* 100–136.

Carey, G. (1987). Big genes, little genes, affective disorder and anxiety: A commentary. *Archives of General Psychiatry, 44,* 486–491.

Clifford, C. A., Hooper, J. L., Fulker, D. W., & Murray, R. M. (1984). A genetic and environmental analysis of a twin family study of alcohol use, anxiety and depression. *Genetic Epidemiology, 1,* 63–79.

Coryell, W., Endicott, J., Andreassen, N. C., Keller, M. B., Clayton, P. J., Hirschfeld, R. M. A., Scheftner, W. A., & Winokur, G. (1988). Depression and panic attacks: The significance of overlap as reflected in follow-up and family study data. *American Journal of Psychiatry, 145,* 293–300.

Crowe, R. R., Noyes, R., Wilson, A. F., Elston, R. C., & Ward, L. J. (1987). A linkage study of panic disorder. *Archives of General Psychiatry, 44,* 933–937.

Crown, S., & Crisp, A. H. (1966). A short clinical diagnostic self-rating scale for psychoneurotic patients. The Middlesex Hospital Questionnaire (M.H.Q.). *British Journal of Psychiatry, 116,* 33–37.

Eysenck, H. J. (1959). Maudsley personality inventory. London: University of London.

Eysenck, H. J., & Prell D. B. (1951). The inheritance of neuroticism: An experimental study. *Journal of Mental Science, 97,* 441–465.

Freedman, D. G. (1965). An ethiological approach to the genetic study of human behavior. In S. G. Vandenberg (Ed.), *Methods and goals in human behavior genetics.* New York: Academic Press.

Freedman, D. G. (1974). *Human infancy: An evolutionary perspective.* Hillsdale, NJ: Erlbaum.

Freedman, D. G. (1976). Infancy, biology, and culture. In L. P. Lipsitt (Ed.), *Developmental psychobiology: The significance of infancy.* Hillsdale, NJ: Erlbaum.

Freedman, D. G., & Keller, B. (1963). Inheritance of behavior in infants. *Science, 140,* 196–198.

Geer, J. H. (1965). The development of a scale to measure fear. *Behavior Research and Therapy, 3,* 45–53.

Goldsmith, H. H., & Gottesman, I. I. (1981). Origin of variation in behavioral style: A longitudinal study of temperament in young twins. *Child Development, 52,* 91–103.

Jardine, R., Martin, N. G., & Henderson, A. S. (1984). Genetic covariation between neurotiscism and the symptoms of anxiety and depression. *Genetic Epidemiology, 1,* 89–107.

Kendler, K. S., Heath, A., Martin, N. G., & Eaves, L. J. (1986). Symptoms of anxiety and depression in a volunteer twin population: The etiological role of genetic and environmental factors. *Archives of General Psychiatry, 43,* 213–221.

Kendler, K. S., Heath, A., Martin, N. G., & Eaves, L. J. (1987). Symptoms of anxiety and symptoms of depression: Same genes, different environments? *Archives of General Psychiatry, 44,* 451–457.

Langinvaionio, H., Kaprio, J., Koskenvuo, M., & Lonngvist, J. (1984). Finnish twins reared apart: 3. Personality factors. *Acta Geneticae Medicae et Gemellologiae, 33,* 259–264.

Last, C. G., Strauss, C. C., & Francis, G. (1987). Comorbidity among childhood anxiety disorders. *Journal of Nervous and Mental Disease, 175,* 726–730.

Lienert, G. A., & Reisse, H. (1961). Ein korrelationanalytischer Beitrag zur genetischen Determination des Neurotizismus. *Psychologische Beitrage, 7,* 121–130.

Martin, N. G., Jardine, R., Andrews, G., Heath, A. C. (1988). Anxiety disorders and neurotiscism: Are there genetic factors specific to panic? *Acta Psychiatrica Scandinavica, 77,* 698–706.

Merikangas, K. R., Prusoff, B. A., & Weissman, M. M. (1988). Parental concordance for affective disorders: Psychopathology in offspring. *Journal of Affective Disorders, 15,* 279–290.

Neale, M. C., & Fulker, D. W. (1984). A bivariate biometric analysis of year data obtained from twins and their parents. *Acta Geneticae Medicae et Gemellologiae, 33,* 273–286.

Pedersen, N. L., Friberg, L., Floderius-Myhrhed, B., McClearen, G. E., & Plomin, R., (1984). Swedish early separated twins: Identification and characterization. *Acta Geneticae Medicae et Gemellologiae, 33,* 243–250.

Rose, R. J., & Ditto, W. B. (1983). A developmental-genetic analysis of common fears from early adolescence to early adulthood. *Child Development, 54,* 361–368.

Rose, R. J., & Kaprio, J. (1988). Frequency of social contact and intrapair resemblance of adult monozygotic cotwins—or does share experience influence personality after all? *Behavior Genetics, 18,* 309–329.

Shields, J. (1962). *Monozygotic twins brought up apart and brought up together.* Oxford: Oxford University Press.

Shields, J., & Slater, E. (1966). La similarité du diagnostic chez les jumeaux et la problème de la specificité biologique dans les nervoses et les troubles de la personalité. *Evolutione Psychiatrie, 31,* 441–451.

Thomas, A., & Chess, S. (1984). Genesis and evolution of behavioral disorders: From infancy to early adult life. *American Journal of Psychiatry, 141,* 1–9.

Thomas, A., Chess, S., & Birch, H. G. (1968). *Temperament and behavior disorders in children.* New York: New York University Press.

Torgersen, A. M. (1981). Genetic factors in temperamental individuality. *Journal of American Academy of Child Psychiatry, 20,* 702–711.

Torgersen, A. M. (1987). Longitudinal research on temperament in twins. *Acta Geneticae Medicae et Gemellologiae, 36,* 145–154.

Torgersen, A. M. (1989). Genetic and environmental influences on temperamental development: A longitudinal study of twins from infancy to adolescence. In S. Doxiadis (Ed.), *Early influences shaping the individual.* New York: Plenum.

Torgersen, S. (1979). The nature and origin of common phobic fears. *British Journal of Psychiatry, 134,* 343–351.

Torgersen, S. (1981). Environmental childhood similarity and similarity in adult personality and neurotic development in twin pairs. In L. Gedda, P. Parisi, & W. E. Nance (Eds.), *Twin research: Vol. 3. Intelligence, personality, and development.* New York: Liss.

Torgersen, S. (1983). Genetic factors in anxiety disorders. *Archives of General Psychiatry, 40,* 1085–1089.

Torgersen, S. (1985). Hereditary differentiation of anxiety and affective neuroses. *British Journal of Psychiatry, 146,* 530–534.

Torgersen, S. (1986). Childhood and family characteristics in panic and generalized anxiety disorder. *American Journal of Psychiatry, 43,* 630–632.

Torgersen, S. (1989). *Comorbidity of major depression and anxiety disorders in twin pairs.* Manuscript submitted for publication.

Van Valkenburg, C., Akiskal, H. S., Puzantian, V., & Rosenthal, T. (1984). Anxious depressions: Clinical, family history, and naturalistic outcome—comparison with panic and major depressive disorders. *Journal of Affective Disorder, 6,* 67–82.

Weissman, M. M., Leckman, J. R., Merikangas, K. R., Gammon, G. D., & Prusoff, B. A. (1984). Depression and anxiety disorders in parents and children: Results from the Yale Family Study. *Archives of General Psychiatry, 41,* 845–852.

White, R., & Lalouel, J.-M. (1988). Chromosome mapping with DNA markers. *Scientific American, 258,* 40–48.

Young, J. P. R., Fenton, C. W., & Lader, M. J. (1971). The inheritance of neurotic traits: A twin study of the Middlesex Hospital Questionnaire. *British Journal of Psychiatry, 119,* 393–398.

CHAPTER 8

Childhood Separation Anxiety Disorder and Adult-Onset Agoraphobia: Review of Evidence

Bruce A. Thyer

Among the many major advances to be found in the DSM-III (American Psychiatric Association, 1980) and the DSM-III-R (American Psychiatric Association, 1987) is an overt commitment to describe psychopathology using atheoretical terms whenever possible and to base diagnostic criteria on the findings of empirical clinical research studies whenever such information is available. These developments have not been without their critics, but on balance the DSM-III-R seems to provide a giant step in advancing the field of mental health nosology from the realm of clinical anecdote to that of controlled empiral inquiry.

Apart from providing phenomenological descriptions of abnormal behavior, the DSM-III-R also contains specific criteria whose presence or absence, in many diagnostic categories, may be reliably ascertained. As a consequence, the interrater reliabilities in psychiatric diagnosis have been substantially improved in comparison with those obtainable through using the DSM-II. In addition to the specific diagnostic criteria, the DSM-III-R contains with it additional commentary pertaining to age-of-onset information, the projected course, complications, prevalence, sex ratio, familial pattern, predisposing factors, and associated features of the various disorders. In addition, some information is provided for most disorders pertaining to potential differential diagnoses. All these features serve to make the DSM-III-R an extremely useful document (see chapter 2).

As indicated in chapter 2, the substantial changes found in the DSM-III-R is a radical reworking of the general category labeled "anxiety disorders." In the DSM-III there were separate diagnoses for panic disorder (subsumed under the larger category of "anxiety states"), agoraphobia with panic attacks and agoraphobia without panic attacks both being subcategories of "phobic disorders." In the DSM-III-R, we find a major category labeled "panic disorder," with a subtype labeled as "panic disorder with agoraphobia." The associated agoraphobic avoidance may be categorized as either mild, moderate, severe, in partial remission, or in full remission. Panic attacks themselves are similarly described. This revision properly places the experience of panic attacks as the driving force behind much of the clinical symptomatology labeled "anxiety."

The new category of panic disorder with agoraphobia applies to all patients who have met the diagnostic criteria in the past for agoraphobia with panic attacks, and experienced the onset of their problems with pathological anxiety in the form of one or more, usually a random series, of apparently spontaneous panic attacks. Panic attacks are sudden episodes of acute fear with an onset of usually several minutes or less, culminating in intense feelings of somatic anxiety and psychological distress, up to and including fears of dying or of going crazy. The usual course of events seems to be that after experiencing one or more episodes of apparently spontaneous panic, the afflicted individuals begin to avoid places where panics occurred in the past. If panics continue to occur over the course of time, usually extending many months, such individuals began to avoid entering into situations in which *if* a panic attack did occur, they could not escape quickly or help might be unavailable. It is common to see the initial development of limited phobias secondary to this fear of a panic attack, such as expressway driving or driving on high bridges, or of heights, crowds, or enclosed spaces. Such phobias tended to persist and spread with the continued experience of panic attacks until the person became truly polyphobic and in many cases sought refuge by retreating to the home, thus leading to the stereotype of the housebound agoraphobic. It is important to note that this progression is driven by the experience of panics, thus the decision in the DSM-III-R to label the disorder "panic disorder" and subsume under it a form called "panic disorder with agoraphobia," in recognition that very few agoraphobics do not have this phenomenon labeled "panic attacks."

To date there is no widely accepted biological or psychological theory of panic attacks, certainly none with substantial empirical support. The DSM-III-R suggests, however, that "Separation anxiety disorder in childhood and sudden loss of social supports or disruption of important interpersonal relationships apparently predispose to the development of this disorder" (American Psychiatric Association, 1987, p. 237), with respect to panic disorder and agoraphobia. In turning to the commentary on separation anxiety disorder, the DSM-III-R notes that "In most cases the disorder develops after some life stress, typically a loss, the death of a relative or pet, an illness of the child or a relative, or a change in the child's environment, such as a school change or a move to a new neighborhood" (American Psychiatric Association, 1987, p. 60). It is unclear from the empirical literature how this separation anxiety hypothesis came to be included in the diagnostic commentary of the DSM-III-R, yet this contention was previously noted in the DSM-III, which contended that "Separation anxiety disorder in childhood and sudden object loss apparently predispose to the development of . . . agoraphobia and panic disorder" (American Psychiatric Association, 1980, p. 226, 231). The hypothesis that separation anxiety is etiologically related or a selective precursor to the development of adult-onset agoraphobia or panic disorder is not a clinically unimportant contention. Indeed, the separation anxiety hypothesis (SAH) is beginning to have an impact on the treatment planning of agoraphobic individuals (Friedman, 1985).

A further illustration of the salience of the separation anxiety hypothesis with respect to the treatment of the clinically anxious or agoraphobic client may be found in major psychiatric reference books. For example, Freedman, Caplan, and Sadock (1976) suggest that "When faced with a patient with anxiety neurosis, the therapist must ask himself two questions: What inner drive is the patient afraid of? What are the consequences he fears from its expression? In neurotic conflicts the drives are either sexual or aggressive in nature. The consequences the patient fears determines the quality of the anxiety that he experiences. Anxiety falls into four major categories; superego anxiety, castration anxiety, separation anxiety, and id or impulse anxiety. . . . Separation anxiety refers to the stage of the somewhat older but still preoedipal child who fears the loss of love or even abandonment by his parents if he fails to control his impulses in conformity with their standards and demands" (p. 612). These authors go on to recommend psychodynamically oriented psychotherapy to treat the agoraphobic or anxiety neurotic, such treatment being aimed at ameliorating the underlying conflicts giving rise to anxious symptomatology. It should be noted that at the time these recommendations were made and even today there is not yet any scientifically credible evidence suggesting that psychodynamically oriented psychotherapy is of benefit to either individuals suffering from panic disorder or from agoraphobia.

Given that the DSM-III-R is purportedly an atheoretical and empirically supported document, it remains to be seen whether the separation anxiety hypothesis is supported by empirical research to a sufficient extent to warrant its inclusion in the DSM-III and potential inclusion in the DSM-IV.

PHENOMENON OF SEPARATION ANXIETY

Among the many developmentally related fears that may make their appearance and disappearance at reasonably predictable times during childhood and adolescence, the phenomenon of separation anxiety is well recognized. Campbell (1986, p. 37) defines the developmental use of the term separation anxiety as the "protest at the mother's departure, distress caused by her absence, and anxiety about her anticipated absence." Such separation anxiety commonly makes its appearance toward the end of the infant's first year, and its genesis has been usually related to ethological factors, in the sense that as the child becomes more mobile about this time frame, separation anxiety has adaptive significance in protecting the infant from being alone and subject to harm. Topographically, separation anxiety is manifested by crying, wailing, and other signs of protest on the absence of the mother or other significant caregiver, and seeking/searching behavior in the absence of the caregiver. Separation fears appear to peak between the ages of 9 to 13 months and occur among children all over the world (Marks, 1987). For most children, separation anxiety begins to decrease after about 2½ years of age. True experimental studies on the traumatic effects of infant separation experiences among humans are impossible to conduct for ethical reasons. There is an extensive animal literature, well reviewed by Marks (1987), who also describes the experimental separation experience literature with human infants, but these typically involve relatively benign separation manipulations.

With the passage of time, most children, through a process of progressively longer and gradual separation experiences that are not accompanied by aversive consequences, become less and less fearful of such separations from significant caregivers, and become a relatively autonomous child at 3 to 5 years of age.

SAD

The DSM-III-R contains a section entitled "Disorders Usually First Evident in Infancy, Childhood or Adolescence," and has a subsection labeled "Anxiety Disorders of Childhood or Adolescence" (American Psychiatric Association, 1987). The first anxiety disorder of childhood listed is labeled "separation anxiety disorder" and refers to "excessive anxiety, for at least two weeks, concerning separation from those to whom the child is attached. When separation occurs, the child may experience anxiety to the point of panic. The reaction is beyond that expected for the child's developmental level. Onset of the disorder is before age 18" (p. 58). With this disorder the anxiety-evoking stimulus seems to be the actual or anticipated absence of a significant caregiver, but like the other phobic disorders is an unreasonable fear out of proportion to the demands of the situation. Children who meet the diagnostic criteria for SAD often worry that their significant caregivers will leave and not return, or may be harmed. Other common, unrealistic, and persistent worries are that the child may be harmed or kidnapped. These fears are often accompanied by avoidance behaviors typical of other phobic disorders such as reluctance or refusal to go to school, reluctance or refusal to go to sleep, generalized avoidance of being alone, the expression of various somatic complaints (e.g., headaches, stomachaches, etc.) to be near the major attachment figure, significant expression of distress when their parent or other caregiver is actually absent, or other signs of upset in anticipation of such absences such as tantrums, pleas not to leave, or crying. The DSM-III-R indicates that for the diagnosis of SAD to be made, the defining features must have their onset before the age of 18, persist for at least a 2-week period, and not be associated with any psychotic disorder or a pervasive developmental disorder.

A differential diagnosis for SAD is relatively easy to make given the specificity of the anxiety-evoking stimuli as centered around major attachment figures. In overanxious disorder for example, the child's fears and concerns are not specifically centered around the parents or other caregivers. In avoidant disorder, the condition is similar to an exaggerated version of shyness, and the conspicuous attachment to parents is also usually not present. In so-called school phobia or school refusal, the dependent behaviors of the child are usually absent during weekends when it is not incumbent on them to go to school.

The initial onset of SAD in adolescence or later is quite rare, but the condition may persist for many years. In its severest form, SAD may completely incapacitate the child and interfere with significant areas of psychosocial functioning. There are no known patterns of premorbidity associated with the onset of SAD, the condition is apparently equally common in boys and girls, and it may run in families.

The empirical research literature in the treatment of SAD is relatively meager. In their recent review of the topic, Thyer and Sowers-Hoag (1988) located a total of 11 studies describing the treatment of children with symptoms related to SAD. All but two of these studies were case reports or single-subject designs with relatively low internal validity. Fortunately, children who meet the diagnostic criteria for SAD do seem to respond well to a program of gradual real-life exposure therapy similar to that which has been shown to be effective in the treatment of a variety of other phobic disorders (Thyer, 1987). In fact, the only treatment approach that has any evidence of being helpful in the treatment of SAD are the behavior therapies; virtually no research evidence supports the use of psychoanalytic or psychodynamic treatments (Edelson, 1985; Lewis, 1986).

Does Childhood SAD Predispose to Agoraphobia?

Before reviewing clinical research on the SAH it is important to outline the limitations of this review. Several studies have examined the concordance between the history of childhood school phobia, and adult panic disorder or agoraphobia, given the common view that school phobia represents a relatively pure form of childhood SAD (Berg, Marks, McGuire, & Lipsedge, 1974; Deltito, Perugi, Maremmani, Mignani, & Cassano, 1986; Gittelman & Klein, 1980, 1984, 1985; Gittelman-Klein & Klein, 1971, 1973) (see chapter 5). Even if it were found that a history of school phobia were selectively associated with adult-onset agoraphobia, such evidence could not be viewed as corroborative of the SAH because it has recently been shown that SAD and school phobia possess several significant distinguishing characteristics and are best viewed as two separate conditions (Last, Frances, Hersen, Kazdin, & Strauss, 1987). In any event, the preceding studies examining the association between a history of school phobia and adult-onset agoraphobia suffer from several methodological shortcomings such as the use of retrospective and nonblind interviews that lack validation data, and, more important, the studies have produced ambiguous findings. A history of school phobia has *not* been clearly shown to be especially prevalent among adult panic disorder or agoraphobic patients.

Apart from the evidence indicating that school phobia and SAD are distinct conditions, it has now become increasingly clear that school phobia symptomatology may arise from several diverse etiological mechanisms (Thyer & Sowers-Hoag, 1986). For example, school phobic behavior may arise from a true phobic reaction to some aspect of the school, such as a frightening bully or intimidating teacher. Second, so-called school phobia *may* also arise from true SAD experienced by a child, with phobiclike reactions to separation being present in other circumstances apart from those attendant to going to school. Third, school phobia may be a positively reinforced operant response, wherein whining, crying, tantruming, or somatic complaints on the part of the child may be rewarded by the mother through solicitous attention throughout the day as the child stays home. Differential diagnoses for the apparently school phobic child, other than SAD or phobic disorder, may be overanxious disorder or avoidant disorder of childhood or adolescence (Last & Strauss, 1990). Hence there are at least five possible mechanisms for symptomatically similar behaviors that could be labeled school phobia. It is clearly a mistake to refer to school phobia as a "pure culture" of SAD, as Klein (1981) has contended, and for the preceding reasons the inconclusive body of research on school phobia and agoraphobia is not reviewed here.

Another line of research has been pursued by Gittelman-Klein and Klein (1971) who treated school phobic children with the tricyclic antidepressant imipramine, a drug with demonstrated effectiveness in the treatment of the panic attacks, associated with panic disorder and agoraphobia. Gittelman-Klein and Klein, concluding that imipramine exerted a beneficial effect on school phobia, reasoned that the similarity in pharmacological response between school phobic children and adults suffering from panic attacks argued for the equivalence of these two conditions. This is basically a specious line of reasoning in that apart from having antipanic properties, imipramine is also known to be an effective treatment for enuresis and depression, and also has a mildly sedating effect. Aspirin works extremely well in relieving the pains caused by a toothache, a headache, or an earache secondary to infection. One would not argue that a toothache and a headache are etiologically related because they exhibit a similar positive response to a single medication. Furthermore, in a study conducted by an independent team of investigators (Berney et al., 1981), clomipramine, a heterocyclic antidepressant, was not found to help school phobic children. The dose in this second study was somewhat lower than that used by Gittelman-Klein and Klein, but to date their report is the only one demonstrating the effectiveness of an antipanic compound in the treatment of school phobia and should be viewed as tentative at present.

Other lines of evidence that may have some potential bearing on the SAH include the extensive animal literature and the smaller body of research using human subjects, which demonstrates the deleterious effects of infantile separation experiences on subsequent adult development and behavior. Such studies may reveal evidence that can at best only indirectly support or refute the SAH. Accordingly, this line of inquiry is also disregarded.

More than 30 years ago, Bowlby (1961) speculated that traumatic maternal separations experienced by children render them vulnerable to the subsequent adult development of anxiety disorders. Earlier, Freud had contended that anxiety is a response to the danger of losing a significant other, or "object" (1959). A similar but more specific hypothesis was set forth about the same time as Bowlby by Klein and Fink (1962), who contended that adult panic attacks were etiologically related to a history of childhood SAD. Several anecdotal reports seemed to support these hypotheses (Frances & Dunn, 1975; Rhead, 1969; Roth, 1959; Stamm, 1972; Wangh, 1967), as did some more systematic inquiries involving structured interviews with adult anxiety disorder patients pertaining to histories of childhood separation anxiety (Klein, 1964; Mendel & Klein, 1969). One difficulty with using such anecdotal reports based on clinical and structured interviews with adult agoraphobics is that the patient's recollections of separation-related experiences are of unknown validity. In addition, clinicians or research interviewers who are not "blind" with respect to the patient's diagnostic status or hypotheses of the research may selectively guide the course and content of interviewing and questioning in a way that unintentionally elicits separation-related material. A further consideration is that there are no known protocols for reliably and validly diagnosing the presence of childhood separation disorder in histories of adult anxious patients or of adults without an anxiety disorder. Structured verbal intervals or pencil-and-paper surveys may obviate some of these concerns but do so at the expense of flexibility.

The assessment of life events in general is known to be fraught with difficulties. For example, even if the presence or absence of certain historical events in an individual's past can be reliably ascertained, the relative degree of stress or trauma that the event elicited may vary greatly among individuals experiencing similar events (Zimmerman, 1983). At times it is unclear whether certain life events assessed in a research study are truly salient to traumatic separation experiences or separation anxiety.

In undertaking this review of empirical studies on the SAH, it seemed that a fairly limited number of research strategies were employed. These are individually reviewed subsequently, in rough order of their robustness and specificity as a potential tool to falsify or corroborate the separation anxiety hypothesis.

Research Strategy 1

Demonstrate that a history of separation anxiety disorder is present in a significant number of agoraphobics: This approach is among the simplest (and weakest) of the available strategies that may be used to investigate the validity of the SAH. Clinicians and researchers who have employed it qualitatively include Roth (1959), Wangh (1967), Rhead (1969), Stamm (1972), Frances and Dunn (1975), Klein and Fink (1962), and Klein (1964). Typically, these authors reported their informal clinical impressions and observations about the presumptive dynamics operative with the agoraphobic patients they had worked with, often just one or two individuals. On a somewhat larger scale, the report of Klein (1964) is typical. Of 32 hospitalized agoraphobic patients, approximately half reported a history of severe separation anxiety during their childhood. In another report, Mendel and Klein (1969) found a history of childhood SAD present reported by 4 out of 8 agoraphobics with an onset of agoraphobia before age 21, and by 4 out of 17 agoraphobics with an agoraphobia onset after age 21 (for a total of 8 out of 25 patients).

Breier, Charney, and Heninger (1986) employed an intensive, structured face-to-face interview to obtain information on the antecedents of the adult-onset of agoraphobia ($n = 55$) and panic disorder ($n = 5$). Eleven of their 60 patients reported a history of childhood SAD, and 15 had been separated from either parent for 1 month or more during childhood. Related findings were reported by Coryell, Noyes, and Clancy (1983) who found that 28% of their sample of panic disorder patients had experienced similar childhood parental separation from one or both parents.

Thorpe and Burns (1983) conducted a national survey in the United

Kingdom of sufferers from agoraphobia, obtaining a sample of 963 respondents. Approximately 38% of their sample "appear to have been separated from their parents for a variety of reasons (illness, divorce, military service, etc.), for at least one period of 3 months or longer" (Thorpe & Burns, 1983, p. 21). These authors also reviewed the general issue of whether or not especially "dependent" individuals are more likely to develop agoraphobia. They concluded that "Although some interesting hypotheses have been advanced between agoraphobia and dependency, a clear consensus is lacking" (Thorpe & Burns, 1983, p. 41).

Deltito et al. (1986) examined the histories and diagnoses of 150 patients referred for pathological anxiety. Twenty-five met the criteria for agoraphobia with panic attacks, and 14 had pure panic disorder. These 39 patients were divided into three groups: panic disorder without school phobia related to separation anxiety, agoraphobia without such school phobia, and agoraphobia with a history of school phobia. The authors claimed to carefully elicit features of separation anxiety in assessing so-called school phobia, avoiding the potential confounds that may occur if this variable is not assessed. No patients with panic disorder reported a history of school phobia/SAD, whereas 15 or 25 agoraphobics reported such a history.

The difficulty with such studies is the lack of methods to validly diagnose separation anxiety disorder of childhood among present-day adults (the same may be said for diagnosing school phobia). The problem of possible atypical clinical samples, clinician/researchers biases, selective recall, and patients' posthoc attributions, all combine to render such data suspect. Furthermore, it is unclear what the incidence of SAD may be among patients with other psychiatric disorders, or among the general population. This latter problem leads to the following, more robust, methods of evaluating the validity of the SAH.

Research Strategy 2

Show that a history of separation anxiety disorder is present in a significant number of agoraphobic/panic disorder patients, and not among patients with other anxiety disorders: Raskin, Peeke, Dickman, and Pinsker (1982) compared the developmental and childhood histories of 17 patients with panic disorder and 16 with generalized anxiety disorder. Information was gathered via blind semistructured psychiatric interviews. The authors found that "Both groups had a similar incidence of early loss, separation anxiety disorder in childhood, and separations as precipitants of anxiety" (Raskin et al., 1982, p. 689). This obviously argues against the notion that SAD is a selective precursor to agoraphobia or panic disorder in adulthood. Only 6 of 17 panic disorder and 4 of 16 generalized anxiety disorder patients reported a history of childhood SAD.

Klein, Zitring, Woerner, and Ross (1983) and Zitrin, Klein, Woerner, and Ross (1983) retrospectively diagnosed the presence or absence of childhood separation anxiety disorder among 58 adult agoraphobic and 59 simple phobic patients. Apparently 50% of the agoraphobics reported a history of childhood SAD, versus only 27% of the simple phobics, a statistically significant difference. In an updated version of their research in this area, Gittelman and Klein (1984) present further data that indicate that this history of SAD is only selectively associated with adult-experienced agoraphobia among women, not men. Such histories were reported by 6 of 19 male agoraphobics and 6 of 15 male simple phobics, versus 23 of 39 female agoraphobics and 10 of 44 female simple phobics, a statistically significant gender difference. In a further report of this patient series, Gittelman and Klein (1985) conclude that "In both childhood and adolescence, agoraphobic patients have significantly more separation anxiety than patients with simple phobia. However, this group difference appears entirely due to the high prevalence of separation anxiety in female agoraphobics. Thus, a history of separation anxiety disorder does not appear to be related to agoraphobia in the men, but it seems to be among the women" (pp. 398–399). This represents a significant modification in the SAH by two of its strongest original supporters. It is possible that these apparent differences also may not withstand further empirical scrutiny, given that prior studies have shown few meaningful differences between male and female agoraphobics with respect to symptomatology and personality (Mavissakalian, 1985).

Thyer, Nesse, Cameron, and Curtis (1985) examined the separation anxiety histories of 44 agoraphobics and 83 simple phobics, using a self-report questionnaire. On none of the instruments' 14 items (e.g., "How much were you upset by being left with babysitters?") did the agoraphobics score significantly higher than the simple phobics, leading these authors to conclude that childhood separation anxiety problems are not a significant precursor to adult-onset agoraphobia, and that the SAH should not appear in future revisions of the DSM-III. Thyer, Nesse, Curtis, and Cameron (1986) replicated this study using a sample of 23 patients with panic disorder and 28 simple phobics, reaching conclusions similar to their earlier work (Thyer et al., 1985).

Bruch, Heimberg, Berger, and Collins (1987) conducted a questionnaire survey of 21 social phobics and 22 agoraphobics and, although finding several historical variables that distinguished the two groups, found that a history of SAD was not reported to a greater extent among the agoraphobics.

In a more selective test of the SAH, Thyer, Himle, and Fischer (1988) examined the incidence of parental deaths, and patient ages at the time of such deaths, among groups of patients with agoraphobia ($n = 40$), panic disorder ($n = 40$), and simple phobia ($n = 40$). The overall incidence of parental deaths was low in all three patient groups, and there were no significant differences among them either in terms of the incidence or in patient ages at the time of these deaths. The authors again conclude that "There is no good evidence that parental death, object loss, or a history of separation anxiety disorder or school phobia uniquely disposes one to the development of panic disorder or agoraphobia" (Thyer et al., 1988).

On balance it seems clear that, regardless of the incidence of childhood SAD in adult agoraphobics, the childhood phenomenon cannot be said to be a *selective* precursor to the adult disorder.

Research Strategy 3

Show that a history of separation anxiety disorder is present in a significant number of agoraphobic/panic disorder patients, relative to individuals without an anxiety disorder: Buglass et al. (1977) found that 30 agoraphobic patients could not be distinguished from a group of 30 matched general-practice patients assessed with pencil-and-paper scales measuring positive, negative, or ambivalent feelings toward one's parents. Related to this study, Parker (1979) retrospectively assessed parental bonding patterns in matched groups of agoraphobics ($n = 40$), social phobics ($n = 40$), and adult offenders ($n = 132$). Compared with adult offenders, social phobics scored both parents as low on caring and high on overprotection, whereas agoraphobics differed from offenders only in scoring lower in parental care. Social phobics appeared to have a greater history of attachment disturbance than agoraphobics, a result at odds with the SAH. Parker concluded that "The view that agoraphobics have experienced maternal overprotection was thus not supported by either study of a categorical agoraphobic group or examination of the intensity of agoraphobic symptoms against degree of maternal overprotection" (1979, p. 560).

Thyer, Himle, and Miller-Gogoleski (1989) replicated the study of Thyer et al. (1988), using a community-based sample of agoraphobia self-help–group members. The incidence of either maternal or paternal deaths was not found to differ, when 43 agoraphobics were compared with 39 nonanxious controls. Because parental death is specifically mentioned in the DSM-III-R as a precursor to SAD, and the sudden disruption of important interpersonal relationships is purportedly associated with the onset of agoraphobia, Thyer, Himle, and Miller-Gogoleski (1989) concluded that the SAH was not supported by their findings.

Tennant, Hurry, and Bebbington (1982) report the results of a survey of

800 members of a South London community that assessed, among other factors, the prevalence of anxiety and depressive states, and histories of childhood separation experiences. A semistructured interview format was employed. It was found that 43% of their community sample reported experiencing various forms of traumatic childhood separation. Psychiatric "morbidity" occurred among 40% of those reporting a traumatic separation experience, and among 32% of those who had not been separated. It was further found that separation experiences were more strongly associated with subsequent depression, not anxiety, and that the "incidence of depression, anxiety, or of depression plus anxiety were not significantly greater in any of the four separated groups than in those not separated" (Tennant et al., 1982, p. 479).

This latter study provides a crucial bit of data relevant to investigating the SAH. Apparently traumatic separation experiences are quite common among the general population (43%). Thus uncontrolled studies employing research strategies 1 and 2, described earlier, or strategy 4 later, which obtained incidences of separation anxiety in the histories of adult agoraphobics equivalent to or lower than this 43% benchmark, may be in reality only assessing the normal level of such experiences in the general population.

Apparently experiencing some variation of separation anxiety problems in childhood is a relatively common occurrence and not one that reliably distinguishes agoraphobics from individuals without anxiety disorders.

Research Stragegy 4

Demonstrate that significant life events involving loss or separation occur shortly before the onset of agoraphobia/panic disorder: Roth (1959) reported the results of his analysis of 135 agoraphobic patients, finding that 37% of the patients experienced the onset of their agoraphobia following the sudden illness of a closely related person, 31% following the patient's own illness or experiencing an acute threat, and often after circumstances that threatened one's marriage.

Doctor (1982) conducted a survey study of 404 agoraphobics (mostly from California) enrolled in a professional treatment program, and elicited information pertaining to "life circumstances" associated with the onset of their disorder. Although the largest category of life circumstances that appeared to precede agoraphobia immediately seemed related to "separation and loss" (31% of the sample so reporting), Doctor concluded that "the heterogeneity of stress situations suggests that factors associated with poor stress management rather than any specific stress itself are what contribute to the development of agoraphobia" (1982, pp. 209–214).

Ost and Hugdahl (1983) examined the histories of 80 agoraphobics using a structured questionnaire. Only 12% of their sample could recall any evident precipitating factors, and "stressful life events like the death of a relative or separation from a partner occurred less often" (Ost & Hugdahl, 1983, p. 627) than events such as somatic disorders or exhaustion at work.

Last, Barlow, and O'Brien (1984) conducted detailed clinical interviews with 58 agoraphobics in an attempt to isolate the occurrence of significant life events immediately before the onset of their disorder. Most reported calamitous experiences, such as interpersonal conflict, miscarriages, hysterectomies, and so on. Reports of the patients having experienced the death or illness of a significant other, however, only occurred among 16% of their sample. Other types of stressful experiences were far more common.

Roy-Byrne, Geraci, and Uhde (1986a) assessed the experience of recent loss among 33 panic disorder patients, using a validated life events scale, for the 1-year period before the onset of their first panic. Eleven patients reported such major losses (e.g., death of a parent, divorce, etc.), and 22 had not. The authors concluded that "the occurrence of severe loss before the onset of panic attacks in patients with panic disorder is not related to the severity of subsequent anxiety symptoms but does appear to be related to the subsequent occurrence of a major depression" and that "the occurrence of a major loss (e.g., death of a loved one) in patients with panic disorder may confer an increased risk for a subsequent 'secondary' depression without influencing the course of the primary anxiety symptomatology (e.g., frequency of panic attacks)" (Roy-Byrne et al., 1986a, p. 1034).

These studies assessing the experience of significant life events in the histories of agoraphobic/panic disorder patients may ultimately shed some light on the validity of the SAH, which suggests that the "sudden loss of social supports or disruption of important interpersonal relationship" (American Psychiatric Association, 1987, p. 237) are selective precursors to these conditions. Such information may only be properly interpreted, however, when the incidence of similar stressful life events occurring in the lives of the general population is known. The following two research strategies attempt to take this factor into account.

Research Strategy 5

Demonstrate that life events involving loss or separation experiences are present in the recent histories of a significant number of agoraphobic/panic disorder patients, prior to the onset of their disorder, and not among patients with other psychiatric disorders: Persson and Nordlund (1985) compared 73 agoraphobics versus 31 social phobics (all women) on a variety of demographic variables.

Agoraphobia was reportedly more associated with the patients' mothers working outside the home during the patient's childhood, and the experiencing of a loved one's death as a precipitant for their disorder.

Finlay-Jones and Brown (1981) reported that the recent experience of life events related to loss was more strongly associated with the subsequent development of a depressive disorder rather than an anxiety disorder. The latter conditions seemed more often to be preceded by life events involving true elements of danger. These authors provide a thorough review of the research evidence examining the relationships between stressful life events and the onset of psychiatric disorders such as anxiety and depression. These additional studies also support Finlay-Jones and Brown's contention that "severe loss was a causal agent in the onset of anxiety disorders" (1981, p. 803). The results of research strategy 5 seem to have yielded ambiguous results, with respect to the validity of the SAH.

Research Strategy 6

Demonstrate that life events involving loss or separation occur in the recent histories of a significant number of agoraphobic/panic disorder patients, and not among individuals without a psychiatric disorder: Solyom, Silberfeld, and Solyom (1976) used questionnaires and semistructured interviews to assess the presence of pathological maternal overprotection among the mothers of agoraphobic patients ($n = 21$), comparing them with the responses from 47 normal controls. The authors concluded that "The results of this study are inconclusive. Evidence of a relationship between a mother's overprotective behaviour and the development of agoraphobia in her child is not definitive" (Solyom et al., 1976, p. 111).

This research strategy was also followed by Faravelli, Webb, Ambonetti, Fonnesu, and Sessarego (1985) who interviewed 31 agoraphobics and 31 normal controls for the occurrence of significant and supposedly traumatic life events. A total of 38 such events were elicited from the agoraphobic patients versus 14 from the control (examples included such events as separation experiences, parental death, divorces, etc.), a statistically significant difference. A structured interview was employed to obtain the historical material.

Faravelli et al. (1985) retrospectively assessed life events occurring 12 months before the onset of a panic disorder patient's ($n = 23$) first reported panic attack, relative to those of a match ($n = 23$) healthy control group. The two groups were virtually identical in terms of their experienced life events (as assessed by frequency and severity) for the entire year before the patients' onset of panic attacks, except for the 2-month period immediately before the first panic attack (9 patients had such events versus 1 control subject). Examples of such events included experiencing a serious illness in oneself or a loved one, or the death of a cohabiting relative.

Roy-Byrne, Geraci, and Uhde (1986b) compared the responses of 44 panic disorder patients with those of 44 matched healthy controls to a well-validated life events inventory and other methods of assessing stressful life circumstances. The authors report that "In contrast to the subjects in previous studies, these patients with panic disorder did not report a greater number of events involving separation or loss" (Roy-Byrne et al., 1986b, p. 1426).

A further research stragegy that would come close to being definitive, apart from the six reviewed previously, would be to obtain matched samples of children with and without separation anxiety disorder, and to follow them longitudinally for 2 to 3 decades. If the children with separation anxiety developed agoraphobia/panic disorder to a significantly greater extent than the control children without separation problems, the SAH would then be reasonably confirmed. For a variety of reasons, financial among them, this approach has not yet been undertaken. Last (personal communication, 1988), however, recently obtained funds from the NIMH to follow children with SAD and other childhood anxiety disorders longitudinally.

CONCLUSION

The preceding six research strategies are noted in Table 8.1, along with the relevant studies that seem to support or disconfirm the separation anxiety hypothesis. Most of these individual studies (19 out of 30) describe results that do not support the SAH of agoraphobia or panic disorder. Furthermore, the bulk of those that seem to collaborate the SAH are studies with relatively low internal validity (e.g., lack of control groups).

At this stage of empirical inquiry the available evidence does not seem to justify the contention found in the DSM-III-R that a history of childhood SAD is a selective and specific precursor to the adult onset of agoraphobia or panic disorder. Furthermore, no study has yet shown that in instances wherein SAD or sudden object loss have occurred in the histories of such adults that these factors are in any way salient to the disorder's course, prognosis, or response to treatment.

It is clearly incumbent on the supporters of the SAH to gather additional empirical data to corroborate their contentions and to justify the inclusion of diagnostic commentary that is not empirical in nature. To the extent that such data are not forthcoming, the field of psychiatric nosology will retain vestiges of being a politicized process and not a truly scientific one.

TABLE 8.1 Summary of Empirical Research Findings on the Separation Anxiety Hypothesis

Research strategy	Study findings	
	Corroborative	Disconfirming
1	Klein & Fink (1962)	Mendel & Klein (1969)[a]
	Klein (1964)	Coryell et al. (1983)
	Wangh (1969)	Thorpe & Burns (1983)
	Rhead (1969)	Breier et al. (1986)
	Stamm (1972)	
	Frances & Dunn (1975)	
2	Klein et al. (1983)[b]	Raskin et al. (1982)
	Zitrin et al. (1983)	Thyer et al. (1985)
	Gittelman & Klein (1984)	Thyer et al. (1986)
	(partially)	Thyer, Himle, & Fischer (1988)
	Gittelman & Klein (1985)	
	(partially)	
3	None	Buglass et al. (1977)
		Parker (1979)
		Tennant et al. (1979)
		Thyer, Himle, & Miller-
		Gogoleski (1989)
4	Roth (1959)	Doctor (1982)
		Ost & Hugdahl (1983)
		Last et al. (1984)
		Roy-Byrne et al. (1986a)
5	Persson & Nordlund (1985)	Finlay-Jones & Brown (1981)
6	Faravelli et al. (1985)	Solyom et al. (1976)
	Faravelli (1985)	Roy-Byrne et al. (1986b)

[a]Although the authors interpreted their findings as supportive, the incidence of separation experiences reported by their patients did not exceed those of nonpatients, as established by Tennant et al. 1979.
[b]This series of four articles actually reports on the results of a single longitudinal study.

Gittelman is clearly correct in her conclusion that "The retrospective, follow-back studies of adult patients with anxiety disorders are inconsistent in suggesting a specific association between adult panic or agoraphobic disorders and childhood separation anxiety" (1986, p. 121). It is time our diagnostic nomenclature accurately reflects such findings.

ACKNOWLEDGMENT:

Preparation of this chapter was facilitated by a NIMH Faculty Scholar Award (MH-19079).

REFERENCES

American Psychiatric Association. (1980). *Diagnostic and statistical manual of mental disorders* (3rd ed.). Washington, DC: Author.

American Psychiatric Association. (1987). *Diagnostic and statistical manual of mental disorders* (3rd ed., rev.). Washington, DC: Author.

Berg, I., Marks, I. M., McGuire, R., & Lipsedge, M. (1974). School phobia and agoraphobia. *Psychological Medicine, 4*, 428–434.

Berney, T., Kolvin, I., Bhate, S., Garside, R., Jeans, J., Kay, B., & Scarth, L. (1981). School phobia: A therapeutic trial with clomiprimine and short-term outcome. *British Journal of Psychiatry, 138*, 110–118.

Bowlby, J. (1961). Childhood mourning and its implications for psychiatry. *American Journal of Psychiatry, 118*, 481–498.

Breier, A., Charney, D. S., & Heninger, G. R. (1986). Agoraphobia with panic attacks: Development, diagnostic stability and course of illness. *Archives of General Psychiatry, 43*, 1029–1031.

Bruch, M. A., Heimberg, R. G., Berger, P., & Collins, T. M. (1987, November). *Familial and developmental origins of social evaluative concerns in social phobics and agoraphobics.* Paper presented at the annual meeting of the Association for Advancement of Behavior Therapy, Boston, MA.

Burglass, D., Clarke, J., Henderson A. S., & Presley, A. A. (1977). A study of agoraphobic housewives. *Psychological Medicine, 7*, 73–86.

Campbell, S. B. (1986). Developmental issues in childhood anxiety. In R. Gittelman (Ed.), *Anxiety disorders of childhood* (pp. 24–57). New York: Guilford.

Coryell, W., Noyes, R., & Clancy, J. (1983). Panic disorder and primary unipolar depression: A comparison of background and outcome. *Journal of Affective Disorders, 5*, 311–317.

Delitito, J. A., Perugi, G., Maremmani, I., Mignani, V., & Cassano, G. B. (1986). The importance of separation anxiety in the differentiation of panic disorder from agoraphobia. *Psychiatric Developments, 3*, 227–236.

Doctor, R. M. (1982). Major results of a large-scale pretreatment survey of agoraphobics. In R. L. DuPont (Ed.), *Phobia: A comprehensive survey of modern treatments* (pp. 203–214). New York: Brunner/Mazel.

Edelson, M. (1985). Pyschoanalysis, anxiety and the anxiety disorders. In A. H. Tuma & J. Maser (Eds.), *Anxiety and the anxiety disorders* (pp. 633–644). Hillsdale, NJ: Erlbaum.

Faravelli, C. (1985). Life events preceding the onset of panic disorder. *Journal of Affective Disorders, 9*, 103–105.

Faravelli, C., Webb, T., Ambonetti, A., Fonnesu, F., & Sessarego, A. (1985). Prevalence of traumatic early life events in 31 agoraphobia patients with panic attacks. *American Journal of Psychiatry, 142*, 1493–1494.

Finlay-Jones, R., & Brown, G. W. (1981). Types of stressful life events and the onset of anxiety and depressive disorders. *Psychological Medicine, 11*, 803–811.

Frances, A., & Dunn, P. (1975). The attachment-autonomy conflict in agoraphobia. *International Journal of Psychoanalysis, 56*, 435–439.

Freedman, A. M., Kaplan, H. I., & Sadock, B. J. (1976). *Modern synopsis of com-*

prehensive textbook of psychiatry (2nd ed.). Baltimore, MD: Williams & Wilkins.

Freud, S. (1959). *Inhibitions, symptoms and anxiety.* New York: Norton. (Original work published in 1929)

Friedman, S. (1985). Implication of object-relations theory for the behavioral treatment of agoraphobia. *American Journal of Psychotherapy, 34,* 525–540.

Gittelman, R. (1986). Childhood anxiety disorders: Correlates and outcome. In R. Gittelman (Ed.), *Anxiety disorders of childhood* (pp. 101–125). New York: Guilford.

Gittelman, R., & Klein, D. F. (1980). Separation anxiety in school refusal and its treatment with drugs. In L. Hersov & I. Berg (Eds.), *Out of school* (pp. 321–341). New York: Wiley.

Gittelman, R., & Klein, D. F. (1984). Relationship between separation anxiety and panic and agoraphobic disorders. *Psychopathology, 17*(Suppl. 1), 56–65.

Gittelman, R., & Klein, D. F. (1985). Childhood separation anxiety and adult agoraphobia. In A. H. Tuman & J. Maser (Eds.), *Anxiety and the anxiety disorders* (pp. 389–402). Hillsdale, NJ: Erlbaum.

Gittelman-Klein, R., & Klein, D. F. (1971). Controlled imipramine treatment of school phobia. *Archives of General Psychiatry, 25,* 204–207.

Gittelman-Klein, R., & Klein, D. F. (1973). School phobia: Diagnostic considerations in the light of imipramine effects. *Journal of Nervous and Mental Diseases, 156,* 199–215.

Klein, D. F. (1964). Delineation of two drug-responsive anxiety syndromes. *Psychopharmacologia, 3,* 397–408.

Klein, D. F. (1981). Anxiety reconceptualized. In D. F. Klein & J. Rabkin (Eds.), *Anxiety: New research and changing concepts* (pp. 235–263). New York: Raven.

Klein, D. F., & Fink, M. (1962). Psychiatric reaction patterns to imipramine. *American Journal of Psychiatry, 119,* 432–438.

Klein, D. F., Zitrin, C. M., Woerner, M. G., & Ross, D. C. (1983). Treatment of phobias: 2. Behavior therapy and supportive psychotherapy: Are there any specific ingredients? *Archives of General Psychiatry, 40,* 139–145.

Last, C. G., Barlow, D. H., & O'Brien, G. T. (1984). Precipitants of agoraphobia: Role of stressful life events. *Psychological Reports, 54,* 567–570.

Last, C. G., Francis, G., Hersen, M., Kazdin, A. E., & Strauss, C. C. (1987). Separation anxiety and school phobia: A comparison using DSM-III criteria. *American Journal of Psychiatry, 144,* 653–657.

Last, C. G., & Strauss, C. C. (1990). School refusal in anxiety disordered children and adolescents. *Journal of the American Academy of Child and Adolescent Psychiatry, 29,* 31–35.

Lewis, M. (1986). Principles of intensive individual psychoanalytic psychotherapy for childhood anxiety disorders. In R. Gittelman (Ed.), *Anxiety disorders of childhood* (pp. 233–255). New York: Guilford.

Marks, I. M. (1987). *Fears, phobias and rituals.* New York: Oxford University Press.

Mavissakalian, M. (1985). Male and female agoraphobics: Are they different? *Behaviour Research and Therapy, 23,* 469–471.

Mendel, J. & Klein, D. F. (1969). Anxiety attacks and subsequent agoraphobia. *Comprehensive Psychiatry, 10,* 476–478.

Ost, L. G., & Hugdahl, K. (1983). Acquisition of agoraphobia, mode of onset and anxiety response patterns. *Behaviour Research and Therapy, 21,* 623–631.

Parker, G. (1979). Reported parental characteristics of agoraphobics and social phobias. *British Journal of Psychiatry, 135,* 555–560.

Persson, G., & Nordlund, C. L. (1985). Agoraphobics and social phobics: Differences in background factors, syndrome profiles and therapeutic response. *Acta Psychiatrica Scandinavia, 71,* 148–159.

Raskin, M., Peeke, H. V., Dickman, W., & Pinsker, H. (1982). Panic and generalized anxiety disorders: Developmental antecedents and precipitants. *Archives of General Psychiatry, 39,* 587–589.

Rhead, C. (1969). The role of pregenital fixations of agoraphobics. *Journal of the American Psychoanalytic Association, 17,* 848–861.

Roth, M. (1959). The phobic anxiety-depersonalization syndrome. *Proceedings of the Royal Society of Medicine, 52,* 587–595.

Roy-Byrne, P. P., Geraci, M., & Uhde, T. W. (1986a). Life events and course of illness in patients with panic disorder. *American Journal of Psychiatry, 143,* 1033–1035.

Roy-Byrne, P. P., Geraci, M., & Uhde, T. W. (1986b). Life events and the onset of panic disorder. *American Journal of Psychiatry, 143,* 1424–1427.

Solyom, L., Silberfeld, M., & Solyom, C. (1976). Maternal overprotection in the etiology of agoraphobia. *Canadian Psychiatric Association Journal, 21,* 109–113.

Stamm, J. (1972). Infantile trauma, narcissistic injury, and agoraphobia. *Psychiatric Quarterly, 46,* 254–272.

Tennant, C., Hurray, J., & Bebbington, P. (1982). The relationship of childhood separation experiences to adult depressive and anxiety states. *British Journal of Psychiatry, 141,* 475–482.

Thorpe, G. L., & Burns, L. E. (1983). *The agoraphobic syndrome.* New York: Wiley.

Thyer, B. A. (1987). *Treating anxiety disorders: A guide for human service professionals.* Newbury Park: Sage.

Thyer, B. A., Himle, J., & Fischer, D. (1988). Is parental death a selective precursor to either panic disorder or agoraphobia? A test of the separation anxiety hypothesis. *Journal of Anxiety Disorders, 2,* 333–338.

Thyer, B. A., Himle, J., & Miller-Gogoleski, M. A. (1989). The relationship of parental death to panic disorder: A community-based replication. *Phobia Practice and Research Journal, 2,* 29–36.

Thyer, B. A., Nesse, R. M., Cameron, O. G., & Curtis, G. C. (1985). Agoraphobia: A test of the separation anxiety hypothesis. *Behaviour Research and Therapy, 23,* 75–78.

Thyer, B. A., Nesse, R. M., Curtis, G. C., & Cameron, O. G. (1986). Panic disorder: A test of the separation anxiety hypothesis. *Behaviour Research and Therapy, 24,* 209–211.

Thyer, B. A., & Sowers-Hoag, K. M. (1986). The etiology of school phobia: A behavioral approach. *School Social Work Journal, 10,* 86–98.

Thyer, B. A., & Sowers-Hoag, K. M. (1988). Behavior therapy for separation anxiety disorder. *Behavior Therapy, 12,* 205–233.

Wangh, M. (1959). Structural determinants of phobia. *Journal of the American Psychoanalytic Association, 7,* 675–695.

Wangh, M. (1967). Psychoanalytic thought on phobia: Its evolution and its relevance for therapy. *American Journal of Psychiatry, 123,* 1075–1080.

Zimmerman, M. (1983). Methodological issues in the assessment of life events: A review of issues and research. *Clinical Psychology Review, 3,* 339–370.

Zitrin, C. M., Klein, D. F., Woerner, M. G., & Ross, D. C. (1983). Treatment of phobias: 1. Comparison of imipramine hydrochloride and placebo. *Archives of General Psychiatry, 40,* 125–138.

CHAPTER 9

Expression and Treatment of Obsessive-Compulsive Disorder in Childhood, Adolescence, and Adulthood

Greta Francis and Janet Borden

DIAGNOSTIC PICTURE

According to the DSM-III-R (American Psychiatric Association, 1987), the cardinal feature of OCD is recurrent obsessions or compulsions of sufficient severity to cause distress or impairment in functioning, or to be excessively time-consuming. Obsessions are persistent thoughts, images, or impulses that, at least initially, are experienced as unwanted, intrusive, and senseless. Attempts are made to ignore, neutralize, or suppress the obsessions. The individual recognizes that the obsessions are a product of his or her mind (e.g., not thought insertion). Compulsions refer to purposeful behaviors that are performed in a stereotyped manner or repeated according to certain rules. Although the compulsion is performed as a way to decrease or prevent distress, the activity either is excessive or unrealistic. Typically the person recognizes that the compulsive behavior is problematic; however, this may not be true for very young children or individuals with overvalued ideas.

EPIDEMIOLOGY

Course

The course of OCD generally is chronic and unremitting in adults (American Psychiatric Association, 1987; Turner & Beidel, 1988). Black (1974) reported that the initial course of OCD was static or progressively worsening in 57% of cases, episodic in 13%, and fluctuating in 30%. In our

148

experience, once individuals develop the full OCD syndrome, the course may become more episodic. This appears to represent a difference of severity of symptoms, however, rather than an actual absence of symptoms. Given the paucity of epidemiological studies of childhood OCD (see chapter 3), we know little about the course of OCD in children. It has been suggested that approximately one half of adolescent OCD cases remit (Warren, 1960), an intriguing finding that merits further study.

Age at Onset

OCD generally begins in late adolescence or early adulthood (Rachman, 1985), with 65% of patients developing the disorder before age 25 (Rasmussen & Tsuang, 1986), and 80% before age 30 (Emmelkamp, 1982). There is some indication that there is a peak period of maximal incidence from ages 18 to 25 (Turner & Beidel, 1988). Other researchers have suggested that there are in fact two peak periods, from ages 12 to 14 and from ages 20 to 22 (Rasmussen & Tsuang, 1986). These data are based on a limited number of subjects and require replication, however. In a recent five-site epidemiological study of OCD (Karno, Golding, Sorenson, & Burnam, 1988), the mean age of onset ranged from 20.9 years to 25.4 years across the sites, with a mean age of onset overall of 22.7 years.

Cases of childhood OCD also have been reported (e.g., Francis, 1988; Rapoport, 1986; Rapoport et al., 1981). McCarthy and Foa (1988) estimated that 1% of child psychiatry inpatient cases are OCD. Cases of the disorder have been reported in children as young as 3 years old (Hollingsworth, Tanguay, Grossman, & Pabst, 1980; Judd, 1965). This suggests that although the full syndrome most often emerges in the adolescent to early adulthood period, it can also be present in childhood.

Incidence and Prevalence

The prevalence of OCD historically has been difficult to elucidate. DSM-III (American Psychiatric Association, 1980) reported that the disorder was rare in the general population. With the publication of DSM-III-R (American Psychiatric Association, 1987), the disorder was said to be relatively common in "mild forms" in the general population (see chapter 3). Apparently the shift was due, at least in part, to the results of the ECA study, a collaborative effort sponsored by NIMH to determine the prevalence of 15 specific disorders including OCD (Myers et al., 1984; Robins et al., 1984). The results of the ECA study indicated that the prevalence of OCD in the population was approximately 2% to 3% (Robins et al., 1984; Turns, 1985). Myers et al. (1984) reported a 6-month point prevalence of 1.6%. The most recent estimates come from a five-community study (Karno et al., 1988), which finds a lifetime prevalence of OCD in 1.9 to 3.3% of the population and a 6-month point prevalence of 0.7 to 2.2%. These figures were based on lay diagnoses, and concern has been expressed regarding the unexpectedly high prevalence (e.g., Flament et al., 1988). Nonetheless, in adult populations, OCD appears more prevalent than previously expected.

Regarding the prevalence of OCD among children, as noted earlier, McCarthy and Foa (1988) estimate that 1% of child psychiatry inpatients are diagnosed as having OCD. Judd (1965) reported five cases of childhood OCD based on a retrospective chart inspection of 405 patients, yielding a prevalence of 1.2%. Another retrospective chart examination of 8,000 inpatient and outpatient psychiatric referrals found only 17 cases of OCD, or a prevalence of 0.2% (Hollingsworth et al., 1980). Two studies have investigated the prevalence in unselected populations. Based on 2,000 unselected 10- and 11-year-olds, seven children were identified as having OCD features, a prevalence of 0.3% (Rutter, Tizard, & Whitmore, 1970). More recently, Flament and colleagues reported a current prevalence of 1% and a lifetime prevalence of 1.9% in an unselected population (Flament et al., 1988).

Sex Ratio

Among adults diagnosed with OCD, there appears to be a slight increase in the number of women as compared with men. In a review of 11 studies, Black (1974) reported a minor female preponderance (51.3%). Rasmussen and Tsuang (1986) also found a slight difference with more females diagnosed OCD than males (52.9%). In the ECA study, the prevalence for women was slightly higher (3% versus 2% for men). The results of the most recent epidemiological study (Karno et al., 1988) also report this difference with approximately 53% of OCD cases being female. Overall, the difference is slight, and prevalence appears fairly equal between males and females (Marks, 1987). Interestingly, when OCD patients are categorized primarily by the nature of their rituals (e.g., washers versus checkers), the differences in sex ratio may become more pronounced. For example, Rachman and Hodgson (1980) found a 6:1 female to male ratio among OCD "cleaners." Marks (1987) also found that 66% of "cleaners" were female, with some apparent increase in the percentage of males with what has been termed "obsessional slowness."

At the present time, it appears premature to speculate whether there are similar gender differences among children with OCD. Hollingsworth et al. (1980) reported that 75% of referred OCD children were male. This was based on 17 cases. Marks (1987) and Flament et al. (1985) also reported a preponderance of males among children referred for treatment of OCD. In an adolescent sample, however, prevalence among males and females is approximately equal and similar to that seen in an adult population (Flament et al., 1988).

CASE EXAMPLES

Doubt/Checking: Adult

Mr. E. is a 52-year-old married white male who presented with a 30-year history of intrusive thoughts concerning whether or not he had harmed another individual. These doubts were pervasive and occupied a significant portion of his day. For example, Mr. E. questioned whether or not he had been involved in his father's death owing to the fact that his father died following an argument between the two men. This doubt persisted for years and led Mr. E. to seek reassurance from numerous individuals including requesting his mother to write a letter stating that indeed he had not caused his father's death. He carried the letter in his pocket at all times and read it numerous times daily. Mr. E. also questioned whether he had harmed other individuals. One pervasive doubt centered around a small child playing on the corner by a stop sign. Mr. E. was concerned that a rock had been propelled by his truck, striking the child, as he resumed driving after the stop. The doubt became so consuming as to lead Mr. E. eventually to search the neighborhood repeatedly to find evidence that the child was still alive.

Doubt/Checking: Adolescent

Mark is a 17-year-old white male who presented with a 5-year history of intrusive thoughts regarding forgetting to complete important daily tasks. As such, his doubts were pervasive and included multiple situations. He spent most of his time ruminating about the potential disastrous consequences of his perceived oversights. For example, while driving to the outpatient clinic, Mark worried almost constantly that he might run out of gas even though the gas gauge indicated that the tank was full. He began to doubt that the gas gauge was working properly and interpreted any "unusual" noise as evidence that the gauge was broken. This worry would lead him to pay less attention to his driving, thus causing him to doubt whether he was following traffic rules correctly. Mark spent a considerable amount of time checking the car, at times stopping in the middle of a drive to examine various parts of the car. Other intrusive thoughts centered on social situations. Mark was extremely concerned that his social behavior was somehow misinterpreted by others. For example, after talking with a classmate about a homework assignment, Mark would fear that he had given the classmate incorrect information or that he had been rude. Mark frequently sought reassurance from his parents and siblings, and initially would call his therapist several times per day to confirm his next appointment or to clarify his in vivo therapeutic tasks.

Contamination/Washing: Adult

Ms. B. is a 33-year-old single female whose cleaning rituals resulted in significant personal and occupational interference. Ms. B. lived with her parents and brother. Her behavior caused family conflict and resulted in Ms. B. losing her job as she was frequently late to or absent from work. When she presented for treatment, she had been engaging in excessive cleaning since high school, with a steady increase in the time spent in daily cleaning. Before leaving home for any reason, she engaged in a 3-hour cleaning ritual that consisted of a 2-hour shower in which she used between one and four bars of soap, and washed her hair approximately 15 times per shower. She brushed her teeth five times per day with five applications of toothpaste. In addition, she rinsed her mouth with mouthwash for 10 to 15 minutes, using 10 to 20 large bottles of mouthwash per week. To complete the rinsing process, she straddled the bathtub to drink from the tub faucet. Ms. B. also washed her hands 20 to 40 times per day and used tissues to open doors and touch objects after her hands were washed. She used excessive detergent (one box per week) and insisted that her clothing be washed separately from that of other family members. Both the washer and dryer were scrubbed with disinfectant before clothing could be placed in them. If clothing touched any outside surface of the washer or dryer, it was washed again.

Contamination/Washing: Child

Justin is a 7-year-old white male who lives with his parents and two younger brothers. Historically, he was described as a somewhat difficult infant, toddler, and preschooler who did not tolerate major changes well. Around age 6, when Justin started elementary school, the parents noticed that he began to express frequent concerns about germs. Justin would come home from school in tears complaining that other kids were "germy" if they did things like cough without covering their mouths or sneeze without using a tissue. Justing began to wash his hands excessively and dab large quantitites of liquid soap onto his hands in a protective fashion before going to school. He refused to touch objects that had been used by "germy" kids. In school, he developed the habit of spitting into his shirt collar whenever anyone did anything that he considered "germy." In the wintertime, Justin often suffered from severely chapped skin because of his excessive use of water. When describing these behaviors, Justin referred to them as "habits." He recognized that other kids did not do such things, and was concerned that other kids would discover them and make fun of him. Although his parents initially hoped that Justin would grow out of these behaviors, they became quite concerned as the problems persisted.

Ordering: Adult

Mr. C is a 51-year-old married male who described himself as "picky" for as long as he could remember. He described a lifelong pattern of compulsive character-istics such as excessive attention to detail, stubbornness, and being a "workaholic." Mr. C. reported the onset of ritualistic behaviors shortly after starting his own business. These rituals tended to wax and wane, apparently as a function of stress. The rituals involved the ordering of his possessions. Mr. C. required that all of his clothing be organized in a particular fashion with articles hung in a complex arrangement by color and style. Clothing in drawers was required to be in a certain order. For example, socks were arranged by colors. Books also were required to be in a certain order on the shelf and to be equally spaced from the edge of the shelf. Mr. C. became angered by any possession being out of its intended order. His insistence on order resulted in significant interpersonal difficulties and also made it difficult for him to keep employees in his business.

Ordering: Adolescent

Roseanne is a 14-year-old female who presented with pervasive OCD symptoms with an onset at age 9. She lived with her intellectually limited mother, autistic 13-year-old sister, language-disordered 4-year-old brother, and various maternal realtives. Her father died when she was 11 years old. Most of Roseanne's compulsions involved elaborate rule making and ordering. In fact, there appeared to be no aspect of her life that was not governed by these compulsions, and she virtually was unable to engage in spontaneous behavior. Roseanne's day was organized according to a rigid hourly schedule. One of the more bizarre examples of the schedule was her daily 48-minute visits to five peers. If one of the peers was unable or, more commonly, unwilling to visit with her, she went back home immediately to wait, with an alarm clock, for the next scheduled visit time. Roseanne also exhibited a complicated eating ritual that included the consumption of only certain foods at certain times. Each meal began with a sip of beverage and was followed by a rigid cycle of three bites of meat, bread, vegetable, and dessert. Food was chewed for the amount of time required for her to sing a popular commercial jingle to herself. Although Roseanne's functioning in most domains was quite impaired because of the comprehensiveness of her compulsive behavior, she was very reluctant to acknowledge this fact and maintained initially that her way of behaving was something that would be good for other children to learn.

TREATMENT OF OCD

Behavior Therapy: Adults

In their review of the behavioral treatment literature on OCD, Foa, Steketee, and Ozarow (1985) concluded that exposure and response prevention are the treatment of choice for OCD patients, with greater than 70% of patients being significantly improved following treatment. Procedurally, exposure brings the patient into contact with the feared stimuli, and response prevention keeps the patient from engaging in ritualistic behavior. The goal of the procedure is to achieve both within- and between-session habituation, or extinction of the anxiety response (Foa et al., 1985).

Meyer (1966) combined exposure and response prevention in the treatment of OCD patients. With a series of 15 patients, Meyer and colleagues (Meyer & Levy, 1973; Meyer, Levy & Schnurer, 1974) reported 10 of 15 (66%) of patients were significantly improved, and 5 of 15 (33%) were moderately improved. In another uncontrolled investigation, Foa and Goldstein (1978) treated 23 OCD patients, with 80% being improved or much improved at a 15-month follow-up period. These promising results argued for the efficacy of exposure and response prevention in a population previously assumed refractory to treatment.

Several controlled studies have also been completed. Rachman and colleagues (Hodgson, Rachman, & Marks, 1972; Rachman, Hodgson, & Marks, 1971; Rachman, Marks, & Hodgson, 1973; Roper, Rachman, & Marks, 1975) compared relaxation to exposure and response prevention in the treatment of OCD. In sum, across these studies, of those patients treated with exposure and response prevention, 11 were much improved, 12 were improved, and 7 had no change. Patients treated with relaxation showed no improvement.

Collectively, this research began to show the efficacy of the behavioral intervention of exposure plus response prevention. A natural question that arose was whether there were differential effects of the two treatments. Foa, Steketee, and Milby (1980) randomly assigned patients to either exposure or response prevention, both being followed by the combined treatment. Results indicated that exposure was superior in reducing the level of anxiety, whereas response prevention was superior in controlling rituals. There were no group differences, however, when the combined treatment results were compared. A later study involved randomly assigning patients to one of three conditions: exposure only, response prevention only, or a combination of the two (Foa, Steketee, Grayson, Turner, & Latimer, 1984). Again, the same results emerged with the combined treatment being more effective than either treatment alone. In fact, a substantial number of subjects treated with the single-component treatments appeared to relapse. Accordingly, it would appear that both exposure to feared stimuli and prevention of ritualistic behaviors are essential in the treatment of OCD.

Several variations of the basic exposure and response prevention paradigm have been examined. The first variation concerns the choice of stimulus presentation. The fearful stimuli can be presented imaginally, in vivo, or using both modalities. In general, in vivo exposure appears superior (Rabavilas, Boulougouris, & Stefanis, 1976; Turner & Beidel, 1988). There are situations in which in vivo exposure is not possible, however, and an imaginal procedure represents an acceptable alternative (Foa, Steketee, Turner, & Fischer, 1980; Steketee, Foa, & Grayson, 1982). As an example, the case of Mr. E. described earlier used imaginal exposure owing to Mr. E.'s fears centering on the potentially disastrous consequences of his behavior (e.g., harming or killing others).

Other variations in the exposure and response prevention procedure include the frequency of sessions, length of sessions, and intensity of the stimuli. Emmelkamp (1987) reported that there was no clear difference between massed versus spaced sessions. Foa et al. (1985) suggest, however, that the length of the interval between sessions is important. They indicate that with shorter intersession intervals, habituation is more likely to occur. The second variation involves the length of the exposure session. Rabavilas, Boulougouris, Stefanis, and Vaidakis (1977) found that prolonged exposure was superior to briefer sessions, and Foa et al. (1985) concluded that total exposure time appears most critical. Finally, the intensity of the stimuli has been examined with results generally concurring that gradual exposure is just as effective as presentation of the maximal feared stimuli (Marks, Hodgson, & Rachman, 1975).

Impressive results have been obtained by using exposure and response prevention in the treatment of adult OCD. A critical issue is the extent to which improvements are maintained. That is, what is the long-term effectiveness of this approach? Based on a compilation of patients treated, Emmelkamp, Hoekstra, and Visser (1985) reported that of 42 patients evaluated 2 to 6 years after treatment with exposure and response prevention (mean = 3.6 years), 24 were much improved, 10 were improved, and 8 were treatment failures.

Approximately 20% to 25% of patients do not respond to this intervention. Foa and colleagues have attempted to identify characteristics associated with treatment outcome. An interesting factor appears to be the age of onset. The younger the individual at onset, the more likely treatment gains are to be maintained (Foa, Grayson, Steketee, & Doppelt, 1983). This finding has implications for children and adolescents with OCD, which require careful investigation. Another important factor is the presence of severe levels of depression, which has been found to impede the process of habituation and, as such, is a detriment to outcome (Foa, 1979; Foa, Steketee, & Groves, 1979). Foa (1979) also noted that patients do not respond well when they present with "overvalued ideation," or the belief that their concerns, fears, and behaviors are rational. This also has important implications for the treatment of children and adolescents given developmental differences in levels of cognitive sophistication and understanding of rational and irrational thought.

Pharmacological Treatment: Adults

Several pharmacological agents have been used in the treatment of adult OCD. A complete review of these studies is beyond the scope of this chapter. The reader is referred to recent reviews by Jenike, Baer, and Minichiello (1987) and Perse (1988) for more complete descriptions of various medication trials with OCD patients.

The current neurobiological hypothesis is that OCD is related in some way to abnormal regulation of brain serotonergic functioning (Charney et al., 1988; Yaryura-Tobias, 1977). Thus, there is interest in pharmacological agents that have potent serotonergic effects. The two medications that have received the most attention to date are clomipramine and fluoxetine.

Clomipramine is a tricyclic antidepressant that is a potent serotonergic reuptake blocker (Zohar, Insel, Zohar-Kadouch, Hill, & Murphy, 1988). Clomipramine was administered in an open trial to patients with various diagnoses, but all with prominent obsessive-compulsive features (Stroebel, Szarek, & Glueck, 1984). Fifteen patients carried a primary diagnosis of OCD. Of these, 80% were improved, with an overall reduction of 60% in obsessive-compulsive symptoms across all patients.

Clomipramine also has been compared with placebo and other antidepressants in the treatment of OCD. Clomipramine was found to be superior to placebo (Montgomery, 1980; Thoren, Asberg, Cronholm, Jornestedt, & Traskman, 1980). The Thoren et al. (1980) study was a 5-week double-blind comparison of clomipramine, nortriptyline, and placebo. Mean reduction on scaled scores of OCD was 42% for clomipramine, 21% for nortriptyline, and 7% for placebo. Clomipramine did not yield changes on a standard OCD inventory, however. The differences between clomipramine and nortriptyline are suggestive that clomipramine resulted in superior outcome; however, they failed to reach conventional levels of statistical significance.

In a 12-week double-blind trial, clomipramine was compared with imipramine (Volavka, Neziroglu, & Yaryura-Tobias, 1985). Clomipramine appeared slightly better in decreasing OCD symptoms; however, the difference was not significant. Similar results were reported by Mavissakalian, Turner, Michelson, and Jacob (1985) in another comparison of clomipramine and imipramine.

Clomipramine also has been compared with amitriptyline in the treatment of OCD in a 4-week double-blind trial (Ananth, Pecknold, Van Den Steen, & Engelsmann, 1981). Clomipramine, but not amitriptyline, produced significant decreases in obsessive symptoms, depression, and anxiety. Clomipramine and desipramine have also been compared (Insel, Mueller, Alterman, Linnoila, & Murphy, 1985; Zohar & Insel, 1987). Results indicated that clomipramine was superior to desipramine on ratings of OC symptoms. Zohar and Insel (1987) reported, however, that although changes in OC symptoms were statistically significant, they accounted for only 28% improvement. In another investigation, clomipramine was compared with desipramine and to zimelidine (another potent serotonergic agonist) (Insel, Mueller, Gillin, Siever, & Murphy, 1985). Again, clomipramine was superior to desipramine, and there were no differences between the desipramine and the zimelidine groups.

Another serotonergic agent receiving attention in the treatment of adult OCD is fluoxetine. Fontaine and Chouinard (1986) conducted a 9-week open clinical trial with seven OCD patients. Significant improvements were reported on a scale measuring OCD symptoms and on a psychiatric global rating scale. In another investigation, a 12-week single-blind trial of fluoxetine resulted in significant improvement of depression and OCD symptoms (Turner, Jacob, Beidel, & Himmelhoch, 1985).

Two recent investigations have examined fluvoxamine, a unicyclic antidepressant that inhibits serotonin reuptake (Perse, Greist, Jefferson, Rosenfeld, & Dar, 1987; Price, Goodman, Charney, Rasmussen, & Heninger, 1987). In the Price et al. (1987) study, 10 OCD patients were treated in a single-blind treatment with fluvoxamine. Six of the 10 were judged to be improved on a global rating, but changes on an inventory designed to measure OCD symptoms showed less improvement. In a double-blind crossover trial, fluvoxamine was compared with placebo (Price et al., 1987). Results indicated that approximately 80% of subjects receiving fluvoxamine improved on measures of OCD symptoms, depression, and anxiety.

Collectively, these results suggest that certain medications have some impact on the condition of patients with OCD. Yet, approximately 70% of patients relapse on termination of clomipramine (Ananth, 1986), suggesting that OCD symptoms are not eliminated when medication is the sole treatment. An intriguing finding is that certain serotonergic agonists are useful with adult OCD patients, whereas zimelidine is not. A simplistic view of the mechanisms of action of these medications is that they increase the functional level of serotonin. If this were the case, zimelidine should produce similar outcomes as the other serotonergic agonists. Recently, some researchers have speculated that the mechanisms of action also involve noradrenergic functioning and also rely on the specificity of binding (Insel, Mueller, Alterman, et al., 1985; Turner & Beidel, 1988).

Medication appears to offer a useful treatment option for adults with OCD. The utility has yet to equal that seen with exposure and response prevention, however (Perse, 1988). To date, studies have not been conducted to compare the two modes of intervention directly. In a sequential design, Turner, Beidel, Stanley, and Jacob (1988) examined fluoxetine, and exposure and response prevention. Exposure and response prevention followed a 12 week fluoxetine trial. Fluoxetine appeared most effective in patients with higher levels of depression and anxiety, whereas the behavioral intervention was more "universally effective." Other researchers have challenged this view and claimed that clomipramine, for example, has specific antiobsessional properties (Insel, Murphy, Cohen, Alterman, Kilts, & Linnoila, 1983). A randomized comparison of the two modes of intervention clearly is needed. Another option with OCD patients is to combine pharmacological and behavioral treatments. This would appear relevant in cases in which levels of depression would impede the habituation process.

Behavior Therapy: Children and Adolescents

There have been few accounts of the behavioral treatment of childhood OCD in the literature. There currently are no controlled studies of psychosocial treatment for OCD in children. Available case studies and single case design reports suggest that strategies developed for adults, namely exposure and response prevention, have been successfully used with children (e.g., Bolton, Collins, & Steinberg, 1983; Mills, Agras, Barlow, & Mills, 1973; Stanley, 1980). For example, Mills et al. (1973) evaluated, via an ABAB design, the use of response prevention to treat a 15-year-old hospitalized boy who evidenced elaborate bedtime and morning rituals. Following a 12-day baseline monitoring phase, response prevention was applied to the bedtime rituals. The adolescent was told that he would no longer be allowed to engage in the bedtime rituals. During the response-prevention phase, a staff member remained in the bedroom with the adolescent during the night. Within 10 days, bedtime rituals stopped. In addition, the authors noted a concomitant decrease in morning rituals, even though these rituals had not been a target of treatment. During the return to baseline phase, although the staff member no longer remained in the room with the adolescent during the night, he did not exhibit any bedtime or morning rituals. According to the authors, treatment gains were maintained for approximately 8 weeks following discharge. The adolescent then began to engage in a new series of bathing rituals, however. Further outpatient treatment, which consisted of response prevention implemented by the parents, reportedly was successful in reducing the bathing rituals.

Stanley (1980) presented a case study of an 8-year-old, obsessive-compulsive girl treated using response prevention. The child exhibited a variety of problematic bedtime rituals including performing tasks 3 times each (e.g., dressing and undressing, fluffing her pillow, singing) and repeatedly checking on the location of her toys. The parents implemented a response prevention procedure that led to elimination of the rituals within 2 weeks and maintenance of these gains at 1-year follow-up.

McCarthy and Foa (1988) presented a case study of a 13-year-old male using imaginal exposure, in vivo exposure, and response prevention. The boy presented with obsessive worries about causing injury to his family, failing in school, and being teased by peers. To "neutralize" these fears, he engaged in several compulsive behaviors such as excessive rehearsal of school work, repeated head and arm movements, and repetition of behaviors that occurred simultaneously with the obsessive thoughts (e.g., brushing his teeth). He had previously been treated unsuccessfully with supportive therapy and clomipramine. Treatment consisted of 15 outpatient sessions over a 3-week period followed by 1 week of intensive, home-based treatment. A reward system also was used to increase treatment compliance. The authors presented data indicating elimination of obsessions and compulsions that was maintained at 1-year follow-up.

Extinction procedures also have been used in the treatment of childhood OCD. Hallam (1974) described the use of extinction to treat a 15-year-old hospitalized female with a 3-year history of compulsive reassurance-seeking behaviors (i.e., repetitive questions about whether people were saying nasty things about her). The initial phase of treatment consisted of instructing staff to respond to her questions by saying "I can't answer that." This strategy reportedly made no impact on the frequency of her compulsive reassurance seeking. As such, an extinction procedure was started in which staff was instructed to ignore her questions by turning or looking away, and redirecting conversation. At first, the adolescent was described as highly agitated and anxious; however, within 4 weeks, the reassurance seeking behavior had been eliminated. Halfway through the extinction phase, a response cost procedure was added in which the adolescent lost 1 minute of recreation time for each reassurance-seeking question asked. Although this study presented a promising approach to the treatment of compulsive reassurance seeking in an adolescent, the case study design and lack of pretreatment baseline data make it difficult to evaluate the results empirically.

In an attempt to expand on Hallam's (1974) work, Francis (1988) conducted a within-series single case study of the use of extinction to treat an 11-year-old boy with OCD. The child was seen on an outpatient basis, and treatment was implemented by the parents. The child presented with persistent obsessive worries about death and dying as well as frequent compulsive reassurance-seeking behavior. He often voiced fears of dying from various diseases and persistently asked, "Am I going blind?"; "Do you think I will throw up?"; and "Am I going to die?" The parents were instructed to monitor his reassurance-seeking questions 4 times per day. During the 8-day baseline phase, the parents were instructed to respond in their usual way to the child, which consisted of them attempting to reassure him. The 8-day extinction phase consisted of the parents ignoring all reassurance-seeking questions by looking or turning away, and redirecting the conversation. The therapist maintained frequent telephone contact with the family during this phase. The return to baseline phase lasted for 5 days and consisted of a resumption of parents' attention to the reassurance-seeking behavior. The onset of this phase occurred spontaneously when the parents began attending to the reassurance-seeking behavior at a time when several family members were ill. Of note, the family illness persisted for another 5 days following the predetermined end of this phase. The return to extinction phase lasted for 20 days and consisted of the reimplementation of the extinction procedure. A 1-month follow-up assessment was conducted in which the parents monitored the child's behavior for 3 days.

Results indicated that the extinction procedure was successful in decreasing the frequency of reassurance-seeking behavior to zero within 6 days. During the withdrawal of extinction, the child's behavior worsened dramatically, at which time reassurance seeking was occurring at a rate higher than that seen during baseline. Once extinction was reimplemented, the frequency of reassurance-seeking behavior fell to zero within 12 days, and remained at zero for 9 consecutive days and at the 1-month follow-up.

It is important to emphasize that the few available behavioral treatment studies of childhood OCD have shown short-term treatment successes. Given the chronic and disabling nature of OCD, future researchers need to evaluate the long-term efficacy of such treatment strategies.

When treating children and adolescents, primary caregivers need to be involved in therapy. Moreover, the child's school may also need to be involved to generalize treatment gains. Teachers may need to be instructed to extinguish compulsive reassurance seeking or require nonritualistic completion of school tasks. Children also may need more encouragement to complete treatment tasks than adults and thus can benefit from reward systems to increase compliance. Finally, it is important to keep self-monitoring simple enough that the child is able to complete it accurately. In the case of young children, the parent likely will serve as the sole data collector.

Pharmacological Treatment: Children and Adolescents

Few data currently are available attesting to the effectiveness of pharmacological agents in the treatment of OCD in children and adolescents. Clomipramine is the only pharmacological treatment that has been evaluated systematically for OCD youngsters (Flament et al., 1985; Rapoport, Elkins, & Mikkelson, 1980). Flament et al. (1985) conducted a double-blind, crossover design study comparing clomipramine hydrochloride and placebo. Subjects consisted of 19 OCD youngsters between the ages of 10 and 18 years (mean age = 14.5 years) who had experienced significant OCD symptoms for at least 1 year. The average duration of illness was 4 years. Children with psychosis, mental retardation, or primary affective disorder were excluded from the study. All youngsters but one had a past history of psychiatric treatment for OCD, and one half of the sample had not responded to previous treatment with tricyclic antidepressants. The children participated in a 1-week baseline monitoring phase followed by 10 weeks of clomipramine or placebo, each of which was administered for 5 weeks. The mean dose of clomipramine was 141 mg per day. Children and their parents also received supportive psychotherapy. No formal behavior therapy was conducted. Clomipramine yielded a decrease in obsessional behavior that was independent of baseline depression levels. Clomipramine did not produce full recovery of obsessive symptoms, however. At the end of treatment, 26% of youngsters were described as unchanged or only slightly improved, 64% of youngsters were described as moderately or much improved, and 10% were described as symptom free. There was no change in global measures of depression or anxiety. Unfortunately, the authors provided no information about the kind of compulsive behaviors exhibited by the youngsters so it is impossible to assess the effect of clomipramine on compulsions.

CONCLUSION

OCD in adults clearly is better understood than OCD in children and adolescents. There appears to be remarkable similarity in OCD symptom presentation across the lifespan. The disorder typically emerges in late adolescence or early adulthood; however, there are reported cases of OCD in young children. Although the disorder in adults invariably is chronic and unremitting, there is suggestion that the disorder in adolescents may remit. Slightly more adult females present with OCD than do adult males. By contrast, there is not sufficient data in the child and adolescent literature to make definitive statements regarding sex ratio. In both adult and child populations, it is difficult to determine prevalence rates of OCD. The adult treatment literature consists of controlled investigations of behavioral and pharmacological therapies. Exposure and response prevention clearly have been shown to be effective treatments for OCD in adults. Medications such as clomipramine and fluoxetine also have been shown to be effective, although their utility is not equal to that seen with behavioral interventions. By contrast, the child treatment literature consists primarily of case reports, and there are no controlled group investigations of behavioral treatments. The use of strategies such as exposure, response prevention, and extinction has yielded promising short-term treatment efficacy. Similarly, there is suggestive evidence that clomipramine may be helpful in decreasing obsessive symptomatology in OCD youngsters. In the adult literature there is a need for relatively sophisticated comparative controlled group studies of behavioral versus pharmacological interventions. Given the paucity of information currently available about OCD in children, future directions for research include controlled group assessment and treatment studies.

REFERENCES

American Psychiatric Association. (1980). *Diagnostic and statistical manual of mental disorders* (3rd ed.). Washington, DC: Author.

American Psychiatric Association. (1987). *Diagnostic and statistical manual of mental disorders* (3rd ed., rev.). Washington, DC: Author.

Ananth, J. (1986). Clomipramine: An antiobsessive drug. *Canadian Journal of Psychiatry, 31,* 253–258.

Ananth, J., Pecknold, J., Van Den Steen, N., & Engelsmann, F. (1981). Double-blind comparative study of clomipramine and amitriptyline in obsessive neurosis. *Progress in Neuro-Psychopharmacology and Biological Psychiatry, 5,* 257–262.

Black, A. (1974). The natural history of obsessive neurosis. In P. H. Hoch & J. Zubin (Eds.), *Obsessional states* (pp. 19–54). London: Metheun.

Bolton, D., Collins, S., & Steinberg, D. (1983). The treatment of obsessive-compulsive disorder in adolescence: A report of 15 cases. *British Journal of Psychiatry, 142,* 456–464.

Charney, D. S., Goodman, W. K., Price, L. H., Woods, S. W., Rasmussen, S. A., & Heninger, G. R. (1988). Serotonin function in obsessive-compulsive disorder: A comparison of the effects of tryptophan and m-chlorophenylpiperazine in patients and healthy subjects. *Archives of General Psychiatry, 45,* 177–185.

Emmelkamp, P. M. G. (1982). *Phobic and obsessive-compulsive disorders: Theory, research, and practice.* New York: Plenum.

Emmelkamp, P. M. G. (1987). Obsessive-compulsive disorders. In L. Michelson & L. M. Ascher (Eds.), *Anxiety and stress disorders: Cognitive-behavioral assessment and treatment* (pp. 310–331). New York: Guilford.

Emmelkamp, P. M. G., Hoekstra, R. J., & Visser, S. (1985). The behavioural treatment of obsessive-compulsive disorder: Prediction of outcome at 3.5 years follow-up. In A. Brenner (Ed.), *Psychiatry: The state of the art* (Vol. 4). New York: Plenum.

Flament, M. F., Rapoport, J. L., Berg, C. J., Sceery, W., Kilts, C., Mellstrom, B., & Linnoila, M. (1985). Clomipramine treatment of childhood obsessive-compulsive disorder. *Archives of General Psychiatry, 42,* 977–983.

Flament, M. F., Whitaker, A., Rapoport, J. L., Davies, M., Berg, C. Z., Kalikow, K., Sceery, W., & Shaffer, D. (1988). Obsessive-compulsive disorder in adolescence: An epidemiological study. *Journal of the American Academy of Child and Adolescent Psychiatry, 27,* 764–771.

Foa, E. B. (1979). Failures in treating obsessive-compulsives. *Behavior Research and Therapy, 17,* 169–176.

Foa, E. B., & Goldstein, A. (1978). Continuous exposure and complete response prevention in the treatment of obsessive-compulsive neurosis. *Behavior Therapy, 9,* 821–829.

Foa, E. B., Grayson, J. B., Steketee, G. S., & Doppelt, H. G. (1983). Treatment of obsessive-compulsives: When do we fail? In E. B. Foa & P. M. G. Emmelkamp (Eds.), *Failures in behavior therapy.* New York: Wiley.

Foa, E. B., Steketee, G., Grayson, J. B., Turner, R. M., & Latimer, P. R. (1984). Deliberate exposure and blocking of obsessive-compulsive rituals: Immediate and long-term effects. *Behavior Therapy, 15,* 450–472.

Foa, E., Steketee, G. S., & Groves, G. A. (1979). Use of behavioral therapy and imipramine: A case of obsessive-compulsive neurosis with severe depression. *Behavior Modification, 3,* 419–430.

Foa, E. B., Steketee, G., & Milby, J. B. (1980). Differential effects of exposure and response prevention in obsessive-compulsive washers. *Journal of Consulting and Clinical Psychology, 48,* 71–78.

Foa, E. B., Steketee, G. S., & Ozarow, B. J. (1985). Behavior therapy with obsessive-compulsives: From theory to treatment. In M. Mavissakalian, S. M. Turner, & L. Michelson (Eds.), *Obsessive-compulsive disorder: Psychological and pharmacological treatment.* New York: Plenum.

Foa, E. B., Steketee, G. G., Turner, R. M., & Fischer, S. C. (1980). Effects of imaginal exposure to feared disasters in obsessive-compulsive checkers. *Behavior Research and Therapy, 18,* 449–455.

Fontaine, R., & Chouinard, G. (1986). An open clinical trial of fluoxetine in the treatment of obsessive-compulsive disorder. *Journal of Clinical Psychopharmacology, 6,* 98–101.

Francis, G. (1988). Childhood obsessive-compulsive disorder: Extinction of compulsive reassurance seeking. *Journal of Anxiety Disorders, 2,* 361–366.

Hallam, R. S. (1974). Extinction of ruminations: A case study. *Behavior Therapy, 5,* 565–568.

Hodgson, R. J., Rachman, S., & Marks, I. M. (1972). The treatment of chronic obsessive-compulsive neurosis: Follow-up and further findings. *Behaviour Research and Therapy, 10,* 181–189.

Hollingsworth, C. E., Tanguay, P. E., Grossman, L., & Pabst, P. (1980). Long-term outcome of obsessive-compulsive disorder in childhood. *Journal of the Academy of Child and Adolescent Psychiatry, 19,* 134–144.

Insel, T. R., Mueller, E. A., Alterman, I., Linnoila, M., & Murphy, D. L. (1985). Obsessive-compulsive disorder and serotonin: Is there a connection? *Biological Psychiatry, 20,* 1174–1188.

Insel, T. R., Mueller, E. A., Gillin, C., Siever, L. J., & Murphy, D. L. (1985). Tricyclic response in obsessive-compulsive disorder. *Progress in Neuro-Psychopharmacology and Biological Psychiatry, 9,* 25–31.

Insel, T. R., Murphy, D. L., Cohen, R. M., Alterman, I., Kilts, C., & Linnoila, M. (1983). Obsessive-compulsive disorders. *Archives of General Psychiatry, 40,* 605–612.

Jenike, M. A., Baer, L., & Minichiello, W. E. (1987). Somatic treatments for obsessive-compulsive disorders. *Comprehensive Psychiatry, 28,* 250–263.

Judd, L. L. (1965). Obsessive compulsive neurosis in children. *Archives of General Psychiatry, 25,* 298–304.

Karno, M., Golding, J., Sorenson, S., & Burnam, A. (1988). The epidemiology of obsessive-compulsive disorder in five US communities. *Archives of General Psychiatry, 45,* 1094–1099.

Marks, I. M. (1987). *Fears, phobias and rituals.* New York: Oxford University Press.

Marks, I. M., Hodgson, R., & Rachman, S. (1975). Treatment of chronic obsessive-compulsive neurosis by in vivo exposure. *British Journal of Psychiatry, 136,* 1–25.

Mavissakalian, M., Turner, S. M., Michelson, L., & Jacob, R. G. (1985). Tricyclic antidepressants in obsessive-compulsive disorder: 2. Antiobsessional or anti-depressant agents? *American Journal of Psychiatry, 142,* 572–576.

McCarthy, P. R., & Foa, E. D. (1988). Obsessive-compulsive disorder. In M. Hersen & C. G. Last (Eds.), *Child behavior therapy casebook.* New York: Plenum.

Meyer, V. (1966). Modification of expectations in cases with obsessive rituals. *Behaviour Research and Therapy, 4,* 273–280.

Meyer, V., & Levy, R. (1973). Modification of behavior in obsessive-compulsive disorders. In H. E. Adams & P. Unikel (Eds.), *Issues and trends in behavior therapy.* Springfield, IL: Charles C Thomas.

Meyer, V., Levy, R., & Schnurer, A. (1974). A behavioral treatment of obsessive-compulsive disorders. In H. R. Beech (Ed.), *Obsessional states.* London: Metheun.

Mills, H. L., Agras, W. S., Barlow, D. H., & Mills, J. R. (1973). Compulsive rituals treated by response prevention: An experimental analysis. *Archives of General Psychiatry, 38,* 524–529.

Montgomery, S. A. (1980). Clomipramine in obsessional neurosis: A placebo con-trolled trial. *Pharmacology and Medicine, 1,* 189–192.

Myers, J. K., Weissman, M. M., Tischler, G. L., Holzer, C. E., Leaf, P. J., Orvaschel, H., Anthony, J. C., Boyd, J. H., Burke, J. D., Kramer, M., & Stoltzman, R. (1984). Six-month prevalence of psychiatric disorders in three communities. *Archives of General Psychiatry, 41,* 959–967.

Perse, T. (1988). Obsessive-compulsive disorder: A treatment review. *Journal of Clinical Psychiatry, 49,* 48–55.

Perse, T. L., Greist, J. H., Jefferson, J. W., Rosenfeld, R., & Dar, R. (1987). Fluvoxamine treatment of obsessive-compulsive disorder. *American Journal of Psychiatry, 144,* 1543–1548.

Price, L. H., Goodman, W. K., Charney, D. S., Rasmussen S. A., & Heninger, G. R. (1987). Treatment of severe obsessive-compulsive disorder with fluvoxamine. *American Journal of Psychiatry, 144,* 1059–1061.

Rabavilas, A. D., Boulougouris, J. C., & Stefanis, C. (1976). Duration of flooding sessions in the treatment of obsessive-compulsive patients. *Behaviour Research and Therapy, 14,* 349–355.

Rabavilas, A. D., Boulougouris, J. C., Stefanis, C., & Vaidakis, N. (1977). Psy-chophysiological accompaniments of threat anticipation in obsessive-compulsive patients. In C. D. Spielberger & I. G. Sarason (Eds.), *Stress and anxiety* (Vol. 4). New York: Wiley.

Rachman, S. J. (1985). An overview of clinical and research issues in obsessive-compulsive disorders. In M. Mavissakalian, S. M. Turner, & L. Michelson (Eds.), *Obsessive-compulsive disorders: Psychological and pharamacological treatment* (pp. 1–47). New York: Plenum.

Rachman, S. J., & Hodgson, R. J. (1980). *Obsessions and compulsion.* Englewood Cliffs, NJ: Prentic Hall.

Rachman, S., Hodgson, R., & Marks, I. M. (1971). The treatment of chronic obsessive-compulsive neurosis. *Behaviour Research and Therapy, 9,* 237–247.

Rachman, S., Marks, I. M., & Hodgson, R. (1973). The treatment of obsessive-compulsive neurotics by modelling and flooding in vivo. *Behaviour Research and Therapy, 11,* 463–471.

Rapoport, J. L. (1986). Childhood obsessive-compulsive disorder. *Journal of Child Psychology and Psychiatry, 27,* 289–295.

Rapoport, J., Elkins, R., Langer, D. H., Sceery, W., Buchsbaum, M. S., Gillin, J. C., Murphy, D. L., Zahn, T. P., Lake, R., Ludlow, C., & Mendelson, W. (1981). Childhood obsessive-compulsive disorder. *American Journal of Psychiatry, 138,* 1545–1554.

Rapoport, J., Elkins, R., & Mikkelson, E. (1980). Clinical controlled trial of chlorimipramine in adolescents with obsessive-compulsive disorder. *Psychopharmacological Bulletin, 16,* 61–63.

Rasmussen, S. A., & Tsuang, M. T. (1986). Epidemiology and clinical features of obsessive-compulsive disorder. In M. A. Jenike, L. Baer, & W. E. Minichiello (Eds.), *Obsessive-compulsive disorders: Theory and management* (pp. 23–44). Littleton, MA: PSG.

Robins, L. N., Helzer, J. E., Weissman, M. M., Orvaschel, H., Gruenberg, E., Burke, J. D., & Regier, D. A. (1984). Lifetime prevalence of specific psychiatric disorders in three sites. *Archives of General Psychiatry, 41,* 949–958.

Roper, G., Rachman, S., & Marks, I. M. (1975). Passive and participant modeling in exposure treatment of obsessive-compulsive neurotics. *Behavior Research and Therapy, 13,* 271–279.

Rutter, M., Tizard, J., & Whitmore, K. (1970). *Education, health, and behavior.* London: Longmans.

Stanley, L. (1980). Treatment of ritualistic behavior in an eight-year-old girl by response prevention: A case report. *Journal of Child Psychology and Psychiatry, 21,* 85–90.

Steketee, G. S., Foa, E. B., & Grayson, J. B. (1982). Recent advances in the treatment of obsessive-compulsives. *Archives of General Psychiatry, 39,* 1365–1371.

Stroebel, C. F., Szarek, B. L., & Glueck, B. S. (1984). Use of clomipramine in treatment of obsessive-compulsive symptomatology. *Journal of Clinical Psychopharmacology, 4,* 98–100.

Thoren, P., Asberg, M., Cronholm, B., Jornestedt, L., & Traskman, L. (1980). Clinical treatment of obsessive-compulsive disorder: 1. A controlled clinical trial. *Archives of General Psychiatry, 37,* 1281–1285.

Turner, S. M., & Beidel, D. C. (1988). *Treating obsessive-compulsive disorders.* New York: Pergamon.

Turner, S. M., Beidel, D. C., Stanley, M. A., & Jacob, R. B. (1988). A comparison of fluoxetine, flooding, and response prevention in the treatment of obsessive-compulsive disorder. *Journal of Anxiety Disorders, 2,* 219–225.

Turner, S. M., Jacob, R. G., Beidel, D. C., & Himmelhoch, J. (1985). Fluoxetine treatment of obsessive-compulsive disorders. *Journal of Clinical Psychopharmacology, 5,* 207–212.

Turns, D. M., (1985). Epidemiology of phobic and obsessive-compulsive disorders among adults. *American Journal of Psychotherapy, 39,* 360–370.

Volavka, J., Neziroglu, F., & Yaryura-Tobias, J. A. (1985). Clomipramine and imipramine in obsessive-compulsive disorder. *Psychiatry Research, 14,* 83–91.

Warren, W. (1960). Some relationships between psychiatry and children and adults. *Journal of Mental Science, 106,* 815–826.

Yaryura-Tobias, J. A. (1977). Obsessive-compulsive disorders: A serotonergic hypothesis. *Journal of Orthomolecular Psychiatry, 6,* 317–326.

Zohar, J., & Insel, T. R. (1987). Obsessive-compulsive disorder: Psychobiological approaches to diagnosis, treatment, and psychophysiology. *Biological Psychiatry, 22,* 667–687.

Zohar, J., Insel, T. R., Zohar-Kadouch, R. C., Hill, J. L., & Murphy, D. L. (1988). Serotonergic responsivity in obsessive-compulsive disorder. *Archives of General Psychiatry, 45,* 167–172.

CHAPTER 10

Developmental Issues in Measurement of Anxiety

Deborah C. Beidel and Melinda A. Stanley

A central characteristic of living organisms is their capacity for maturation and change. Although the most common conceptualization of development is one of improvement, growth also encompasses aging and the consequent decline in abilities. As reflected by the chapters in this book, maturation is more than just a physical process. It includes changing cognitive skills, behavioral abilities, and emotional expressions.

The biology of growth and decline highlights one of the most debated issues in developmental psychology and presents special challenges for those who wish to study psychopathology. The conceptual debate centers on whether development consists of one continuous process or is more properly characterized by discrete, and perhaps unrelated, stages (Overton & Reese, 1981). For example, based on research from the Fels Institute, variation in infant behaviors was not predictive of behavior patterns at ages 6 to 10 (Kagan, 1980), and for some investigators, this has implied little stability in behavioral expression (Klein & Lasky, 1978). Others have considered continuity as the rate of change in the developmental function of a particular variable rather than persistence of a particular behavior (McCall, 1977). Similarly, for Kagan (1980), continuity is the persistence of a psychological construct or attribute. A related concept is stability, or normative stability, most often defined as the degree to which individuals retain their ranks on a particular dimension relative to others in the normative group (McCall, 1977). For these investigators, it is not a specific behavior but a lasting tendency to behave in a certain manner that defines continuity.

Psychological constructs such as anxiety or an anxious temperament have been considered continuous and stable characteristics. Thus, those who possess "anxious traits" should retain this quality throughout their lifetime, and in any particular group, the individual's place within the normal distribution should remain stable despite maturation and aging.

The challenge faced by psychologists, however, is to demonstrate this continuity despite the discontinuity brought about by changing specific environmental or situational demands, or physical, cognitive, and behavioral capabilities (Lerner, Hertzog, Hooker, Hassibi, & Thomas, 1988). For those who conduct psychological assessments, recognition that an emotional state may be expressed in a dramatically different fashion at different ages is important for constructing and conducting valid assessments and in interpreting the results. In fact, the construct may be obscured if inappropriate assessment methods are used. The purpose of this chapter is to discuss the assessment of anxiety in light of general development. The chapter is divided into several parts. First, the influence of maturation on "normal" developmental fears is examined. Second, the contribution of physical, cognitive, and behavioral maturation both to the expression of anxiety and implementation of specific assessment procedures is addressed. This review is focused largely on the childhood and adolescent populations. After the available literature in each area is reviewed, practical considerations for improving the assessment of anxiety are discussed.

CONTINUITY AND DISCONTINUITY IN ANXIETY AND FEAR

There is evidence to demonstrate that individuals differ in the degree to which they possess "anxious qualities" and that these differences persist across an extended period. Research on the consistency of these behaviors has led to the use of terms such as an anxious temperament (Thomas & Chess, 1981), behavioral inhibition (Kagan, 1982), and anxiety proneness (Spielberger, Pollans, & Worden, 1984). The supporting data are derived from studies using self-report inventories, behavioral observations, and psychophysiological assessment methods. For example, based on parental observations, data from the New York Longitudinal Study revealed that an anxiety affect factor (derived from a temperament survey) showed stability across the initial 12-year developmental period (age 1–12 years; $r = .97$). Kagan and his colleagues have conducted longitudinal studies assessing the stability of "behavioral inhibition," a temperamental variable characterized by physical withdrawal when in the company of an unfamiliar woman, unfamiliar toys, and temporary separation from the mother. The signs used to identify behavioral inhibition included extended speech latencies before interaction with the unfamiliar woman, immediate retreat from the woman, close proximity to mother, and cessation of play and speech. These behaviors are clearly reminiscent of an anxious temperament (Kagan, 1982). Uninhibited children show the opposite pattern. A complete review of these studies is not within the scope of this chapter, and the reader is referred to the studies by Kagan and his colleagues (Garcia-Coll, Kagan, & Reznick, 1984; Kagan, 1982; Kagan, Reznick, Clarke, Snidman, & Garcia-Coll, 1984; Kagan et al., 1987; Reznick et al., 1986).

To summarize the findings of the Kagan group, behaviorally inhibited and uninhibited children have been followed during a 5-year period, and there appears to be remarkable stability both for the initial classification of these children at 21 months, and their behavioral and psychophysiological responses in laboratory and school settings 5 years later. The authors have reported a high degree of consistency for group differences in heart rate, heart rate variability, behavioral inhibition with strange adults and peers, and limited social interactions in school. Follow-up assessments have replicated the initial findings that inhibited children have higher heart rates, less heart rate variability, and fewer socially engaging behaviors than the noninhibited children. Similar consistency has been reported for the other variables, suggesting continuity for this psychological construct.

Consistency of reactivity to stressful events also has been demonstrated in studies of rhesus monkeys (Suomi, 1986). Behavioral and physiological individual differences can be detected at infancy, and remain stable through the periods of adolescence and young adulthood. As noted by Suomi (1986), the *type* of behavioral reaction may change with increasing development but not the tendency for the distress to occur. For example, infant rhesus monkeys react to separation with panic, protests, and a high frequency of "coo" vocalizations, whereas adolescent rhesus monkeys respond with agitated, stereotypic activity and silence (Mineka, Suomi, & Delizio, 1981). Continuity in the probability of the occurrence, but discontinuity in its expression highlights the importance of attention to maturational processes when assessing anxiety across the lifespan.

The influence of maturation also is evident when the "normal developmental sequence" of human fear responses is examined. These are fears that appear almost universally in children, are considered to be part of normal development and not the result of traumatic conditioning, and disappear without intervention. The sequential appearance of these fears is not arbitrary but keyed to the child's development, and, particularly, cognitive development. Generally, the developmental sequence of normal childhood fears encompasses four categories: primitive reactivity, separation anxiety, stranger fear, and specific object or event fear (Campbell, 1986; Werry & Amen, 1980). Infants are frightened by loss of support; sudden, intense, and unexpected noises, and heights. One- and 2-year-old children fear strangers, separation, and injury. Preschool children fear imaginary creatures, animals, and the dark. Elementary school children fear school, supernatural events, and physical danger (Barrios, Hartmann, & Shigetomi,

1981). Social fears, bodily injury, school performance, economic and poli-
tical catastrophes are common fears of older children and adolescents.

Using a developmental perspective, the onset of these fears can be
traced to the achievement of corresponding sensorimotor and cognitive
milestones. The reader is referred to Campbell (1986) for a comprehensive
discussion, but one example is provided as an illustration. Five-month-old
infants, when left alone with a stranger, appear calm and show heart rate
responses indicating attention to and interest in the unfamiliar person.
Nine-month-old infants placed in the same situation, however, respond
with fearful facial expressions, gaze aversion, and heart rate increases,
which in combination suggest the experience of fear (Campos, Emde,
Gaensbauer, & Henderson, 1975). Important maturational changes that
occur within these 4 months include the development of object permanence (Donaldson, 1978) and basic memory capacities necessary to
allow the infant to distinguish the familiar from the unfamiliar (Campbell,
1986). It is likely that these maturational changes provide a necessary
foundation for the onset of stranger fear and separation anxiety. This
discussion illustrates several important points. First, the onset of certain
fears is dependent on the maturational stage of the organism. To date,
most of the developmental literature has addressed the development of
cognitive abilities that are linked to the onset of fear. Although important,
other maturational processes, such as physical development, also affect
the form of the anxious responses. Second, just as the acquisition of
language in the young child replaces crying as a means of communication,
so too expressions of fear may change with increased developmental
capacities. As noted by Suomi (1986), despite changes in the expression,
the tendency for the emotion to occur may remain stable, however. The
challenge for valid assessment is to understand developmental changes
which may camouflage the expression of this attribute if inappropriate
models or procedures are used. In the remainder of this chapter, we will
focus more specifically on physical, cognitive and behavioral development,
how maturation may affect the expression of anxiety, and the necessity to
alter the assessment strategy to take account of the developmental processes.

PHYSICAL MATURATION AND
PSYCHOPHYSIOLOGICAL ASSESSMENT

The individual's physical development is the most obvious sign of maturation. Conceptually, the physiological system can be divided into three
parts: affective (sensory input), effective (motor output), and central (integrative) processes. Psychophysiologists have focused most of their

attention on changing central or cognitive capacities (Porges & Fox, 1986), and certainly developmental psychologists have emphasized changing cognitive capabilities to explain normal developmental fears. Maturation throughout the sensorimotor system, however, is likely to play a large role in the expression of emotions. Therefore, to understand the importance of physical development fully, maturation of the affector and effector systems must receive equivalent attention with central integrative processes. The field of developmental psychophysiology most clearly reflects this commitment by assuming "that there is a dynamic interplay between the continuously changing nervous system and the changing effector system" (Porges & Fox, 1986, p. 611). This review of physical maturation will be limited to systems commonly used in the detection or expression of anxiety, namely, the cardiovascular and electrodermal systems.

As has been noted elsewhere, there are few studies addressing psychophysiological assessment of anxious emotional states in children (Beidel, 1988; Beidel & Turner, 1988). Yet in comparison to information available from adults, the psychophysiological responses of infants and toddlers often assume additional importance given the infants' restricted verbal abilities. Similarly, few, if any studies have examined physiological responses of anxious geriatric populations. Although not directed specifically at fear, there is a body of literature that has assessed somatic responses to novel or stressful stimuli. Basically, these are orienting response studies in which the cardiovascular or electrodermal system has served as the primary dependent variable. Infants' heart rate responses to these tasks, for example, have been used to suggest the existence of primitive reactivity, which has been cited as the first fear in infancy. In the next section, the characteristics of the orienting response, the deviations that are seen often in neonatal subjects, and the ways in which changing physiological development influences the presentation of this response are examined. In the subsequent section, the relationship of age to electrodermal activity likewise is evaluated.

Evolution of Orienting Response

The orienting response is a general attentional state on the part of the organism that enhances the ability to process information. The experimental paradigm most commonly used to assess orienting is one in which a stimulus is presented and responses to the event are recorded. In adults, stimuli of high intensity usually produce defensive or protective responding on the part of the organism, whereas those of low intensity usually produce an orienting response. A primary characteristic of the orienting response is a pattern of cardiac deceleration. Cardiac acceleration is representative of defensive responding. These differential responses are seen commonly in adult subjects. Neonates, however appear, to respond to stimulation of any intensity of duration with cardiac acceleration (Berg & Berg, 1979; Graham & Clifton, 1966), thus leading to the suggestion that any environmental change is associated with defensive (fearful) responding. Although not evident at birth, cardiac-orienting responses appear within the first few months of life and by approximately 12 weeks of age resemble those of adults (Graham et al., 1970). This shift has been attributed to developmental changes in the cardiovascular or nervous system.

Complex systems, such as the cardiovascular system, undergo a series of changes during a lifetime. There are changes in the end-organ components of the system, such as increasing rigidity of the arteries, and decreasing pumping capabilities of the heart, as well as other changes reflecting maturation and decline in various parts of the nervous system that affect cardiovascular functioning. The basic evolution of the cardiovascular system includes (a) basal heart rate decreases and blood pressure increases from infancy through adulthood, and (b) heart rate reactivity that decreases with age. Resting heart rates do begin to decline during the same period that the orienting response appears, although this change has been addressed empirically and appears to have little impact on the emergence of the orienting response (Graham et al., 1970). Thus, researchers have turned their attention to the developing nervous system.

Changes in the orienting response have been assumed to reflect central neural development. For example, certain startle reflexes are not fully developed at birth. Blinking in response to loud tones or air puffs does not reach adult latency, form, and amplitude until the child is 6 years old (Clay & Ramseyer, 1976). This reflex is dependent on neuronal transmission across many synaptic sites, and its initial absence has been suggested as representing a central neuronal pathway immaturity (Berg & Berg, 1979). Some psychophysiologists have used the slowly maturing startle reflexes to propose the existence of a central-processing system, called the transient detection system. This system would be responsible for recognizing the "transient" nature of stimuli such as those used to assess orienting (Graham, 1984). Without this system, all events are treated as sustained (long playing) and thus activate defensive responding. The absence of functional central-processing mechanisms at birth could explain the existence of "primitive reactivity" inasmuch as all events would be perceived as sustained. With neuronal maturation and expanding synaptic connections, the transient detection system would evolve, allowing discrimination between brief and sustained responses and differential infant response to various types of stimulation. There is a great deal of evidence to support the existence of this system (see Berg & Berg, 1979). Other more parsimonious explanations for the onset of the orienting response also have been postulated, however.

First, neural development also occurs outside the central nervous system. As part of the parasympathetic nervous system, the vagus nerve is important in maintaining cardiovascular homeostasis. Increases in arterial blood pressure lead to reflexive decreases in heart rate and blood pressure in an effort to "stabilize" the cardiovascular system (Larsen, Schneiderman, & Pasin, 1986). Control of this heart rate decrease is the function of the vagus nerve. The vagal nerve also has been implicated in the deceleratory heart rate responses evoked through external stimulation (Porges & Fox, 1986). Developmentally, the vagus undergoes changes in diameter and myelination, most of which occur during the last 3 months of gestation, but some minor changes continue to occur postterm. Even these minor changes, however, may play an important role in explaining the onset of cardiac-orienting responses in neonates. In fact, Porges and Fox (1986) suggest that maturation of the vagal nerve, which results in increased tonic control, also can explain the change in evoked heart rate responses, and invoking an extensive reorganization in central-processing mechanisms may be unnecessary.

In addition to peripheral neural development, an important consideration when evoking orienting responses is the use of proper testing conditions. One difficulty in testing neonates is doing so when the baby is in a quiet, alert state. Graham et al. (1970) had to assess more than 100 infants to obtain 12 who remained quiet and alert during the session. Even so, these researchers still failed to detect an orienting response in infants less than 12 weeks old. Other investigators have reported that under these same conditions, however, neonates do respond to novel tones with a slight decelerative response, although the magnitude is greatly diminished when compared with older infants (Porges & Fox, 1986). The finding that a minimal response sometimes can be elicited when the state of the infant is carefully controlled suggests that peripheral development cannot be ignored. Indeed, the onset of distinct cardiovascular deceleration more clearly coincides with the final stages of vagal development than with the much later development of startle reflexes. Based on these data, Porges and Fox (1986) suggested that the shift in cardiac-orienting response occurs as a result of changes in the "brain-vagus-heart" axis. Thus, increased myelination of the vagus nerve and improved vagal tone, perhaps in combination with maturation of the central nervous system, provides the most satisfactory explanation of this changing phenomenon.

Primitive Reactivity and Orienting Response

How does the development of the orienting response relate to the assessment of anxiety in children? As noted earlier, the emotional state of infants and toddlers often must be observed from their somatic and behavioral reactions. The neonates' defensive reactions to the presentation of novel events might suggest that they are incapable of discriminating between those events that are meant to signal attention and those that signal danger. As noted by Bowlby (1973), an overgeneralization of danger, and thus primitive reactivity, may serve to protect the infant until such time as certain neurological systems have the opportunity to develop. There is a possibility that part of the "primitive reactivity," however, may be a function of presenting stimuli when the neonate is in a suboptimal state of alertness. If this is so, then the notion that any stimulus presentation, regardless of intensity or duration, produces fearful responding in neonates will have to be reevaluated. Obviously, this issue requires further experimentation. Nevertheless, this discussion highlights several issues concerning the assessment of anxiety. First, the assessment requires that the subject be in an alert, restful state. During the first few weeks of life, this may be difficult to achieve. Second, changes in cardiac response should not necessarily be attributed immediately to development of the central nervous system. This cognitive bias may cause peripheral neural developments that affect the cardiovascular system, such as that associated with the vagus nerve, to be overlooked.

Heart Rate as Anxiety Indicator

Although resting heart has little impact on maturation of the orienting response, heart rate plays a large role in psychophysiological assessments of anxiety. The results of studies that have assessed the heart rate response of anxious children indicate that their heart rates increased when placed in anxiety-producing situations. For example, a multiphobic child had an increase in heart rate when climbing a ladder or approaching a blood-soaked pillowcase, but not while taking a test (Van Hasselt, Hersen, Bellack, Rosenbaum, & Lamparski, 1979). Children with clinically significant test anxiety manifested significantly larger pulse rate increases than their nonanxious peers when taking a test or reading aloud before a small audience (Beidel, 1988). As noted earlier, behaviorally inhibited children (a concept that appears reminiscent of anxiety) had higher heart rates and less heart rate variability than nonbehaviorally inhibited children during cognitive and social interaction tasks (Reznick et al., 1986). Although there appear to be heart rate reactivity differences when children are grouped according to anxiety or behavioral inhibition, reliability trials based on samples of anxious children have yet to be conducted. With respect to behavioral inhibition, Reznick et al. (1986) reported a correlation of .58 when heart rates at ages 4 and 5½ were compared, but only .15 between heart rates at 21 months and 5½ years. Similarly, heart rate variability at 5½ years was more highly correlated with variability at 4 years (.64) than at 21 months (.39). Although differences in method of heart rate assessment at 21 months and the latter times partially may have accounted for the lower correlations, another reason for the decrease in reliability with increasing time intervals may be maturation. Obviously, all organisms do not mature in a lock-step fashion, and across longer time intervals, the general unevenness of development could be reflected in lower correlations. In support of this contention, data based on a sample of children unselected for anxiety suggested higher baseline correlations across shorter (girls tested 10.4 months apart, $r = .80$) than longer intervals (boys tested 41 months apart, $r = .58$; Matthews, Rakaczky, Stoney, & Manuck, 1987), although these data are inconclusive owing to the use of two different samples.

As noted earlier, resting heart rates do decline with increasing age. Heart rates of 6-week-old neonates averaged 153.6 beats per minute (BPM) (Graham et al., 1970), whereas heart rates of adults range from 60 to 80 BPM. In contrast, blood pressure increases with age (Berenson, 1980). Significant changes can occur in childrens' resting heart rates and blood pressures across a 4-year period (Matthews et al., 1987). At age 10.4 years, average baseline blood pressure readings of 96/61 mmHg and 81 BPM were recorded for a group of boys compared with baselines of 112/65 mmHg and 69 BPM when reassessed 41 months later. Recognition that baseline values change is important because within short intervals, it can be difficult to determine if declines reflect maturation or adaptation to the laboratory setting. For example, in the same paper cited earlier, Matthews et al. (1987) reported that across a 10-month interval, there was a significant decline in girls' baseline heart rates (75.9 BPM to 67.7 BPM), although there was no change in baseline blood pressures. As noted by the authors, the heart rate decline could have been due to either the effect of repeated testing or maturation.

Data interpretation can become quite complicated when treatment, repeated testing, and maturation effects must be addressed. If decreases in heart rate occur from pretreatment to posttreatment for both the treatment and control groups, the influence of maturation and repeated testing must be considered. One way to address this issue would be to conduct a series of assessment sessions over a short timespan (e.g., 1 week). This would allow for an assessment of possible repeated testing effects within a time frame too limited for maturational change to be a factor.

Interplay of Somatic and Cognitive Factors

This issue of repeated testing effects underscores the notion that some subjects, particularly those that are anxious, may react unfavorably to the laboratory setting. One aspect of this "reactivity" may be increased heart rate during baseline periods. For example, although the sample size was too small to permit statistical analyses, unpublished data from our clinic revealed laboratory baseline heart rate values of 93.4 BPM for children with overanxious disorder compared with 86.9 BPM for children with "uncomplicated" test anxiety, and 87.1 BPM for normal controls, all of whom were the same age (mean = 9.1 years). It is unclear if this difference represents a valid difference in resting heart rate values or an anxious response on the part of the overanxious children to the upcoming laboratory assessment. Heart rate data presented by Reznick et al. (1986) support the latter interpretation. Inhibited children at 5½ years of age had significantly higher heart rates during baseline and quiet periods than the noninhibited children. As noted by these authors, this was the first age at which group differences at these "nontask" assessment points were noted. The authors suggested that increased cognitive abilities allowed the children to anticipate future events, which may have been reflected in increased heart rate. If, as Kagan et al. (1987) suggests, these behaviorally inhibited children possess a biological vulnerability, maturing cognitive abilities may allow this temperament to be expressed as worry and anticipation of the future. Thus, in addition to physical development, cognitive maturation may play an important role in interpreting the physiological parameters of the anxiety response.

Electrodermal Activity in Anxious Subjects

Another common somatic measure of anxious emotion is electrodermal response. The body contains two kinds of sweat glands: eccrine and apocrine. Apocrine glands, found in the genital and underarm areas primarily respond to stressful conditions. Eccrine glands, found over most of the rest of the body, are involved in temperature regulation. The eccrine glands located in the soles of the feet and the palms of the hands, however, react less to heat and more to external stimulation (Porges & Fox, 1986). Studies with premature infants demonstrate an inability for emotional sweating to occur before 36 to 37 weeks of conceptual age, suggesting that this is when these glands mature (Harpin & Rutter, 1982). Psychophysiological assessment at these sites can include measurement of tonic levels or phasic responses. Tonicity is a measure of the individual "at rest," whereas phasic response is a change in the resting level that occurs as a result of an event.

The anxiety literature is replete with studies demonstrating differences between anxious and nonanxious adults based on tonic level and phasic responses (e.g., Nietzel & Bernstein, 1981). The use of these variables to assess anxiety in children is quite rare (Beidel & Turner, 1988). Borkovec (1970) assessed the skin conductance responses to psychopathic, neurotic, and normal boys when presented with tone stimuli. Because the purpose of this study was to confirm the hypothesis of decreased autonomic reactivity in the psychopathic group, the neurotic and normal groups were combined, thus yielding a nonpsychopathic versus a psychopathic comparison. The psychopathic group was less reactive to the stimuli than the nonpsychopathic group. The response of the neurotic group alone, which would most closely resemble an anxious group, was not presented, thus it is unclear if these boys were more responsive than the normal controls. Several other studies in which children were categorized based on a self-report measure of anxiety reported that skin conductance variables were assessed (Finch, Kendall, & Garrison, cited in Finch & Kendall, 1979; Melamed, Yurcheson, Fleece, & Hawes, 1978), but either did not describe the results or found that no relationship existed between anxiety and electrodermal activity.

In addition to the use of polygraph procedures, another method of assessing electrodermal activity is the palmar sweat index. In this procedure, the palm is pressed onto specially treated paper, and the prints are rated to determine the degree of emotional arousal. These ratings, though subjective, have been used to document increases in emotionality. For example, Lore (1966) measured changes in children's palmar sweat prints before and after listening to a "scary" story, and found a higher amount of sweating after the scary story was read. Melamed et al. (1978) found a significant correlation between the palmar sweat index assessed during a dental examination and children's self-report of dental fears. There appears to be some validity for the use of this index. Its subjective rating system, however, has given it limited appeal among researchers. First, the prints are rated by comparisons across the entire sample. In addition, the prints are sensitive to the amount of hand pressure used to make them. Therefore, differing degrees of hand pressure can alter the amount of sweat recorded, allowing the possibility that firm hand pressure can be misinterpreted as high emotionality.

Aging and Electrodermal Responses

Similar to the heart rate literature described earlier, the relationship between anxiety and electrodermal response appears to be partially mediated by age. Most studies that have examined age-related differences have used orienting and conditioning paradigms to study the effects of age, and, like cardiovascular studies, have been limited to normal or unselected populations. In general, these studies reveal electrodermal activity attenuation with increasing age. For example, younger subjects (mean = 25.3 years) had higher electrodermal tonic levels during rest periods and habituation trials than an older age group (mean = 69.5 years), although there were no age differences in habituation rate or phasic response magnitude (Catania, Thompson, Michaelewski, & Bowman, 1980). In contrast, other studies have shown a difference in the magnitude of the phasic response when different age groups were assessed. For example, response magnitude was greater in younger subjects, when children (age 11 years), young adults (20.5 years), and aged adults (68 years) were studied (Morrow, Boring, Keough, & Haesley, 1969), although it was unclear if the term "younger" referred to just the children, or the children and young adults combined. In a sample composed of women (Plouffe & Stelmack, 1984), older women (aged 71 years) had smaller phasic responses and lower tonic levels than younger women (aged 19.9 years). Similar to the Catania et al. (1980) study, there were no age differences in the number of trials until habituation.

Electrodermal responding has been used as a measure of a subject's emotional state, with higher tonic levels indicative of higher "arousal." Thus, age differences in tonic level and phasic response magnitude might be constructed as evidence of reduced "emotionality" among geriatric populations. A mitigating factor, however, is that the number of active sweat glands at various body sites decreases as age increases. A full-term baby has an active sweat gland density in the thigh region that is 6 times that of an adult (Foster, Hey, & Katz, 1969). Based on a count of active sweat glands in the index finger, the number of active glands per 10 mm^2 of skin decline from 29 per 10 mm^2 in white males aged 20 to 39, to 27 per 10 mm^2 in white males age 40 to 60, to 18 per 10 mm^2 in white males older than age 60. The differences between the latter two groups was significant (Juniper & Dykman, 1967). Catania et al. (1980) also found a significantly greater number of sweat glands in subjects who were 25.3 years old (180 in the perferred hand and 210.1 in the nonpreferred hand) compared with subjects who were 69.5 years old (67 in the preferred hand and 74.9 in the nonpreferred hand). From these data, as well as others, it is apparent that the lower tonic levels found in older adults is at least partially a function of fewer glands available to produce sweating, the medium used to conduct the electrical current.

Explanations of the age-related changes in phasic responses are somewhat more complicated. Phasic responses are often considered to be indirect indicators of cognitive processing. As noted by Morrow et al. (1969), early conditioning studies reported decrements in reflexive responding, which correlated with increasing age. These studies were based on simple conditioning paradigms and thus could not differentiate response attentuation owing to aging peripheral organs versus reduced conditionability owing to declining central-processing abilities. More recent studies have used differential conditioning procedures that would allow this type of discrimination to be made (e.g., Morrow et al., 1969). For example, in this study there were no differences between the groups based on a differential conditioning paradigm, in that both ages had larger responses to the CS+ stimulus than to the CS– stimulus. This supports the interpretation that decreased phasic responses in older subjects are due to peripheral end-organ deterioration, specifically a decline in the number of active sweat glands rather than a decrease in central-processing capabilities. Other studies also support this interpretation (c.f., Plouffe & Stelmack, 1984). Again, as in cardiovascular-orienting studies, methodological nuances may clarify the nature of age-related changes. In fact, Catania et al. (1980), who did not find any decrease in phasic responses in aged subjects, suggested that the decreases found in other studies may have been a function of the specific assessment method that was used. The constant voltage procedure used by Catania et al. (1980) appears to provide a more direct measure of skin conductance than does the constant current method used in other studies. According to these authors, although the constant voltage method depends only on the conductance in each individual pathway, the constant current method also depends on the number of available pathways. As the total number of pathways decreases, more current is forced into those remaining. Thus, in aged skin, more current is forced into fewer pathways, resulting in higher densities, which can injure the sweat glands or reduce glandular functioning. Direct comparisons between these methods based on different aged samples are needed. Based on the explanations provided by Catania et al. (1980), however, it appears that age-related differences in phasic responses might be avoided if the most direct assessment method is used.

Psychophysiological assessment with anxious children is an emerging field, and in addition to the theoretical issues discussed earlier, there are practical considerations that must be addressed. First, there is the unfamiliarity of a laboratory setting. Although this also may be true for adults, it is likely that many more children will be unfamiliar with the concepts of research investigations and the use of polygraph equipment. Thus, a "pre-assessment" visit during which the child can see the functions of the equipment may be useful in acclimating the child to the laboratory environment. Second, the issue of extraneous movement during the assessment procedures necessitates consideration by the researcher. Because young children appear less able to inhibit movements than adults (see behavioral assessment section), movement detectors may be helpful in detecting physiological data that may be movement artifacts. Also, the length of baseline assessment requires careful consideration. Studies conducted in our laboratory suggest that 20-minute baseline periods, often necessary for adaptation, cannot be tolerated by children below the age of 8 (Turner, Beidel, & Epstein, 1988). Finally, the type of stimuli used with young children deserves consideration. For example, we have found that a picture of a snake with bared fangs was an appropriate stimulus for habituation studies of fear with 8-year-olds but created such extreme distress in a 6-year-old that the experiment could not be conducted.

To summarize the somatic literature, it appears that physical maturation and decline play a significant role in the validity of cardiovascular and electrodermal responses. First, although immature central-processing systems may contribute to these deviant responses, peripheral end organs also continue to mature after birth. With respect to electrodermal responses, the influence of age on the effector system (i.e., the sweat glands) makes it difficult to use these particular responses as a valid developmental index of psychological or central nervous system processing (Porges & Fox, 1986). Second, it appears that data collection parameters may play a role in the response characteristics. This includes the state of the organism (Porges & Fox, 1986), the data collection method (Catania et al., 1980), and research designs that can address the differing effects of treatment, adaptation, and maturation. Third, the lack of electrodermal studies with neonates and infants may be due to some practical difficulties (Porges & Fox, 1986). For example, these authors reported that even very small electrodes can be sensitive to movement artifacts, making it difficult to determine if the recorded activity was a result of electrode pressure or a valid phasic response. Furthermore, smaller diameter electrodes necessitate adjustments in current density to avoid producing an electrical current that is irritating to the skin. Fourth, although research with neonates may be impractical, assessments with anxious children and adolescents are still needed. Thus far, most maturational data are based on samples of normal subjects. It is not clear, for example, if resting cardiovascular values or maturational changes are different for anxious subjects. Fifth, because of the potential for changing baselines as a result of maturation, change scores or residualized scores, and not absolute values, may constitute more appropriate data for statistical analyses. Finally, the influence of age on physiological variables precludes using subjects who differ widely in age within the same sample. For example, using the Matthews et al. (1987) data, children 4 years apart may have significantly different baseline levels. Differences in the number of active sweat glands across adult samples may preclude using samples that vary widely in age. Thus, samples should be as homogeneous as possible, and subjects should be carefully age matched to control groups.

COGNITIVE DEVELOPMENT AND COGNITIVE-SUBJECTIVE ASSESSMENT

Although somatic indices play a central role in the developmental assessment of anxiety, particularly for young children with limited verbal capacities, subjective and cognitive symptoms of anxiety typically are a primary focus in the initial assessments of anxiety and anxiety disorders. In adults, measurement of these variables occurs via clinical interviews amd numerous standardized self-report inventories. When one considers the use of similar strategies with children, however, several question arise: (a) Do children have the capacity to describe themselves as being anxious? (b) If so, do anxiety labels such as fear, embarrassment, and worry mean the same for children as they do for adults? (c) Can children make discriminations between various emotion labels, and with what degree of accuracy are they able to rate the intensity and frequency of subjective-cognitive symptoms? (d) Can children identify cognitions and subjective feeling states as separate (although probably related) concepts? (e) To what edegree, if any, do faulty cognitions play a role in the anxiety experienced by children, as has been suggested to occur in adult samples (Beck & Emory, 1985)? When considering these questions, it probably is more useful to ask at what age children become capable of making various discriminations and judgments rather than focusing on whether they can or cannot perform as adults? In this vein, a developmental perspective of cognitive maturity would address questions regarding the ways in which anxiety in children should be modified and interpreted differently as cognitive development occurs. Before considering these issues explicitly, we shall review very briefly some basic theoretical ideas regarding cognitive development. In addition, we shall describe some of the measures typically used to assess subjective-cognitive symptoms to place the subsequent discussion in a broader perspective.

Cognitive Development

Based on Piaget's theory of cognitive development, children from birth until approximately 18 months function in a sensorimotor realm. They have no awareness during most of this period that they themselves are separate from their environment. As a result, perceptions are guided by extreme egocentrism. It is only during the middle to end of this period that the important concept of object permanence develops (Donaldson, 1978). With the emergence of this concept, an infant begins to perceive external objects as being separate from himself, and becomes capable of experiencing attachment feelings and the concomitant fears of separation (Hoffman, 1981).

Fears reported by children at a later age rely on the cognitive capacity to represent aspects of the environment internally. Without the ability to imagine that dangerous or otherwise feared events might happen, a child would not be likely to report fears of such things as monsters or ghosts. The ability to represent objects and events internally develops during the preoperational period that lasts from approximately 18 months to 6 years (Donaldson, 1978). Hoffman (1981) has indicated that internal representation of social events may occur at an even earlier age than ability to do the same with physical objects. Because it is the latter on which Piaget's premises were established, we might expect children within an even earlier phase of the preoperational period to be capable of cognitive representation of social objects and events. Given the development of language capacity that also occurs during this age range, and the importance of language for the assessment of subjective experiences, most work in the assessment of subjective-cognitive symptoms of anxiety in children is conducted with children who are at least kindergarten age.

The concrete operations period follows and lasts from ages 7 to 11 (Donaldson, 1978). It is during this period that children develop the concept of reversibility and begin to use logic for problem solving, although the latter is still tied strongly to the presence of concrete objects (Donaldson, 1978). This age group typically makes up the middle range of children assessed in the literature to be reviewed here. The oldest groups (children aged 12 or older) usually are considered to be functioning cognitively in the formal operations stage, exhibiting some ability to reason logically without the aid of concrete objects (i.e., ability to work from theoretical hypotheses). It is with the movement into these latter stages that children cease to report fears of imaginary objects and events (e.g., monsters, ghosts) and begin to describe fears of school, physical danger, and negative evaluation.

Measures of Subjective-Cognitive Symptoms

One of the most frequently used self-report inventories is the State-Trait Anxiety Inventory for Children (STAIC; Spielberger, 1973). The scale was originally constructed and standardized for use with children in grades 4 to 6 (aged 9 through 12). The STAIC is composed of two 20-item scales designed to assess separately state and trait anxiety. Several studies have attested to the reliability and validity of this instrument in groups of both normal and emotionally disturbed children aged 9 to 12 (e.g., Finch & Nelson, 1974; Finch, Montgomery, & Deardorff, 1974b; Montgomery & Finch, 1974; Papay et al., 1975; Spielberger, 1973). More recently, Papay and Spielberger (1986) demonstrated that the instrument also had some validity for children in kindergarten, first, and second grades. Internal consistency data, however, suggested that the younger children (in kindergarten and first grade) responded consistently only when the STAIC was administered individually and orally rather than via the more standard group/written format. Second graders, conversely, responded in a consistent manner when the inventory was administered in small groups. These procedural differences probably were necessary based on the limited reading and writing capacities of the younger children.

A second self-report inventory widely used in the assessment of subjective anxiety in children is the Children's Manifest Anxiety Scale (CMAS; Castaneda, McCandless, & Palermo, 1956). The CMAS consists of 42 anxiety items and 11 additional items that comprise a Lie Scale. As with the STAIC, psychometric properties of the CMAS have been examined in both normal and emotionally disturbed children (e.g., Casteneda et al., 1956; Finch, Montgomery, & Deardorff, 1974; Kitano, 1960). A recent revision of the CMAS (RCMAS), entitled, "What I Think and Feel," was developed by Reynolds and Richmond (1978). The RCMAS includes 28 anxiety and 9 lie items, and has been used with children as young as kindergarten age. Early data demonstrated adequate psychometric properties for this revised inventory (e.g., Reynolds, 1980; Reynolds & Richmond, 1978, 1979).

Other less frequently used measures include the Test Anxiety Scale for Children (TASC; Sarason et al., 1960), the Revised Children's Cognitive Assessment Questionnaire (RCCAQ; Zatz & Chassin, 1985), and the Children's Negative Cognitive Error Questionnaire (CNCEQ; Leitenberg, Yost, & Carroll-Wilson, 1986). The latter two inventories were developed specifically to assess cognitive variables, and thus provide a useful addition to the more subjective scales described earlier. Some researchers also have used more open-ended thought-listing techniques to assess cognitions (Beidel & Turner, 1988; Brown, O'Keefe, Sanders, & Baker, 1986). In these procedures, children are asked either to write or say aloud thoughts that occurred to them during some activity. These thoughts then are scored by blind raters according to some a priori criteria. Although psychometric data are quite limited with some of these instruments, clinical intuition suggests that for younger children, administration procedures need to be modified to account for limited reading and writing capacities. These modifications might include oral and individualized administrations, as indicated with research on the STAIC.

Children's Descriptions of Themselves as Anxious

From a variety of sources, it is evident that children describe themselves as being afraid, anxious, or scared as early as 2 to 3 years old (Bretherton et al., 1986). As noted earlier, by preschool age, commonly reported fears include imaginary creatures, animals, and the dark (e.g., Campbell, 1986). In groups of older children (ages 8 to 18), the most frequently reported fear-producing scenarios involve fears of negative evaluation (Brown et al., 1986; Campbell, 1986).

Regarding more generalized subjective reports, children in kindergarten, first, and second grade are able to report anxiety symptoms of both a state and trait nature (Papay & Spielberger, 1986). The validity of these reports was supported by modest negative correlations between STAIC scores and measures of academic achievement. The data further showed that trait anxiety reported by children in kindergarten was significantly lower than that reported by first- and second-graders. As the authors suggested, it may be that such young children have experienced recent elevations in state anxiety as a result of their initial participation in school activities and only later develop higher trait anxiety as a result of persistent experience with heightened situational anxiety. This explanation, however, does not quite fit with other descriptions of anxiety proneness as a tendency to respond to stress in an anxious fashion. Using this conceptualization, it would appear that the "proneness" should precede the state response. An alternative explanation is that kindergartners cannot evaluate accurately the frequency of anxiety symptoms, or have difficulty understanding and using frequency-related concepts such as hardly ever, sometimes, or often. As described subsequently, however, estimates of internal consistency suggested that for children in all three age groups, evaluation of trait anxiety ("how I usually act") may have been easier than evaluation of state anxiety ("how I feel right now").

Other data suggested that children as young as age 6 are capable of making quantitative ratings of anxiety that correlate reasonably well with observers' ratings (LeBaron & Zeltzer, 1984). As discussed later, children's ratings did not correlate quite as strongly with behavioral observations as did observor's ratings. Nevertheless, anecdotal data indicated that when inconsistencies in the two modes of assessment (self-report and behavioral observation) were noted, clinical information explained the apparent desynchrony. For example, the authors reported that one child who appeared to be quite calm during a painful bone marrow aspiration procedure, but who also described himself as rather anxious, was described by his parents as a "stoic" individual who did little complaining but who experienced frequent symptoms such as insomnia, irritability, and nightmares before the medical procedures (LeBaron & Zeltzer, 1984, p. 736). Thus, although the child appeared less anxious than many others, his self-report of higher distress was likely to be accurate.

As an example of the necessity to adapt the rating system to the capabilities of the respondent, children younger than 10 (and any others who had difficulty with the rating procedure) were asked to make ratings of anxiety with the aid of faces drawn to indicate increasing levels of distress (LeBaron & Zeltzer, 1984). Although the authors did not provide data to support the age of 10 as a cutoff (nor did they indicate the criteria on which children were judged to be having difficulty with the rating procedure), one might expect this procedure to be most useful for children who have not yet moved into the formal operations stage. In this latter developmental period, children should have the capacity to represent abstract concepts such as increasing intensity of emotions, and therefore should benefit less from the addition of visual stimuli (i.e., faces) to an affective rating scale. In summary, it appears that children as young as 5 years old are capable of describing themselves as anxious, both regarding specific fears and generalized heightened anxiety. Differences probably exist, however, in the nature and expression of anxiety within different age groups. Also, assessment of subjective anxiety in children requires attention to the mode of assessment to account for variations in reading and writing skills, as well as stage of cognitive development.

Meaning of Anxiety Labels

In a review of data relevant to children's verbal communication of emotions, Bretherton et al. (1986) reported that children as young as 28 months could use emotional labels to describe themselves and others, and understood appropriately the antecedants for feeling scared (e.g., bad dreams, firecrackers, the dark). As children approached age 3, they were able to make further use of emotional labels in social interactions and make-believe games. Between the ages of 3 and 5, they demonstrated increased complexity in their speech and understanding of emotional labels.

As Seidner, Stipek, and Feshbach (1986) reviewed, however, mere learning of a label to describe emotions is necessary but not sufficient for full emotional expression. Reviewing developmental changes in the concepts of pride and embarrassment, Seidner et al. (1986) suggested that three steps occur in the development of emotions. First, a cognitive construct underlying each affective state must develop. Next, a child must learn the cultural rules surrounding the use of labels for these constructs. Finally, situational variables that elicit the emotions are likely to change with development. It is this final proposition that was the target of Seidner et al.'s (1986) investigation, and their data help to shed light on the ways in which emotional labels may have different meanings based on developmental stages. Given the focus of this chapter on anxiety assessment, only the data relevant to the concept of embarrassment is discussed.

Seidner et al. (1986) interviewed adults and children in kindergarten, second, fourth, and sixth grades. Each participant was asked to describe one real and one imagined event that led to the experience of embarrassment. To ensure that the younger children understood the emotional labels used, they were asked to demonstrate the emotion using facial expressions. Thus, criteria one and two noted earlier were appropriately satisfied. Although children in other studies have reported feeling scared at a very young age, Seidner et al.'s data suggested that embarrassment was a relatively unfamiliar concept for children in kindergarten and first grade. Approximately 33% of the kindergarten children and 20% of the first-graders were unable to report an episode in which they had been embarrassed. These data are consistent with other reports that fear of negative evaluation (intrinsic to embarrassment and a core feature of social phobia) is more characteristic of older children.

Other aspects of this study also highlighted developmental differences. First, most adults (94%) described embarrassing situations in which they had control and felt responsible. All groups of children, however, (regardless of age), were more likely to report as embarrassing events those over which they had no control, suggesting that children defined embarrassment somewhat differently from adults. Second, although for at least 45% of the subjects at all age levels (adults and children) the presence of an audience during the reported event was important, adults were less likely to report the explicit presence of an audience than were children. For children, there were no age-related differences in the frequency of audience references. These data implied that adults had more well-developed internal standards of embarrassment that did not require the explicit presence of an audience (Seidner et al., 1986). Finally, with the exclusion of children in kindergarten, adults were less likely to report embarrassing situations based on social comparison with others. Again, this may have been due to relatively robust, internalized standards in adults. Only kindergarten children were equally likely to omit inclusion of social comparison information. Although the authors suggested that it may be early school experiences that instilled in children the importance of social comparison in feeling embarrassed, kindergarten-age children were the least likely to be able even to identify an embarrassing situation. Thus, they may have had only weak knowledge of the general concept.

In summary, the Seidner et al. data provided some support for the contention that even after anxiety labels are part of a child's verbal and conceptual repertoire, there are differences in situational variables that evoke the feeling. These differences cannot be ignored in the assessment of affective states in children since they imply a different basis for subjective anxiety in adults and children of different ages.

Children's Differentiation of Affective States

Because children have some ability to define and understand emotional labels, the next question concerns the degree to which discrimination between various subjective states is possible. For instance, can children differentiate between anxiety and other subjective feelings such as pain that are often related to, but conceptually distinct from affective states? As Sacham and Daut (1981), and Katz, Kellerman and Siegel (1981) indicated, such distinctions are difficult for all individuals to make, but are particularly troublesome for children. In a study designed to examine behavioral and self-report measures of pain and anxiety in children, LeBaron and Zeltzer (1984) asked cancer patients aged 6 to 18 to make subjective ratings of both pain and anxiety before and after undergoing a bone marrow aspiration procedure. The authors' clinical impression was that children had little difficulty telling the difference between being "scared" and "hurt" (p. 737), although neither mean ratings of pain and anxiety, nor correlations between the two were reported. Data were presented, however, indicating that there were no age-related differences in the ratings of either subjective state. Observers also rated anxiety and pain in all patients, and these scores then were correlated with the children's self-ratings. Correlations indicated that observers' and children's ratings of anxiety were more strongly related than the two ratings of pain, although such correlational data tell nothing about the source of any inaccuracies. Certainly, more research is necessary to make any conclusions regarding children's discrimination of anxiety and other nonaffective subjective states.

Another question of interest concerns children's ability to discriminate between various negative affective states. For example, although there are recent data attesting to qualitative differences between children diagnosed as anxious and depressed (Stavrakaki, Vargo, Boodoosingh, & Roberts, 1987), to our knowledge there are few data that address directly children's ability to differentiate subjective states of anxiety and depression. In the Bretherton et al. (1986) data discussed earlier, children as young as 2 to 3 years old described causal consequences of both affective states in ways that indicated some understanding of different situations likely to evoke one of the two feelings. Conversely, the data from a study by Trieber and Mabe (1987) suggested that children aged 6 through 16 (and their mothers) had significant difficulty with discriminations between anxiety and depression. In this study, correlations between self-report measures of anxiety and depression in the children were relatively high regardless of whether raters were the children themselves or their mothers. The data, however, were not analyzed separately based on age of the children and therefore did not allow examination of developmental changes in abilities to make anxiety-depression discriminations.

Because symptoms of anxiety and depression often occur together, the important judgment necessary to discriminate the two states may be intensity of feeling—that is, which of the comorbid experiences is the severest? Papay and Spielberger (1986) provided some data suggesting that intensity of affect may be one of the most difficult subjective judgments to make. Their data regarding internal consistency of the STAIC indicated that responses to the trait-anxiety portion of the scale were more consistent than ratings of state anxiety in children aged 5 to 7. Because the former requires judgments of frequency (i.e., how often do I feel anxious?) while the latter relies on assessments of intensity (i.e., how bad do I feel right now?), Papay and Spielberger proposed that the concept of intensity may be acquired during a later developmental period than the concept of frequency. Such a hypothesis, however, requires further empirical study.

The data reviewed to this point have concentrated primarily on the assessment of subjective feelings of anxiety in children. Another aspect of anxiety assessment involves the extent to which cognitions play a role in the experience of anxiety. Before examining the issue, the age at which children are capable of distinguishing emotion from cognition is addressed.

Differentiation of Emotions and Cognitions

It appears that only one study has attempted to assess directly the developmental changes in children's ability to differentiate feelings from thoughts. Gotterbarn and Cannella (1987) asked children in grades 1, 3, and 5 (aged 6 to 12) to complete two separate tasks. In the first, they were shown pictures and dialogue depicting one of several emotional states (anger, fear, happiness, and sadness). The children then were asked to describe what the character(s) in each vignette were thinking and feeling. In a second task, various cognitive and feeling-oriented statements were read aloud, and children were asked to identify whether each sentence expressed primarily a feeling or a thought.

On both tasks, older children were more accurate in differentiating feelings from thoughts. In general, however, the largest increases in accuracy occurred between grades 1 and 3. In addition, there were modest, but significant, correlations between IQ scores and accuracy on both tasks for all groups of children. Although the data did not apply solely to the assessment of anxiety, they suggested that both age and IQ are probably important variables to take into consideration when asking children to rate separately the subjective and cognitive symptoms of anxiety.

The data further showed that all groups of children had difficulty differentiating "hot cognitions" (Ellis, 1985) from emotions. Hot cognitions were defined as thoughts that are value laden and inevitably lead to emotional experience (e.g., "He should act like I want him to."). "Cool cognitions," conversely, embody only descriptive or observational information and are not value laden (e.g., "She is the only child on the playground"). The former are the types of thoughts most likely to be associated with anxiety (or any emotional experience), and there apparently were no developmental increases in ability to distinguish hot cognitions from emotions.

One important aspect of Gotterbarn and Cannella's (1987) study that merits some attention here was the inclusion of an educational lesson regarding the nature of the differences between thoughts and emotions. This lesson occurred before the children's participation in the two tasks. It is unclear precisely what impact this lesson might have had because no groups of children who were not so educated were included. Of further interest would be the degree to which children could be trained to make thought-emotion distinctions. Also, because the lesson contained no information regarding the differentiation of "hot" and "cool" types of thoughts, it would be of interest to find out if children could be trained to make this type of distinction. Regardless, Gotterbarn and Cannella's data provided some support for the ability of children, at least by grade 3, to make distinctions between thoughts and feelings.

Role of Cognitions in Anxiety

In accordance with the data indicating that children as young as 6 to 7 have more difficulty than older children identifying cognitions as separate from emotions, studies examining cognitive symptoms of anxiety have focused on older children. Brown et al. (1986) asked children aged 8 through 18 to respond to three scenarios depicting stressful events: a visit to the dentist, presentation of an oral report to peers, and any stressful situation from the child's recent past. For each scenario, the child described the kinds of thoughts that might occur (i.e., by imagining that he or she was at the dentist or giving the oral report presently, or by recalling thoughts that had been present during the actual recent stressful event). Cognitions were rated as using coping or catastrophizing mechanisms. Coping thoughts included positive self-talk (e.g., "Be brave"), attention diversion (e.g., thinking about something else), task orientation (e.g., rehearsing what to do or say), relaxation, and thought stopping. Catastrophizing thoughts were representative of a focus on negative affect or pain (e.g., "My heart is pounding, and I feel shaky"), desire to escape or avoid the situation (e.g., "I want to run away"), or a concern about negative consequences (e.g., "Is the dentist trying to kill me?" "Everyone will laugh at me").

Catastrophizing thoughts were fairly common at all ages, and the frequency rarely decreased with age. Alternatively, the frequency of coping cognitions increased with age primarily because of increased use of positive self-talk across all situations. Of most interest here, however, was the relationship between cognitive strategy and anxiety. All children completed the STAIC or the STAI (depending on their age), and scores on the trait anxiety scale were correlated with a general classification of each child as predominantly a coper or catastrophizer. (Thirty-six percent of the children were classified as the former, whereas 64% were categorized as the latter). The copers in general, regardless of age, were those children with lower trait-anxiety scores. Thus, these data provided support that cognitive activity, assessed in children via an open-ended strategy, correlated with their characterological functioning along an anxiety dimension.

A study by Leitenberg et al. (1986) substantiated the notion that anxious children are more likely to exhibit catastrophizing cognitions. Children in grades 4, 6, and 8 completed the CNCEQ, a self-report inventory designed to assess the frequency with which various "cognitive errors" are made by children. Results revealed that children defined as high in evaluation anxiety (on the basis of scores on the TASC) were more likely to catastrophize, overgeneralize, personalize, and make selective abstractions than children low in evaluation anxiety. Again, we have some evidence that cognitive symptoms can be assessed in older children and that they correlate with other symptoms of anxiety. Leitenberg et al. (1986) also demonstrated, however, that these same types of cognitive "errors" were equally common in depressed children and those defined as low in self-esteem. Thus, it remains to be seen whether cognitive symptoms unique to the experience of anxiety can be identified in children. Such an issue is also of significant importance to the adult literature.

In summary, children as young as age 2 to 3 report fearful, and by age 5 are able to use anxiety labels in relatively complex, meaningful ways. It also is apparent, however, that developmental differences exist in the situations likely to elicit anxiety, and in children's ability to use concepts such as frequency and intensity to make anxiety-related judgments. Variations in assessment strategies often are necessary to elicit reasonably accurate subjective ratings. First, the group/written format often used with self-report measures obviously is inappropriate for young children with limited reading and writing skills. Also, visual stimuli can facilitate the subjective-cognitive responses of young children. For example, LeBaron and Zeltzer (1984) used a 5-point scale anchored both by numerals and faces to illustrate increasing degrees of distress. In other areas of developmental research, visual stimuli such as pictures, videotapes, and finger puppets have been used to accompany orally presented scenarios to facilitate children's reports of cognitive activity (e.g., Fincham, 1981; Harris, 1977).

Developmental variations also exist in children's ability to differentiate anxiety from other affective and nonaffective states. Further, the role of cognitions in subjective anxiety probably varies as children become more capable of making discriminations between cognitions and affect. In general, precise developmental differences in subjective cognitive capacities are not always clear, but consideration of a child's level of development is certainly essential to a thorough assessment of anxiety.

MOTORIC-BEHAVIORAL MATURATION AND OVERT-BEHAVIORAL ASSESSMENT

Overt-behavioral expressions of anxiety such as escape from or avoidance of the fearful event are dependent on the individual's physical ability to carry out the responses. As a child matures physically and socially, the behavioral correlates of fearfulness change from gross motoric responses such as crying or running away to more covert expressions such as gaze aversion. Development proceeds in cephalocaudal and proximodistal fashion. Thus, children gain control of neck muscles before leg muscles, and gross motor behaviors evolve before subtler control is possible. Like somatic responses, overt behaviors assume additional importance in the assessment of preverbal children. Assessing the overt signs of anxiety can be accomplished through self-monitoring, observational checklists and rating scales, and standardized behavioral avoidance tests. These procedures have been used with subjects of all ages, although as noted repeatedly throughout this chapter, reliable and valid assessment depends on awareness of maturation and developmental stages. There appear to be few studies that address directly the utility of a particular behavioral assessment procedure for specific age groups, yet the recommendations of child psychopathology researchers suggest that special consideration must be paid to the use of these measures in children. Thus, the practice of indiscriminantly adapting adult anxiety assessment methods for use with children is often inappropriate (Ollendick & Meador, 1984). An extensive discussion of behavioral assessment in children is beyond the scope of this chapter, and the interested reader is referred an excellent review by Ollendick and Meador (1984).

In this section, physical maturation and its effect on behavioral assessment are discussed. Specifically, the impact of maturation on the construction and utility of behavioral rating scales and self-monitoring is addressed. Procedural variations necessary for valid self-monitoring also are presented. Before discussing these specific behavioral assessment strategies, however, changes in the severity and frequency of fearful expressions in young children are examined. In many cases changes in overt behaviors have been attributed to cognitive maturation rather than motoric development. Nevertheless, this review highlights the speed of development and the interplay of cognitive, somatic, and behavioral factors in determining expressions of anxiety and fear.

Children's Changing Behavioral Responses to Fearful Events

Situations such as heights and snakes often have been used as analogues for the study of fear and anxiety in adults, given the frequency with which these fears are reported. Dental fears often have been the target of anxiety assessments with children. Like test anxiety, dental anxiety is fairly common in children, although unlike test anxiety, dental fears have not been related empirically to DSM-III disorders (Beidel & Turner, 1988). The evolution of overt expressions of fear in dental settings was presented by

Winer (1982). Based on the results of 17 studies that used observer rating scales to rate cooperative behavior, three basic conclusions were drawn. First, many children at every age show positive behaviors in dental settings. Few children exhibited physical resistance, forceful crying, or the need for physical restraint during dental examinations. Second, by the age of 4 or 5 all children behave positively. Third, most of the increase in positive behavior occurs between the ages of 3 and 6. Although almost every child behaves positively by the age of 5, there are some data suggesting a tendency for dental anxiety to increase again as children get older including a negative relationship between cooperation during dental procedures and ages 12 to 18 ($r = -.51$; Allan & Hodgson, 1968), and an increase in self-reported fear when comparing junior and senior high school students (Kleinknect, Klepac, & Alexander, 1973). Interestingly, this same bimodal distribution also occurs with test anxiety.

Two developmental-cognitive explanations for the changing nature of these dental fears are offered by Winer (1982). First, perhaps cognitive development between the ages of 3 and 6 allows the child to understand the nature of dental examinations, and this knowledge may serve to lessen the fearful response. This explanation however, does not address the resurgence of this fear during the adolescent years. A second hypothesis is that the fearful expressions exhibited in younger children (ages 2 to 5) when in dental settings may be reflective of their more basic fears including stranger anxiety or separation anxiety. Thus, at this age, the response of children to the dental procedures may reflect distress at separation from mother or being left alone with strangers rather than specific fear of the dentist. As the child outgrows these more basic fears, fearful behavior in dental settings declines as well. The upsurge in older children and adolescents might reflect further increasing cognitive capacities, allowing for anticipation of negative effects (such as painful restorations or extractions). This explanation also fits well with developmental studies of test anxiety in which the first increase in frequency (age 6) coincides with the entry into a strange situation (school), whereas the second upsurge coincides with cognitive capabilities for anticipation of negative events and fear of negative evaluation. Obviously these hypotheses await empirical investigation.

Cognitive developmental explanations often are incomplete, however. For example, although these observer rating scales possess a high degree of interrater reliability (e.g., Vinham, Sengston, & Cipes, 1978), scores on these instruments often do not correlate with physiological or self-report measures of anxiety. Assuming that all of the assessment procedures possess some internal validity, cognitive explanations alone cannot completely account for these data. An alternative explanation that would be more consistent with these data would acknowledge the children's increasing muscular control. Perhaps by the age of 5, children can exert a substantial degree of control over their motor behaviors, and thus their subjective state becomes less observable to others. Physical maturation and social acculturation may allow the individual to exert more control over overtly fearful behaviors. Nonetheless, although social pressures and physical maturation may mask expression, the lack of overt distress does not indicate the absence of anxious emotion.

Evolution of Subtle Anxiety Expressions

The preceding discussion to some extent focuses on the end product of behavioral maturation, that is, at what age are children capable of inhibiting overt expressions of fear? There are data from the developmental literature that are pertinent to the other side of this issue, that is, at what age do covert expressions of fear begin to emerge? It appears that subtle indications of fear can appear at a very early age. Sroufe and Waters (1977) examined the correlation between heart rate accleration and behavioral indicators of stranger fear in 1-year-old infants. The infants' heart rates were recorded, and anxious behaviors were rated on a stranger's entry into a room (both in the home and in a laboratory setting). Across the two conditions, when the infants' overt behaviors (e.g., crying, crawling away, or walking away) were compared, there were no differences based on the stranger's entry, yet heart rate acceleration was significantly more pronounced when strangers approached the infants in the laboratory. When the investigators returned to the videotapes and rated the infants' behavior for subtler indicants of fear (e.g., gaze aversion, furrowed brow, or decreased rate of smiling), however, they found significant correlations between these behaviors and heart rate acceleration.

The positive relationship between these subtle behaviors and accelerated heart rate led the authors to postulate the existence of a less intensive aversive state in the infants that they called wariness and that appears reminiscent of mild fear. Interestingly, the authors noted a temporal relationship between heart rate changes and these subtle behaviors in that stranger approach was followed by heart rate acceleration, which was followed by gaze aversion, which led to a decelerating heart rate. If the child again looked at the stranger, the entire sequence could be repeated. One interpretation of these data is that gaze aversion served a modulatory function by decreasing somatic response to an aversive event (Sroufe & Waters, 1977). Whether the child is cognizant of his or her ability to decrease this state of arousal, and does so intentionally is unclear. Cognitive awareness, however, may not be a necessary prerequisite. The behaviors exhibited by the child are consonant with behavioral theories of fear that emphasize the role of negative reinforcement in the development of escape or avoidance responses. Regardless of the etiological mechanism, these data indicate that children are capable of subtle and apparently functional avoidance behaviors at a very early age.

Development and the Validity of Observer Ratings

The frequency and severity of anxious behaviors can be assessed by the use of observer checklists and rating scales. For children, there are several standardized checklists including the Behavior Problem Checklist (Quay & Peterson, 1967, 1975), the CBCL (Achenbach, 1978; Achenbach & Edelbrock, 1979), and the Louisville Fear Survey Schedule for Children (Miller, Barrett, Hampe, & Noble, 1972). Norms are available for these parental rating scales, and in the case of the CBCL, scoring profiles differ depending on the age and sex of the child. The use of normative data allows the behavior of an individual child to be placed within a "normal" context. In addition, the CBCL scoring profiles reflect clustering of behaviors that can vary when age and gender are considered. In addition to the necessity for normative data and scoring procedures that may be altered to accommodate development, however, attention must be directed to the role of maturation on the content of the observational checklists.

Inattention to physical and social development when constructing behavioral scales can lead to misinterpretation of experimental results. For example, developmental changes in anxious behaviors have been studied in children and adolescents undergoing bone marrow aspiration (BMA) procedures. For example, an Observational Scale of Behavioral Distress (OSBD) was used to make ratings of anxiety and distress on 42 pediatric cancer patients undergoing BMA procedures who were grouped into three age ranges (2 to 6 years, 7 to 12 years, and 13 to 20 years; Jay, Ozolins, Elliot, & Cladwell, 1983). Ratings were made for the occurrence of 11 distressful and fearful behaviors including crying, screaming, physical restraint, verbal resistance, requesting emotional support, muscular rigidity, verbal fear, verbal pain, flailing, nervous behavior, and information seeking. Children between the ages of 2 to 7 were more likely to cry, scream, and have to be physically restrained during the procedure than children in the older groups. In addition, young females were more likely than the other groups to exhibit higher levels of verbal resistance. Furthermore, younger children were somewhat more likely to flail and ask for emotional support than the older groups.

There was also an interaction between age, previous BMA experience, and total OSBD scores. When the effects of age were discounted, there was still a significant relationship between total OSBD scores and number of previous BMAs, with distress scores decreasing as the number of BMA procedures increased. Furthermore, three predictors (age, parental anticipation of the child's pain, and number of previous bone marrow aspirations) accounted for 86% of the OSBD variance. The authors noted that distress levels changed dramatically between the ages of 6 and 7, which according to Piagetian theory is the age when children develop a more logical and realistic understanding of medical procedures. This knowledge may function to reduce anxiety. The authors further suggested that developmental changes in impulse control and gratification of delay allow older children to readily inhibit extreme motoric behavioral responses.

Although these explanations may play a role in the age-related changes of fearful behavioral expressions, data from other investigations reveal that observational checklists can be slanted toward extreme examples of fearful behaviors, thus potentially biasing anxiety assessments (LeBaron & Zeltzer, 1984). Based on items listed in the Procedure Behavior Check List (PBCL; muscle tension, screaming, crying, restraint used, pain verbalized, anxiety verbalized, verbal stalling, and physical resistance), LeBaron and Zeltzer (1984) found that children between the ages of 6 and 9 who were undergoing BMAs were significantly more likely to cry, scream, express verbal anxiety, and need physical restraint than children between the ages of 10 and 18. The older group was more likely to exert greater physical control resulting in fewer emotional outbursts. Thus, the 10 to 18 age group had lower scores on the PCBL than children aged 9 and under. The observers in this study were able to identify two behaviors, however, that had been overlooked by previous investigators and were not part of the PCBL. Flinching and groaning were more common in the older groups than the younger children. When these two behaviors were added to the PBCL scores, the significant differences in behavioral distress between the two groups disappeared. Therefore, when subtler expressions were considered, there did not appear to be any difference in the frequency or severity of the anxiety or pain experienced by the two groups, although the specific anxious and painful behaviors differed. Interestingly, these child-adolescent behavioral differences mirror the infant-adolescent rhesus monkey responses described earlier in this chapter (panic, vocalizations, and high activity in infants vs stereotypic activity and silence in adolescents; Mineka et al., 1981).

Qualitative differences based on age also were reported by Katz, Kellerman, and Sigel (1980). A rating scale similar to that used by the studies described earlier revealed significant age effects in the display of anxious behaviors. Again, older children exhibited fewer types of anxious behaviors than younger children and were more likely to exhibit muscle tension than the younger ones. Generally, anxious behaviors evolved from crying, screaming, and gross motor activity into specific verbal expressions of pain and increased muscle tension. Thus, it is evident that the development of anxious behaviors mirror the progression of more basic motor skills by evolving from general to specific.

Children's Ability to Self-Monitor

Self-monitoring procedures allow for an assessment of the anxious behavior in the context in which it occurs. As noted by Ollendick and Meador (1984), special considerations must be given to the use of these procedures with young children. Limited cognitive abilities and memory capacity argue for the selection of a few well-defined behaviors. Furthermore, descriptions of the behavior or a picture could increase understanding and allow for the assessment of more reliable and valid information. Simple stick figures, such as *COUNTOONS* (Kunselman, 1970) are one example of pictures that have been used to assist children in effectively self-monitoring behaviors, Although the age at which children can begin to self-monitor is not yet clear, it is obvious that skills such as writing and counting are necessary prerequisites. In addition, training in the procedures and the use of prompts will improve the accuracy of monitoring procedures (Ollendick & Meador, 1984).

In summary, development affects the overt expression of anxiety just as it affects the somatic and cognitive realms. Increasing muscular control changes anxious expressions from gross behaviors in which the emotion must be inferred from the context (e.g., crying can signal anger or anxiety) to more specific and direct acts, such as verbally reporting fear. Control of overt behaviors appears at a very early age (Sroufe & Waters, 1977). In the case of high-frequency fears such as dental fears, obvious expressions disappear by the age of 5 or 6 (Winer, 1982), although they are likely to reappear at a later age. It is unclear however, if the meaning of the fearful expression is the same at these two developmental stages.

Naturalistic observations of the behaviors that characterize anxiety at different ages would prevent further occurrences of two common behavioral assessment errors: indiscriminant adaptation of adult procedures, and the application of scales that are "too young" for the population in question. Several investigators have highlighted the need to integrate developmental considerations into the behavioral assessment literature. First, the different scoring profiles for the CBCL illustrate the necessity to consider covariation of behavioral expression by age and gender. Second, further use of normative samples may clarify the onset and evolution of certain fearful expressions. In turn, this information may provide for the development of age-appropriate observer rating scales. Third, consideration of developmental limitations supports the use of prompts that may increase the liklihood that behaviors would be recorded via self-monitoring. The use of colored paper, stars or stickers, and wrist counters may serve as visual prompts, and in the case of wrist counters allow for immediate recording, even in the absence of paper and pencil (Ollendick & Meador, 1984). In addition, the use of bright colors, stickers, and novel objects may pique the child's interest, thus increasing the possibility of compliance. Fourth, as was discussed in the section on psychophysiological assessment, normal controls must be assessed along with anxious children so that the influence of maturation can be documented and controlled. Finally, social rules regarding acceptable expressions of fear and reinforcement of "stoic" behaviors will also influence behavioral expressions, although this will not occur unless the child has the physical capabilities to perform as expected.

CONCLUSIONS

The past 10 years have witnessed an explosion of research directed at the anxiety disorders. This includes the introduction of new diagnostic categories such as social phobia, as well as the recognition that children can suffer from these conditions (American Psychiatric Association, 1980, 1987). The recent recognition and reorganization surrounding the anxiety disorders highlights the need for carefully controlled research directed at psychopathology and treatment issues. The theme of this chapter has been to illustrate the continuity of the anxiety construct and how that continuity may be blurred by an insensitivity to the effects of maturation. There has been an attempt to highlight developmental issues that may impact on the reliability and validity of anxiety assessments, and an attempt to broaden the concept of maturation beyond cognitive development. Based on this review, the following recommendations are proposed.

First, with the recent introduction of childhood anxiety disorders diagnostic categories, there has been an increasing interest in studying the psychopathology of these conditions. As noted earlier, a simple downward extension of adult assessment paradigms often will prove unacceptable. Somatic, cognitive, and behavioral development need to be considered and procedures adjusted accordingly. For example, an impromptu speech task is part of the standard assessment procedure for socially phobic adults treated at the Western Psychiatric Institute and Clinic Anxiety Disorders Clinic (Beidel, Turner, Jacob, & Cooley, 1988). This type of task, however, is outside of the experience of most preadolescent children. Therefore, to study the social phobia in children, a read-aloud task is used. Reading aloud before a group is topographically similar to giving a speech, yet is more in the context of children's everyday experiences. Similar modifications in the use of other behavioral assessments, such as self-monitoring procedures, were discussed earlier.

A second major issue with children is the use of carefully matched control groups. Particularly with studies in which psychophysiological assessment is used, experimental and control subjects should be matched for age, height, weight, and pubertal status. Although matching on all of these variables can become a Herculean task, these factors influence the validity of the resultant data. An alternative method for dealing with these variables would be through statistical control and the use of covariance procedures. Furthermore, some of the caveats that apply to the assessment of children pertain to geriatric patients as well. As the population continues to age, there will be an increasing need for treatment among these patients, and appropriate assessment procedures will be necessary.

Throughout this chapter, somatic, behavioral, and cognitive development have been discussed as if they were relatively independent entities. The decision to do so was based on the necessity to organize the material in some coherent fashion. Obviously, development cuts across these systems and as was noted earlier, improved cognitive abilities can influence somatic expressions of anxiety (Reznick et al., 1987). Thus, the influence of maturation in one system and its impact on expression through a second modality also must be considered. Along with these interactions, the importance of social development must be addressed. Knowledge regarding the rules of emotional expression are a necessary part of data interpretation, although stoic or fearless behaviors require the physical and cognitive abilities to inhibit an anxious response. In the final analysis, it is likely that all of these factors combine, often in a synergistic fashion, to influence the expression of anxiety.

Acknowledgment: Preparation of this chapter was supported in part by NIMH grants #41852, 30915, 18269, and 16884.

REFERENCES

Achenbach, T. M. (1978). The child behavior profile: 1. Boys aged 6–11. *Journal of Consulting and Clinical Psychology, 46,* 478–488.

Achenbach, T. M., & Edelbrock, C. S. (1979). The child behavior profile. 2. Boys aged 12–16 and girls aged 6–11 and 12–16. *Journal of Consulting and Clinical Psychology, 47,* 223–233.

Allan, T. K., & Hodgson, E. W. (1968). The use of personality measurements as a determinant of patient cooperation in an orthodontic practice. *American Journal of Orthodontics, 54,* 433–440.

Barrios, B. A., Hartman, D. B., & Shigetomi, C. (1981). Fears and anxieties in children. In E. J. Mash & L. G. Terdal (Eds.), *Behavioral assessment of childhood disorders* (pp. 259–304). New York: Guilford.

Beck, A. T., & Emery, G., with Greenberg, R. L. (1985). *Anxiety disorders and phobias: A cognitive perspective.* New York: Basic Books.

Beidel, D. C. (1988). Psychophysiological assessment of anxious emotional states in children. *Journal of Abnormal Psychology, 97,* 80–82.

Beidel, D. C., & Turner, S. M. (1988a). Assessing anxious emotion: A review of psychophysiological assessment in children. Unpublished manuscript, University of Pittsburgh.

Beidel, D. C., & Turner, S. M. (1988b). Comorbidity of test anxiety and other anxiety disorders in children. *Journal of Abnormal Child Psychology, 16,* 275–287.

Beidel, D. C., Turner, S. M., Jacob, R. G., & Cooley, M. R. (1988). Assessment of social phobia: Reliability of an impromptu speech task. Unpublished manuscript, University of Pittsburgh.

Berenson, G. S. (1980). *Cardiovascular risk factors in children.* New York: Oxford University Press.

Berg, W. K., & Berg, K. M. (1979). Psychophysiological development in infancy: State, sensory function, and attention. In J. Osofsky (Ed.), *Handbook of infant development* (pp. 238–317). New York: Wiley.

Borkovec, T. D. (1970). Autonomic reactivity to sensory stimulation in psychopathic, neurotic and normal juvenile delinquents. *Journal of Consulting and Clinical Psychology, 35,* 217–222.

Bowlby, J. (1973). *Attachment and loss: Vol. 2. Separation.* New York: Basic Books.

Bretherton, I., Fritz, J., Zahn-Waxler, C., & Ridgeway, D. (1986). Learning to talk about emotions: A functionalist perspective. *Child Development, 57,* 529–548.

Brown, J. M., O'Keefe, J., Sanders, S. H., & Baker, B. (1986). Developmental changes in children's cognition to stressful and painful situations. *Journal of Pediatric Psychology, 11,* 343–357.

Campbell, S. B. (1986). Developmental issues. In R. Gittelman (Ed.), *Anxiety disorders in children* (pp. 24–57). New York: Guilford.

Campos, J. J., Emde, R. N., Gaensbauer, T., & Henderson, C. (1975). Cardiac and behavioral interrelationships in the reactions of infants to strangers. *Developmental Psychology, 11,* 589–601.

Castaneda, A., McCandless, B. R., & Palermo, D. S. (1956). The children's form of the Manifest Anxiety Scale. *Child Development, 27,* 317–326.

Catania, J. J., Thompson, L. W., Michalewski, H. A., & Bowman, T. E. (1980). Comparison of sweat gland counts, electrodermal activity, and habituation behavior in young and old groups of subjects. *Psychophysiology, 17,* 146–152.

Clay, S. A., & Ramseyer, J. C. (1976). The orbicularis oculi reflex in infancy and childhood. *Neurology, 26,* 521–524.

Donaldson, M. (1978). *Children's minds.* New York: Norton.

Finch, A., & Kendall, P. (1979). The measurement of anxiety in children: Research findings and methodological problems. In A. J. Finch & P. C. Kendall (Eds.), *Clinical treatment and research in child psychopathology* (pp. 51–79). New York: Spectrum.

Finch. A. J., Jr., Kendall, P. C., Dannenburg, M. A., & Morgan, J. R. (1978). Effects of task difficulty on state-trait anxiety in emotionally disturbed children. *The Journal of Genetic Psychology, 133,* 253–259.

Finch, A. J., Jr., Montgomery, L. E., & Deardorff, P. A. (1947a). Children's Manifest Anxiety Scale: Reliability with emotionally disturbed children. *Psychological Reports, 34,* 658.

Finch, A. J., Jr., Montgomery, L. E., & Deardorff, P. A. (1974b). Reliability of state-trait anxiety with emotionally disturbed children. *Journal of Abnormal Child Psychology, 2,* 67–69.

Finch, A. J., Jr., & Nelson III, W. M. (1974). Anxiety and locus of conflict in emotionally disturbed children. *Journal of Abnormal Child Psychology, 2,* 33–37.

Finchan, F. (1981). Perception and moral evaluation in young children. *British Journal of Social Psychology, 20,* 265–270.

Foster, K. G., Hey, E. N., & Katz, G. (1969). The response of the sweat glands of the newborn baby to thermal stimuli and to intradermal acetylcholine. *Journal of Physiology, 203,* 13–29.

Garcia-Coll, C., Kagan, J., & Reznick, J. S. (1984). Behavioral inhibition in young children. *Child Development, 55,* 1005–1019.

Gottenbarn, R., & Cannella, C. (1987, November). *The relationship of age, gender, and IQ to children's ability to differentiate thoughts from emotional states.* Paper presented at the annual meeting of the Association for the Advancement of Behavior Therapy, Boston.

Graham, F. K. (1984). An affair of the heart. In M. G. H. Coles, J. K. Jennings, & J. Stern (Eds.), *Psychophysiology: A Festschrift for John and Beatrice Lacey* (pp. 12–29). New York: Van Nostrand Reinhold.

Graham, F. K., Berg, K. M., Berg, W. K., Jackson, J. C., Hatton, H. M., & Kantowitz, S. R. (1970). Cardiac orienting responses as a function of age. *Psychonomic Science. 19,* 363–365.

Graham, F. K., & Clifton, R. K. (1966). Heart-rate change as a component of the orienting response. *Psychological Bulletin, 65,* 305–320.

Harpin, V. A., & Rutter, N. (1982). Development of emotional sweating in the newborn infant. *Archives of Disease in Childhood, 57,* 691–695.

Harris, B. (1977). Developmental differences in the attributions of responsibility. *Developmental Psychology, 13,* 257–265.

Hoffman, M. L. (1981). Perspectives on the difference between understanding people and understanding things: The role of affect. In J. H. Flavell, & L. Ross (Eds.), *Social cognitive development: Frontiers and possible futures* (pp. 1–19). Cambridge: Cambridge University Press.

Jay, S. M., Ozolins, M., Elliott, C. H., & Caldwell, S. (1983). Assessment of children's distress during painful medical procedures. *Health Psychology, 2,* 133–147.

Juniper, K., & Dykman, R. A. (1967). Skin resistance, sweat gland counts, salivary flow, and gastric secretion: Age, race, and sex differences, and intercorrelations. *Psychophysiology, 4,* 216–222.

Kagan, J. (1980). Perspectives on continuity. In O. G. Brim, Jr., & J. Kagan (Eds.), *Constancy and change in human development* (pp. 26–74). Cambridge, MA: Harvard Univerisity Press.

Kagan, J. (1982). Heart rate and heart rate variability as signs of a temperamental dimension in infants. In C. E. Izard (Ed.), *Measuring emotions in infants and children* (pp. 38–66). Cambridge, MA: Cambridge University Press.

Kagan, J., Reznick, J. S., Clarke, C., Snidman, N., & Garcia-Coll, C. (1984). Behavioral inhibition to the unfamiliar. *Child Development, 55,* 2212–2225.

Kagan, J., Reznick, J. S., & Snidman, N. (1987). The physiology and psychology of behavioral inhibition in children. *Child Development, 58,* 1459–1473.

Katz, E. R., Kellerman, J., & Siegel, S. E. (1980). Behavioral distress in children with cancer undergoing medical procedures: Developmental considerations. *Journal of Consulting and Clinical Psychology, 48,* 356–365.

Kitano, H. H. L. (1960). Validity of Children's Manifest Anxiety Scale and the modified revised California Inventory. *Child Development, 31,* 67–72.

Kleinknect, R. A., Klepac, R. K., & Alexander, L. D. (1973). Origins and characteristics of fear of dentistry. *Journal of the American Dental Association, 86,* 842–848.

Kunzelman, H. D. (Ed.) (1970). *Precision teaching.* Seattle: Special Child Publications.

Lang, P. J. (1977). Physiological assessment of anxiety and fear. In J. D. Cone, & R. P. Hawkins (Eds.), *Behavioral assessment: New directions in clinical psychology* (pp. 178–195). New York: Brunner/Mazel.

LeBaron, S., & Zeltzer, L. (1984). Assessment of acute pain and anxiety in children and adolescents by self-reports, observer reports, and a behavior checklist. *Journal of Consulting and Clinical Psychology, 52,* 729–738.

Leitenberg, H., Yost, L. W., & Carrol-Wilson, M. (1986). Negative cognitive errors in children: Questionnaire development, normative data, and comparisons between children with and without self-reported symptoms of depression, low self-esteem, and evaluation anxiety. *Journal of Consulting and Clinical Psychology, 54,* 528–536.

Lerner, J. V., Hertzog, C., Hooker, K. A., Hassibi, M., & Thomas, A. (1988). A longitudinal study of negative emotional states and adjustment from early childhood through adolescence. *Child Development, 59,* 356–366.

Lore, R. (1966). Palmar sweating and transitory anxieties in children. *Child Development, 37,* 115–123.

Matthews, K. A., Rakaczky, C. J., Stoney, C. M., & Manuck, S. M. (1987). Are cardiovascular responses to behavioral stressors a stable individual difference variable in childhood? *Psychopathology, 24,* 464–473.

McCall, R. B. (1977). Challenges to a science of development psychology. *Child Development, 48,* 333–344.

Melamed, B. G., Yurcheson, R., Fleece, E. L., Hutcherson, S., & Hawes, R. (1978). Effects of film modeling on the reduction of anxiety related behaviors in individuals varying in level of previous experience in the stress situation. *Journal of Consulting and Clinical Psychology, 46,* 1357–1367.

Miller, L. C., Barrett, C. L., & Hampe, E. (1974). Phobias of childhood in a prescientific era. In A. Davis (Ed.), *Child personality and psychopathology: Current topics* (pp. 89–134). New York: Wiley.

Mineka, S., Suomi, S. J., & Delizio, R. D. (1981). Multiple separations in adolescent monkeys: An opponent-process interpretation. *Journal of Experimental Psychology: General, 110,* 56–85.

Montgomery, L. E., & Finch, A. J., Jr. (1974). Validity of two measures of anxiety in children. *Journal of Abnormal Child Psychology, 2,* 293–298.

Morrow, M. C., Boring, F. W., Keough, III, T. E., & Haesly, R. R. (1969). Differential GSR conditioning as a function of age. *Developmental Psychology, 1,* 299–302.

Nietzel, M. T., & Bernstein, D. A. (1981). Assessment of anxiety and fear. In M. Hersen, & A. S. Bellack (Eds.), *Behavioral assessment: A practical handbook* (2nd ed. pp. 215–245). New York: Pergamon.

Ollendick, T. H., & Meador, A. E. (1981). Behavioral assessment of children. In G. Goldstein & M. Hersen (Eds.), *Handbook of psychological assessment* (pp. 351–368). New York: Pergamon.

Ollendick, T. H., & Meyer, J. (1984). School phobia. In S. M. Turner (Ed.), *Behavioral theories and treatment of anxiety* (pp. 367–411). New York: Plenum.

Overton, W. F., & Reese, H. W. (1981). Conceptual prerequisites for an understanding of stability—change and continuity—discontinuity. *International Journal of Behavioral Development, 4,* 99–123.

Papay, J. P., Costello, R. J., Hedl, J. J., Jr., & Spielberger, C. D. (1975). Effects of trait and state anxiety on the performance of elementary school children in traditional and individualized multi-age classrooms. *Journal of Educational Psychology, 67,* 840–846.

Papay, J. P., & Spielberger, C. D. (1986). Assessment of anxiety and achievement in kindergarten and first- and second- grade children. *Journal of Abnormal Child Psychology, 14,* 279–286.

Plouffe, L., & Stelmack, R. (1984). The electrodermal orienting response and memory: An analysis of age differences in picture recall. *Psychophysiology, 21,* 191–198.

Porges, S. W., & Fox, N. A. (1986). Developmental psychophysiology. In M. G. H. Coles, E. Donchin, & S. W. Porges (Eds.), *Psychophysiology: Systems, processes, and applications* (pp. 611–625). New York: Guilford.

Quay, H. C., & Peterson, D. R. (1975). *Manual for the Behavior Problem Checklist* Unpublished manuscript.

Reynolds, C. R. (1980). Concurrent validity of What I Think and Feel: The Revised Children's Manifest Anxiety Scale. *Journal of Consulting and Clinical Psychology, 48,* 774–775.

Reynolds, C. R., & Richmond, B. O. (1978). What I Think and Feel: A revised measure of children's manifest anxiety. *Journal of Abnormal Child Psychology, 6,* 271–280.

Reznick, J. S., Kagan, J., Snidman, N., Gersten, M., Boak, K., & Rosenberg, A. (1986). Inhibited and uninhibited children: A follow-up study. *Child Development, 57,* 660–680.

Sarason, S. B., Davidson, K. S., Lighthall, F. F., Waite, R. R., & Ruebush, B. K. (1960). *Anxiety in elementary school children.* New York: Wiley.

Seidner, L. B., Stypek, D. J., & Feshbach, N. D. (1986). A developmental analysis of elementary school-aged children's concepts of pride and embarrassment. *Child Development, 59,* 367–377.

Spielberger, C. D. (1973). *State-Trait Anxiety Inventory for Children: Preliminary Manual.* Palo Alto: Consulting Psychologists Press.

Spielberger, C. D., Pollans, C., & Worden, T. J. (1984). Anxiety disorders. In M. Hersen & S. M. Turner (Eds.), *Handbook of adult psychopathology* (pp. 263–303). New York: Wiley.

Sroufe, L. A., & Waters, E. (1977). Heart rate as a convergent measure in clinical and developmental research. *Merrill-Palmer Quarterly, 23,* 3–27.

Stavrababi, C., Vargo, B., Boodoosingh, L., & Roberts, N. (1987). The relationship between anxiety and depression in children: Rating scales and clinical variables. *American Journal of Psychiatry, 32,* 433–439.

Suomi, S. J. (1986). Anxiety-like disorders in young nonhuman primates. In R. Gittelman (Ed.), *Anxiety disorders of childhood* (pp. 1–23). New York: Guilford.

Thomas, A., & Chess, S. (1977). *Temperament and development.* New York: Brunner/Mazel.

Turner, S. M., Beidel, D. C., & Epstein, L. E. (1988). Emotion, EMG, SCR, and heart rate in anxious children. Unpublished manuscript, University of Pittsburgh.

Van Hasselt, V. B., Hersen, M., Bellack, A. S., Rosenblum, M. D., & Lamparski, D. (1979). Tripartite assessment of the effects of systematic desensitization in a multi-phobic child: An experimental analysis. *Journal of Behavior Therapy and Experimental Psychiatry, 10,* 51–55.

Venham, L., Bengston, D., & Cipes, M. (1977). Children's response to sequential dental visits. *Journal of Dental Research, 56,* 454–459.

Werry, J. S., & Amen, M. G. (1980). Anxiety in children. In G. D. Burrows & B. M. Davies (Eds.), *Handbook of studies in anxiety* (pp. 165–192). Amsterdam: ASP Biological and Medical Press.

Winer, G. A. (1982). A review and analysis of children's fearful behavior in dental settings. *Child Development, 53,* 1111–1133.

Zatz, S., & Chassin, L. (1985). Cognitions of test-anxious children under naturalistic test-taking conditions. *Journal of Consulting and Clinical Psychology, 53,* 393–401.

CHAPTER 11

Conclusions and Future Directions

Cynthia G. Last

In this book, we have attempted to depict a lifespan or developmental approach toward understanding the anxiety disorders. As is evident from the preceding chapters, conceptualizing anxiety disorders in this manner still is in its infancy, thereby explaining the relative lack of empirically rigorous investigations that directly address these issues.

Chapter 1 delineated three main avenues of inquiry that are appropriate to a lifespan perspective: (a) exploring phenomenological differences and similarities among children, adolescents, and adults experiencing the same disorders; (b) observing predictive links between different developmental stages; and (c) investigating the possible intergenerational expression of the same or similar disorders. Conclusions and directions for future research in each of these three areas is delineated subsequently.

PHENOMENOLOGICAL DIFFERENCES AND SIMILARITIES

OCD

As discussed at length in chapter 9, OCD is one of the few, if not the only, anxiety disorders that appears to express itself relatively similarly across the lifespan. Studies of clinically referred children and adolescents with the disorder suggest that these youngsters are similar to their adult counterparts in that (a) obsessions without compulsions are rare, (b) multiple rituals are common, (c) the most common compulsive ritual is washing/cleaning, and (d) comorbid anxiety disorders are common (Last & Strauss, 1989a; Rapoport, 1986). By contrast, OCD youngsters and adults tend to differ in sex distribution and history of affective disorders: in children and adolescents, OCD is more common among boys, and history of depressive disorder is relatively rare (Adams, 1973; Despert, 1955; Hollingsworth, Tanguay, Grossman, & Pabst, 1980; Last & Strauss, 1989a; Rapoport, 1986; Swedo & Rapoport, 1990).

Panic Disorder

As discussed in chapter 1, considerable controversy currently exists regarding whether "spontaneous" panic attacks exist in young (pre-pubertal) children. Several reports have documented cases of panic disorder in *adolescents* (Alessi, Robbins, & Dilsaver, 1987; Last & Strauss, 1989b; Macaulay & Klein Knecht, 1989), but extremely few have done so for young children, and of those few cases, the question of situation-specific panic (e.g., as part of separation anxiety disorder), rather than spontaneous panic, has been raised (see Last & Strauss, 1989b).

As for adults with panic disorder (Hoehn-Saric & McLeod, 1988), panic disorder in adolescents tends to be overrepresented among females (Alessi et al., 1987; Last & Strauss, 1989b; Macaulay & Klein Knecht, 1989). The relatively high comorbid rate for depressive disorder in adult panic disorders (Barlow, DiNardo, Vermilyea, et al., 1986) has yet to be extended to adolescent samples. Last and Strauss (1989b) found a comorbid rate of only 12% for depressive disorders (although lifetime prevalence was considerably higher at 35%). By contrast, Alessi et al. (1987) reported that 70% of their panic-disordered adolescents showed comorbid depressive disorders—however, their sample consisted of inpatient youngsters, which might have accounted for this finding.

GAD

Whether children and adolescents manifest this disorder remains controversial. Recent data from Last, Perrin, Hersen, and Kazdin (1991) indicate that not 1 of 104 youngsters referred to a child and adolescent anxiety disorder clinic met DSM-III-R criteria for GAD. Similar observations have been reported by other researchers in this field (Kendall, personal communication; Silverman, personal communication). As discussed in chapters 1 and 4, whether overanxious disorder is the childhood "version" of GAD remains an empirical question. The issue currently is being raised in relationship to the forthcoming DSM-IV.

Simple and Social Phobias

A key issue in comparing children, adolescents, and adults with phobic disorders is the developmental appropriateness of the fear. Several studies have documented the normative nature of certain specific fears at various age levels (e.g., Ollendick, Matson, & Helsel, 1985). When a phobic disorder is diagnosed (according to DSM-III-R criteria) in children or adolescents, the implication is that the fear is either not age appropriate or more excessive than what would be expected at that age level. The clinical features of phobic disorders in children, adolescents, and adults on the whole are quite similar, with one important distinction: children and adolescents often do not recognize (or at least admit) that their fear is excessive or unreasonable, which is one of the required DSM-III-R criterion for the disorder. DSM-IV will need to grapple with this developmental issue in its revision.

Empirically rigorous studies of clinically referred children and adolescents with phobic disorders are quite rare. Rather, most of the information we currently have relies on follow-back (retrospective) studies of adult phobic patients. Future studies are needed of child and adolescent samples to further understand potential phenomenological similarities and differences for these disorders across the lifespan.

PTSD

Given the recency of the inclusion of PTSD in the DSM system (APA, 1980), it is only during the past decade that research findings have appeared in the literature. Most of these reports have focused on adult populations (see Keane, Litz, & Blake, 1990), although, in the past few years, a few investigations have examined the disorder in children (see Eth, 1990). It appears that the core characteristics of PTSD—reexperiencing the trauma, psychic numbing, and increased arousal—occur in children, adolescents, and adults who are diagnosed with the condition. Young children also may show regressive behavior, however, in addition to the other features of the disorder. Such regressive behavior may include separation or stranger anxiety, use of transitional objects, and enureisis/ encopresis. In addition, unlike their adult counterparts, children who have experienced a traumatic event usually do not exhibit denial or repression of the trauma, and generally do not report "flashbacks" (although they do report intrusive memories). Eth (1990) has speculated that these cognitive differences between children and adults with PTSD may reflect neuropsychological dissimilarities between the two age groups that have as yet been undefined.

PREDICTIVE LINKS

SAD and Panic Disorders

The hypothesis that childhood SAD is a risk factor for the development of adult-onset panic disorder has appeared in the clinical literature for decades. As discussed at length in chapter 8, current empirical data on the whole do not support such a relationship. Recent available data from family (Last, Hersen, Kazdin, Orvaschel, & Perrin, 1991) and follow-up

(Last, Hersen, Kazdin, & Perrin, 1991) studies also do not support such a relationship. As detailed in chapter 6, the lifetime psychiatric history of first-degree relatives of 28 DSM-III-R diagnosed separation anxious children did not reveal an increased rate of panic disorder (2.7%) compared with the first-degree relatives of (a) children with other types of anxiety disorders (0.0%), (b) children with ADHD (2.0%), and (c) children who had never been psychiatrically ill (0.4%). Of interest, elevated rates of panic disorder were found in the first-degree relatives of children with *overanxious disorder* (11.5%). Replication of our findings with larger samples of SAD and OAD children is warranted.

Our recent prospective data also do not support a relationship between SAD and panic disorder. Not one of these youngsters developed panic disorder during the 2-year follow-up period. Of course, extended follow-up, as the children enter late adolescence and early adulthood, may reveal a different pattern of findings.

OAD and GAD

Because of certain phenomenological similarities between childhood and adolescent OAD and adult-onset GAD, a relationship between the two disorders has been suggested. Recent available data from family (Last, Hersen, Kazdin, Oraschel, & Perrin, 1991) and follow-up (Last, Hersen, Kazdin, & Perrin, 1991) studies do not support such a relationship. Again, as detailed in Chapter 6, the lifetime psychiatric history of first-degree relatives of 17 DSM-III-R–diagnosed overanxious-disordered children did not reveal an increased rate of GAD (3.8%) compared with the first-degree relatives of (a) SAD children (4.2%), (b) children with other anxiety disorders (0.8%), (c) ADHD children (2.0%), and never psychiatrically ill children (0.9%). Replication of these results with a larger sample of OAD youngsters is needed.

As for SAD and panic disorders, our prospective data do not support a relationship between OAD and GAD. Not one of these youngsters developed GAD during the follow-up period. Again, extended follow-up may reveal a different pattern of findings.

Childhood Anxiety Disorder and Adolescent-Adult Anxiety Disorder

Whether anxiety disorders in childhood predict the development of additional anxiety disorders in adolescence and adulthood has yet to be determined. Information from adult anxiety-disordered patients in followback or retrospective studies is suggestive but far from conclusive. Our recent prospective follow-up study of DSM-III-R diagnosed anxiety-disordered children indicated that these children were at increased risk for developing additional (new) anxiety disorders relative to normal (never psychiatrically disturbed) children, but that they did not significantly differ from psychopathological control (ADHD) children in risk rates. Thus, it is possible that anxiety disorders are equally likely to develop in adolescents and adults with a childhood history of *any type* of psychiatric disorder, not specifically those with a childhood history of anxiety disorder.

Childhood Anxiety Disorder and Adolescent-Adult Depressive Disorder

A large body of literature has suggested a relationship between anxiety and depressive disorders in both children and adolescents, and adults (e.g., Barlow et al., 1986; Last, Strauss, & Francis, 1987; Strauss, Last, Hersen, & Kazdin, 1988). In our recent prospective, follow-up study, we did not find that anxiety-disordered children were at risk to develop depressive disorders. Given the relatively young ages of the children in the study, however, it is possible that further extended follow-up may reveal a different pattern of results, as the children enter late adolescence and early adulthood.

INTERGENERATIONAL EXPRESSION

OCD

Whether OCD "runs" in families remains inconclusive. Data from our family study showed an increased risk of OCD in the first-degree relatives of children with OCD. These results are consistent with findings from a recent uncontrolled family study of the disorder (Lenane, Swedo, Leonard et al., 1990) and findings from previous genetic research (see chapter 7). As Emmelkamp (1990) has noted, however, although older twin studies found a higher frequency of OCD in MZ cases compared with DZ cases, the studies were far from representative, and more recent studies are too insufficient to draw firm conclusions.

PD

Available data from familial aggregation studies support the notion that panic disorder runs in families (Harris, Noyes, Crowe, & Chaudhry, 1983; Last, Hersen, Kazdin, Orvaschel, & Perrin, 1991). Moreover, as indicated by Torgersen in chapter 7, there is fairly strong evidence to suggest that genetic factors are involved in their transmission.

GAD

Unlike panic disorder, genetic factors do not appear to be involved in the pathogenesis of GAD (see chapter 7). Whether the disorder even "runs" in families remains uncertain. In a family study conducted by Cloninger, Martin, Clayton, and Guze (1982), results showed an excess of "anxiety neurosis" in families of patients with panic disorder but not in those with anxiety disorder *without* panic. In a more recent study, Noyes et al. (1987) found that the frequency of GAD was higher among first-degree relatives of GAD probands compared with controls but *not* when compared with the relatives of panic disorder probands.

Simple and Social Phobias

The role of genetic factors in the development of clinical phobias is inconclusive but suggestive (see chapter 7). In addition to genetic research, there is a relatively large body of data showing significant correlations between children's and mother's fears, as well as children's and sibling's fears. The relationship for phobia *disorders* is less clear, however. In our family study of anxiety-disordered children, neither simple nor social phobic disorders were found to run in families. By contrast, in a family study of adult probands, Reich and Yates (1988) found the prevalence of DSM-III–diagnosed social phobia to be higher in the relatives of social phobics than the relatives of panic disorder patients. Further examination of the intergenerational expression of phobic disorders is warranted.

PTSD

Given the nature of this disorder, one might predict that PTSD has less of a genetic component involved in its pathogenesis. As noted by Keane, Litz, and Blake (1990), however, it may be that certain individuals inherit a psychological vulnerability, through a positive family history, that increases the risk of developing PTSD under stress. To our knowledge, to date only one study has been published that has examined the prevalence of psychiatric illness in the families of PTSD patients (Davidson, Swartz, Storck, Krishnan, & Hammett, 1985). Davidson et al. found that two thirds of the PTSD sample had family histories that were positive for psychopathology, but this rate was no higher (and, in fact, was lower) than rates obtained in depressed (79%) and GAD (93%) samples.

SAD

Family studies of SAD have been rare. More typically, the relationship between agoraphobia (panic disorder) in the adult and SAD in the offspring has been observed. Findings from family concordance studies have been conflicting regarding support for a relationship between SAD and adult agoraphobia/panic disorder. Weissman, Leckman, Merikangas, Gammon, and Prusoff (1984) compared children of women with major depression with or without a history of anxiety disorder and a group of matched normal control subjects, using the family history method to diagnose offspring. Depressed probands with concurrent anxiety disorders were divided into three groups: those with (a) depression and agoraphobia, (b) depression and panic disorder, and (c) depression and generalized anxiety disorder. Results indicated an increased risk of SAD in the offspring of women with depression and panic disorders, with 36.8% of offspring meeting DSM-III criteria for the diagnosis. None of the offspring of normal or depressed-only probands met criteria for SAD. In the other two depression plus anxiety disorder groups, relatively low rates were obtained for SAD, with 11.1% of children of agoraphobic probands and 6.3% of children of GAD probands meeting diagnostic criteria. When the offspring of agoraphobic and panic-disordered women were combined, the risk of SAD decreased to 24.3%, a rate still greater than in the other groups.

Although these data are important, it should be noted that the possible effect of comorbid depressive disorders in the probands cannot be evaluated because a group of offspring of probands with anxiety disorders without depressive disorder were not included in this study. Also, the lack of results for the agoraphobic group is confusing, given that research (and the current DSM-III-R) indicates that agoraphobia and panic disorder are variants of the same disorder. Finally, an attempt by the investigators to replicate their original findings using the family study method (direct interviews of offspring) failed to support previous findings (Mufson, Weissman, & Warner, 1991).

In our family study of relatives of anxiety-disordered children, we investigated whether the first-degree relatives of children with SAD showed an increased risk of panic disorder and SAD. The prevalence of panic disorder in the relatives of SAD children was quite low (2.7%), and did not differ from other anxiety disorder groups, a psychopathological control group, and a normal control group. Childhood history of SAD in the relatives was more prevalent at 10.3%. This rate differed from that observed for relatives of children with other anxiety disorders (3.4%), ADHD children (5.6%), and normal children (4.3%), but *not* from OAD children (18.8%).

OAD

The only study, to our knowledge, to examine the aggregation of over-anxious disorder in families is our recent family study (Last, Hersen, Kazdin, Orvaschel, & Perrin, 1991). A history of OAD was present in 29.8% of the first-degree relatives of OAD children, but this rate did not differ significantly from the rate of OAD present in the relatives of SAD children (23.7%); however, it did differ from rates evident for the relatives of children with other types of anxiety disorders (11.0%), the relatives of ADHD children (10.3%), and the relatives of normal children (8.1%). Additional research investigating this issue remains to be conducted.

Avoidant Disorder

This childhood anxiety disorder has received extremely little research. Available preliminary data from our family study suggests that the disorder does not run in families. Considerably more research is needed in this area before conclusions can be drawn.

FUTURE DIRECTIONS

A lifespan or developmental approach to the study of psychiatric disorders is a relatively new endeavor, still in its "infancy." For the anxiety disorders, empirically rigorous prospective studies of large samples of clinically referred anxious children are sorely needed to address their course and outcome throughout the developmental stages. Alternative measurement and classification systems should be explored for identifying anxiety in prepubertal youngsters, as the phenomenology of anxiety in young children may manifest itself, and thus needs to be assessed or classified differently from adolescents and adults. Finally cross-sectional, large-scale epidemiological investigations of anxiety symptoms and disorders need to be undertaken to further our understanding of normal versus psychopathological anxiety at different stages across the lifespan.

REFERENCES

Adams, P. (1973). *Obsessive children.* New York: Penguin.

Alessi, N. E., Robbins, D. R., & Dilsaver, S. C. (1987). Panic and depressive disorders among psychiatrically hospitalized adolescents. *Psychiatry Research, 20,* 275–283.

Barlow, D. H., DiNardo, P. A., Vermilyea, J. A., et al. (1986). Co-morbidity and depression among the anxiety disorders: Issues in diagnosis and classification. *Journal of Nervous and Mental Disorders, 174,* 63–72.

Cloninger, C. R., Martin, R. L., Clayton, P., & Guze, S. B. (1982). A blind follow-up and family study of anxiety neurosis: Preliminary analysis of the St. Louis 500. In D. F. Klein & J. G. Rabkin (Eds.), *Anxiety: New research and changing concepts* (pp. 137–154). New York: Raven.

Davidson, J., Swartz, M., Storck, M., Krishian, R. R., & Hammett, E. (1985). A diagnostic and family study of posttraumatic stress disorders. *American Journal of Psychiatry, 142,* 90–93.

Despert, L. (1955). Differential diagnosis between obsessive-compulsive neurosis and schizophrenia in children. In P. H. Hoch & J. Zubin (Eds.), *Psychology of childhood.* New York: Grune & Stratton.

Emmelkamp, P. M. G. (1990). Obsessive compulsive disorder in adulthood. In M. Heiser & C. G. Last (Eds.), *Handbook of child and adult psychopathology: A longitudinal perspective* (pp. 221–234). New York: Pergamon.

Eth, S. (1990). Post-traumatic stress disorders in childhood. In M. Heiser and C. G. Last (Eds.), *Handbook of child and adult psychopathology: A longitudinal perspective* (pp. 263–274). New York: Pergamon.

Harris, E. L., Noyes, R., Crowe, R. R., Chaudhry, D. R. (1983). Family study of agoraphobia: Report of a pilot study. *Archives of General Psychiatry, 40,* 1061–1064.

Hoehn-Saric, R., & McLeod, D. R. (1988). Panic and generalized anxiety disorders. In C. G. Last & M. Heiser (Eds.), *Handbook of anxiety disorders* (pp. 109–126). New York: Pergamon.

Hollingsworth, C., Tanguay, P., Grossman, L., & Pabst, P. (1980). Long-term outcome of obsessive-compulsive disorders in childhood. *Journal of the American Academy of Child Psychiatry, 19,* 134–144.

Keane, T. M., Litz, B. T., & Blake, D. D. (1990). Post-traumatic stress disorder in adulthood. In M. Heiser and C. G. Last (Eds.), *Handbook of child and adult psychopathology: A longitudinal perspective* (pp. 275–291). New York: Pergamon.

Last, C. G., Hersen, M., Kazdin, A. E., Orvaschel, H., & Perrin, S. (1991). Anxiety disorders in children and their families. *Archives of General Psychiatry, 48,* 928–934.

Last, C. G., Hersen, M., Kazdin, A. E., & Perrin, S. (1991). *Prospective study of anxiety disordered children.* Manuscript submitted for publication.

Last, C. G., Perrin, S., Hersen, M., & Kazdin, A. E. (1991). *DSM-III-R anxiety disorders in children: Sociodemographic and clinical characteristics.* Manuscript submitted for publication.

Last, C. G. & Strauss, C. C. (1989a). Obsessive-compulsive disorder in childhood. *Journal of Anxiety Disorders, 3,* 295–302.

Last, C. G., & Strauss, C. C. (1989b). Panic disorder in children and adolescents. *Journal of Anxiety Disorders, 3,* 87–95.

Last, C. G., Strauss, C. C., & Francis, G. (1987). Comorbidity among childhood anxiety disorders. *Journal of Nervous and Mental Disease, 175,* 726–730.

Lenane, M. C., Swedo, S. E., Leonard, H., et al. (1990). Psychiatric disorders in first degree relatives of children and adolescents with obsessive compulsive disorders. *Journal of the American Academy of Childhood Adolescent Psychiatry, 29,* 407–412.

Macauley, J. L., & Klein Knecht, R. A. (1989). Panic and panic attacks in adolescents. *Journal of Anxiety Disorders, 3,* 221–241.

Mufson, L., Weissman, M. M., & Warner, V. (1991). *Depression and anxiety in parents and children: A direct interview study.* Manuscript submitted for publication.

Noyes, R., Clarkson, C., Crowe, R. R., Yates, W. R., & McChesney, C. M. (1987). A family study of generalized anxiety disorders. *American Journal of Psychiatry, 144,* 1019–1024.

Ollendick, T. H., Matson, J. L., Helsel, W. J. (1985). Fears in children and adolescents: Normative data. *Behavior Research and Therapy, 4,* 465–467.

Rapoport, J. L. (1986). Annotation childhood obsessive compulsive disorder. *Journal of Child Psychology and Psychiatry, 27,* 289–295.

Reich, J., & Yates, W. (1988). Family history of psychiatric disorders in social phobia. *Comprehensive Psychiatry, 29,* 72–75.

Strauss, C. C., Last, C. G., Hersen, M., & Kazdin, A. E. (1988). Association between anxiety and depression in children and adolescents with anxiety disorders. *Journal of Abnormal Child Psychology, 15,* 57–68.

Swedo, S. E., & Rapoport, J. L. (1990). Obsessive compulsive disorder in childhood. In M. Heiser and C. G. Last (Eds.), *Handbook of child and adult psychopathology: A longitudinal perspective* (pp. 211–220). New York: Pergamon.

Weissman, M. M., Leckman, J. F., Merikangas, K. R., Gammon, G. D., & Prusoff, B. A. (1984). Depression and anxiety disorders in parents and children: Results from the Yale Family Study. *Archives of General Psychiatry, 41,* 845–852.

Index

Adjustment disorder, 81, 115
Adolescents, anxiety in, 3, 43; *see also*
    Children, anxiety in
  coping methods for, 46
  dental, 192
  fears, 42, 70–71, 170
  obsessive-compulsive disorder, 43,
    50–51, 149, 151, 153, 204
  overanxious disorder, 4, 5, 43, 69
  panic disorder, 43, 49, 80, 105
  school study of, 43, 46, 50
  separation anxiety, 65, 66
  social phobia, 18, 74
Adoption studies, 114
Adult anxiety instruments, 1; *see also*
    various scales
Affector system, 171
Aggressivity, 47
Agoraphobia, 5, 21, 52, 81–82, 99
  age of onset of, 71, 72, 81
  diagnostic classification of, 11
  and gender, 20, 137
  in high-risk children, 55, 56
  and panic attacks, 129
  and school phobia, 71, 81, 84, 90,
    97, 133, 136
  and separation anxiety hypothesis,
    136–143, 210
Amitriptyline, 156
Animal phobias, 18, 20, 70, 71, 73
Anticipatory anxiety, 17, 176, 192
Antidepressants, 133–134, 156–158,
    160–161
Anxiety
  categories of, 130
  in children, 1–5; *see also* Children,
    anxiety in
  descriptive/psychometric data for,
    18
  DSM diagnosis scheme for, 1, 4; *see
    also* DSM diagnostic categories

intergenerational expression of, 5, 6,
    57–58, 204, 208–211; *see also* Ge-
    netic transmission
  measurement of, 1, 170–198; *see
    also* various scales
  in pediatric patients, 51–52, 194–
    195
  predictive links in, 4–5, 204, 206–
    208
  studies of using DSM-III criteria, 42–
    58
  treatment age for, 18
  twin studies in, 120–122
Anxiety Disorders Interview Schedule
    (ADIS), 14–18
Anxiety labels, 185–186, 190
Anxiety proneness, 109, 168, 184
Anxiety Sensitivity Index, 49
Anxiety-depression relationship, 28–30,
    31, 123–124, 208
Apocrine glands, 176
Attention deficit hyperactivity disorder
    (ADHD), 47, 69, 103–108
Avoidant disorder, 30, 38, 132, 211
  in first-degree relatives, 105
  in high-risk children, 54, 55
  in infants, 194
  prevalence of, 43, 48, 52
  and school phobia, 80

Bayley Infant Behavior Profile, 114
Beck Depression Inventory (BDI), 20
Bedtime rituals, 158
Behavior disorders; *see also* Attention
    deficit hyperactivity disorder
  and fears/worries, 41
  prevalence of, 43, 47, 48
Behavior Problem Checklist, 194
Behavior therapy, 153–155, 158–160
Behavioral assessment, 191, 194–197
  errors in, 196

Behavioral inhibition, 168–169, 174, 176, 198
Blood pressure, 172, 175
Bowlby, J., 134, 174
Brain-vagus-heart axis, 173
British Social Adjustment Guides, 89

Cardiovascular system, 169–176; *see also* Heart rate
developmental changes in, 172, 180
Catastrophizing, 189, 190
Center for Stress and Anxiety Disorder (SUNY Albany), 14
Child and Adolescent Anxiety Disorder Clinic, Western Psychiatric Institute and Clinic, 73, 187
Child Assessment Schedule (CAS), 52, 57, 96
Child Behavior Checklist (CBCL), 24, 47, 51, 194, 196
Child Global Assessment Scale (C-GAS), 47–48
Childhood History Questionnaire, 101
Children, anxiety in, 1–5, 21, 30, 114; *see also* various disorders
bottom-up studies of, 100–109
and developmental stages, 180–190
as different from adult anxiety, 1–2, 21, 27
vs. feelings of pain, 186–187
genetic factors in, 120, 124; *see also* Twin studies
high-risk, 52–58
interventions for, 2
lack of longitudinal studies of, 37, 38, 58
measurement of, 1, 170–198; *see also* various scales
overt signs of, 191–196
prevalence rates for, 43, 58, 105
self-monitoring in, 196–197
self-reports of, 183–185
and somatic complaints, 3, 58, 65, 67, 118, 132, 171–180
symptoms of, 41–42
top-down studies of, 96–99
variables in, 21–24, 40
Children at Risk for Affective Disorders Study, 57
Children's Anxiety Evaluation Form (CAEF), 13, 23

Children's Manifest Anxiety Scale (CMAS), 1, 2, 183
Revised (RCMAS), 23, 24, 183
Children's Negative Cognitive Error Questionnaire (CNEQ), 183, 189–190
Classification, 7, 30, 31, 32, 211
Cleaning rituals, 150, 152, 204
Clomipramine, 134, 156, 157, 158, 159–162
use of in children, 160–161, 162
Cognition, 180–190
and developmental stages, 181–182
vs. emotion, 188–189
errors in, 190
"hot" vs. "cool," 188
and self-report tools, 182–183
Cognitive-Somatic Anxiety Questionnaires (CSAQS), 20
Comorbidity, 24–27, 30–31, 40, 43, 48
Compulsions, 148; *see also* Obsessive-compulsive disorder
Concrete operations period, 182
Conduct disorder; *see* Behavior disorder
Continuity, 167, 168, 197
Coping skills, 46, 82, 189
COUNTOONS, 196

Dark, fear of, 4, 70, 73
Delusion-Symptoms-States Inventory, 119
Dental anxiety, 191–192, 196
Dependency, 82–83
Depressive disorder, 5, 25, 123–124; *see also* Antidepressants, Anxiety-depression relationship
children's ability to recognize, 187
genetic/environmental bases for, 123
and loss, 140
and obsessive-compulsive disorder, 155
in older overanxious-disorder children, 69
in parents, 54, 56, 57, 97–98, 123
Desipramine, 156, 157
Developmental stages, 31–32, 113, 168
and anxiety, 180–190
and cognition, 181–182
and predictive links, 4–5

Diagnostic Interview for Children and
   Adolescents (DICA), 15, 38, 46, 52,
   57
Diagnostic Interview Schedule for
   Children (DISC), 13, 38, 47, 51, 52,
   56
   Addendum for Compulsive Personality Disorder, 50
Diagnostic interviews, 37
"Difficult child cluster," 115
Doubt/checking, 151
DSM diagnostic categories, 1, 3, 4, 7–
   12, 30–32, 63, 128–131, 207–208
   alternatives to, 32
   DSM-II, 8, 9–10, 128
   DSM-III, 8, 9–11, 128, 130
   DSM-III-R, 8, 9, 10–12, 128–131, 142
   DSM-IV, 130, 205, 206
   lack of child/adult differentiation in,
   9
   multiaxial system, 8–9
   and school phobia, 78–80, 90
   studies predating, 38–42
   studies using, 38–58
   validity of; see Validity studies
Dunedin Multidisciplinary Health and
   Development Research Unit (New
   Zealand), 46

Eccrine glands, 176
Effector system, 171
Egocentrism, 181
Electrodermal system, 171, 176–180
   and age, 177–180
Embarrassment, 185–186
Emotional disorders, risk factor for,
   52
Environmental events, 109, 124
   and fear response, 172
   and generalized anxiety disorder,
   121
   in monozygotic twins, 114
Epidemiology, 37, 211
Exclusionary rules (DSM), 11–12, 24,
   27
Exposure therapy, 132, 153–155, 157–
   159, 166
   in children and adolescents, 158–
   159
   imaginal, 155, 159
Extinction procedures, 159, 160, 161

Familiar aggregation, of psychiatric
   disorders, 5, 28, 94–95, 113; see
   also Depression, in parents
   male vs. female relatives in, 106,
   108, 110
   mother–child dyad in, 101, 102, 108,
   209, 210
   and parents' psychiatric diagnoses,
   52–58, 96, 97–99
Family history method, 94, 95, 97, 98,
   104, 108
Family study method, 94, 95, 102, 103,
   108
Fear Questionnaire (FQ), 20, 21
Fear Survey Schedule for Children, 1,
   2, 23, 24, 194
Fearfulness, 114–115, 120
Fears, 3; see also Panic disorder,
   Phobic disorder
   adult-onset, 40–41
   by age group, 18, 40, 63, 169, 183,
   205
   and behavior problems, 41
   changes in, 63–64, 73
   and cognition, 181
   developmental sequence of, 169
   and maturational changes, 170
   specific, 4, 18, 20, 24, 40–42, 73, 74–75
   twin studies of, 118–120
Fink, M., 134
Fluoxetine, 157, 158, 161
Fluvoxamine, 157
Formal operations period, 182
Freud, Sigmund, on anxiety, 134

Gender, in distribution of anxiety disorders, 20, 21–23, 40, 137
   in agoraphobia, 137
   among children, 23, 43, 47, 48, 49
General Health Questionnaire (GHQ),
   87
Generalized anxiety disorder, 20, 207
   in adults, 25, 56–57, 99
   in children, 3, 205
   diagnosis of, 14, 17
   genetic factors in, 121, 124, 209
   onset of, 18
   and school phobia, 81
Genetic linkage studies, 114, 122, 124
Genetic transmission, 109, 113, 124;
   see also Twin studies

Hamilton Anxiety Scale, 14, 20
Headache, 3, 65, 132
Heart rate
    as anxiety indicator, 174–176
    in behavioral inhibition, 169, 174,
        176
    developmental changes in, 172, 173,
        175
    in infants, 170, 171, 172–175, 176
Hypochondriasis, 42, 81

ICD-10 classification, 78, 79, 81
Imipramine, 133, 156
Incidence, in epidemiology, 37
Infancy
    egocentrism in, 181
    somatic response in, 170, 171–173
    stranger fear in, 170, 193
    testing in, 173
    wariness in, 193
Information processing, 171
Insulin-dependent diabetes mellitus,
    51–52
Interview protocols, 12, 95–96; see
    also various interview schedules
Interview Schedule for Children, 13,
    52, 96
IQ, 188

Junior Eysenck Personality Inventory,
    89

Klein, D. F., 134

Language, development of, 182
Leeds Scale, 85, 86, 87
Leyton Obsessive Inventory—Child
    Version (LOI-CV), 50, 51
Life events, assessment of, 134, 140,
    141–142
Lifetime diagnoses, 95

Matching, in experimental subjects,
    198
Maturation
    cognitive, 176
    and continuity, 167, 168, 197
    and fear response, 169, 170, 191–193
    influence of on testing, 175
    physical, 170–180, 190, 193

Middlesex Hospital Questionnaire, 118
Multitract-multimethod assessment
    strategy, 27
Muscular control, 191, 193, 196

Neural development, 172–173
Neuroticism, 115, 117–118, 130
New York Longitudinal Study, 115, 168
Nightmares, 41, 65, 184
NIMH Clinical Research Branch Col-
    laborative Psychobiology of De-
    pression Study, 57
NIMH Diagnostic Interview Schedule
    for Children, 96
Nortriptyline, 156

Observational Scale of Behavioral Dis-
    tress (OSBD), 194, 195
Obsessive thoughts/rituals, 50, 148,
    151, 159
Obsessive-compulsive disorder (OCD)
    in adolescents, 43, 50–51, 149, 151,
        153, 155, 158, 159, 161
    age of onset of, 18, 49, 149, 161
    case examples of, 151–153
    in children, 149, 150, 152, 155, 161,
        204
    and comorbidity, 50, 204
    and depression, 20, 25, 50, 158
    epidemiology of, 148–151
    in first-degree relatives, 106, 107,
        110, 208
    in high-risk children, 54–56
    prevalence of, 149–151, 161
    remission in, 149, 161
    and school phobia, 81
    and socioeconomic status, 20
    treatment of, 153–161
    twin studies of, 121, 208
Ordering, as ritual, 152–153
Orienting response, 171–173
Overanxious disorder (OAD), 4, 38, 66,
    68–70, 132, 205, 207
    in adolescents, 4, 5, 43, 58, 69
    age differences in, 69–70, 74
    comorbidity in, 25, 69
    in first-degree relatives, 101, 106,
        107, 211
    and gender, 23, 47
    in high-risk children, 54, 56, 57, 58
    prevalence of, 48, 52

and school phobia, 80
symptoms of, 68–69
testing for, 24

Palmar sweat index, 177
Panic attack, 49, 56, 121, 129
    in children, 49, 205
    in DSM-III-R, 129
    genetic basis for, 122, 124
    imipramine for, 134
    and phobia, 129
Panic disorder
    in adolescents, 43, 49, 80, 205
    in adults, 25, 99, 205
    with agoraphobia, 20, 129
    in children, 3, 49, 52, 54, 55, 205
    in first-degree relatives, 106, 107,
        108–109
    and gender, 20, 49, 205
    genetic basis for, 122, 208
    in high-risk children, 54–56
    onset of, 18
    and separation anxiety, 129–130,
        136
    and stressful life events, 141–142
    twin studies of, 121–122
Parental death, 138
Parents; see Familial aggregation
Phasic responses, 176, 177–179
    and aging, 178–179
Phobic disorders, 14–15, 70–74, 75,
        205–206; see also Agoraphobia,
        Fears, School phobia, Social
        phobia
    and comorbidity, 25
    and developmental stage, 4, 70, 72–
        73, 74
    and gender, 20
    genetic factors in, 121, 209
    in high-risk children, 54–55, 56
Piaget, Jean, 181, 182
Polygraph, 177, 179
Posttraumatic stress disorder (PTSD),
        81, 206, 209
Predictive links, 4–5, 204
Prevalence, in epidemiology, 37
Primitive reactivity, 171, 172, 174
Problem Behavior Check List (PBCL),
        195
Psychodynamic therapy, 130
Psychopathology

developmental, 3, 32, 167
    symptom prevalence in, 41
Psychophysiology, developmental, 171,
        179, 198
Psychosomatic Symptom Survey
        (PSSS), 20

Reassurance seeking, 159–160
Regressive behavior, 206
Relaxation therapy, 154
Response cost procedure, 159
Response prevention, 153–155, 157–
        159, 161
    in children and adolescents, 158–
        159
Revised Children's Cognitive Assess-
        ment Questionnaire (RCCAQ), 183

Schedule for Affective Disorders and
        Schizophrenia (SADS), 13
    Epidemiological Version, 54
    Lifetime Version, 95
    for School Age Children, 13, 38, 52,
        56, 96, 103
School phobia, 23, 24, 25, 67, 71, 78–
        90, 96–97
    and agoraphobia, 71, 81, 84, 90, 97,
        133, 136
    antidepressant treatment for, 133–
        134
    and birth order, 82–83
    definition of, 88
    differential diagnosis of, 133
    familial aggregation in, 102
    follow-up studies on, 84–87
    in high-risk children, 54–56
    and illness, 79, 89, 90
    onset of, 79, 80, 97
    and school attendance problems,
        87–90
    vs. separation anxiety, 132, 133
    in siblings, 100
    symptoms of, 65, 66, 78
Self-Administered Dependency Ques-
        tionnaire (SADQ), 82, 83
Self-report measurements, in children,
        23–24, 38, 57, 182
Sensorimotor system, 171
Separation anxiety disorder (SAD), 5,
        23, 24, 38, 64–68, 74, 130–143
    age differences in, 65–67

age of onset in, 131, 132
comorbidity in, 25, 98
criteria for, 65, 80, 81
and dependency, 82
differential diagnosis of, 132
DSM-III-R definition of, 131
in first-degree relatives, 100, 107–108, 110
in high-risk children, 54, 56, 57, 58, 98
and maturational changes, 170
and panic disorder, 129–130, 206–207, 210
in pediatric patients, 52
prevalence of, 43, 47, 48, 51–52
and school phobia, 66, 67, 73–74, 79
symptoms of, 66
therapy for, 132
Separation anxiety hypothesis (SAH), 130, 134, 135–143
research strategies employed for, 135–142
Serotonergic agents, 156–158
Skin conductance responses, 176, 179
Social phobia, 18, 20, 74, 81, 138, 197
and dysthymia, 25
in first-degree relatives, 105
prevalence of, 51, 52
vs. simple phobias, 72, 73, 74
Social withdrawal, 48, 65
Socioeconomic status (SES), in distribution of anxiety disorders, 20, 23, 40, 48
Somatic responses, 3, 58, 65, 67, 118, 132, 171–180
Stability, 167, 168
in behavioral inhibition, 169
Startle reflex, 172, 173
State-Trait Anxiety Inventory (STAI), 1, 20

State-Trait Anxiety Inventory for Children (STAIC), 1, 2, 23, 182, 183, 187
and academic achievement, 183
Stick figures, 196
Stomachache, 3, 65, 132
Stranger fear, 169, 170, 193
Stress
animal studies in, 169
dealing with, 46, 139, 189
and emotional disorders, 52
precipitating anxiety, 109, 135, 139, 141
Structured Clinical Interview for DSM-III-R (SCID), 95, 103
Sweat glands, 176, 178, 179, 180

Taylor Manifest Anxiety Scale, 1
Temperament studies, 115, 116
Test anxiety, 174, 176, 192
Test Anxiety Scale for Children (TASC), 183, 190
Tonicity, 176, 178
Transient detection system, 172
Truancy; see School phobia
Twin studies, 113–124
of clinical anxiety, 120–122
of neuroticism, 115, 117–118
of panic attacks, 121
of phobic fears, 118–120
of temperament, 115, 116

Vagus nerve, 173, 174
Validity studies, 18, 24, 27–28, 94

"What I Think and Feel," 183
Worries, 40–41, 69; see also Fears
Wrist counters, 196–197

Zimelidine, 157